Your Body

Biofeedback at its Best

Your Body

Biofeedback at its Best

Beata Jencks, (Ph.D.)

nh Nelson Hall/Chicago

To Arulf,
from whom I learned more
about healthy psychophysiological
responses than from anybody else

And Kim,
without whom this book
would not be what it is

LIBRARY OF CONGRESS CATALOGING IN PUBLICATION DATA
Jencks, Beata.
    Your body—biofeedback at its best.
    Bibliography: p.
    Includes index.
    1. Biofeedback training. I. Title. [DNLM: 1. Bio-
feedback (Psychology). 2. Psychophysiology. WL102
J5ly]
BF319.5.B5J46   152.1'88   77-24618
ISBN 0-88229-351-6
ISBN 0-88229-508-X pbk.

Contents

Illustrations

01809

Tables

Alphabetical List of Abbreviations

ANS   Autonomic Nervous System
ASC   Altered State of Consciousness
CNS   Central Nervous System
EEG   Electroencephalogram
EMG   Electromyogram
GSR   Galvanic Skin Response
PNS   Peripheral Nervous System
PSNS   Parasympathetic Nervous System
SNS   Sympathetic Nervous System

Introduction

Man grasps at almost any aid offered to reduce the stress of life. Dependence on prescribed tranquilizers rose between 1962 and 1972 by 290 percent (Illich 1975), and mechanical biofeedback now offers a button to press instead of a pill to swallow.

"Relax by Biofeedback!" say the instrument advertizers. However, most biofeedback instruments do not relax a person. They can usually only register the tension or relaxation of a relatively small part of body or mind. Relaxation of the forehead muscles does not necessarily imply relaxation of the jaw; nor does relaxation of the arms imply that of the legs. Warming the hands and cooling the forehead may or may not change the temperature of other parts of the body in undetermined ways, and may therefore simply transfer circulatory difficulties instead of ameliorating them.

Modern mechanized and industrialized life has threatened the autonomy of body and mind. Clock time, not hunger, determines eating; artificial illumination, work shifts, and time schedules instead of day and night cycles determine times of sleep and activity; artificial, imagined, and vicarious excitements, not real dangers, stimulate the fight or flight reactions of body and mind. Furthermore, people are motivated and conditioned to get things rather than to do things. Biofeedback machines provide a needlessly dependence-producing substitute for more direct, flexible, selective, and simpler interventions which any person can carry out himself, thus achieving a more independent, self-assured lifestyle.

In a world where stress takes a great toll, man must learn to regain autonomy of body and mind and to determine his own actions and reactions. He must distinguish between the transitive meaning of "to heal," as practiced by physicians and priests, or as achieved by medication, and the intransitive "to heal," by which an ailing person heals himself through his own efforts and natural resources. The distinction must be made between therapy, which means obtaining help from outside, and self-help. To modify voluntarily one's behavior, physiological activity, emotions, and mental processes by self-regulation is frequently possible. Often a person must learn to change his habits, but this can be done without instruments and great expense.

Before anything was known about man's nervous and hormonal systems and their interactions, the skills and teaching of shamans, yogis, priests, and similar adepts were developed by instinct and through practical experience, and the people profited from this knowledge. However, all was esoteric, and transcendental, and clothed in magic.

Since the old skills were so little understood and magic and religious concepts did not appeal to modern medic:ne, the practical advantages of the old arts were largely disregarded and are only now being rediscovered with the renaissance of Yoga and similar methods. However, through self-experimentation, several psychophysiological methods have been developed since the turn of the century. This was usually done by persons who had some defect which was not amenable to medical treatment, or through improvements in the training procedures for professional performers and athletes. Also, several useful methods have been developed from German medical hypnosis and from post-Freudian psychotherapeutic practice in which body and mind are employed directly for reconditioning.

This book is written from the practical point of view. It can be used for self-training, or by therapists in physical therapy, psychotherapy, or nursing, with individuals or groups.

The reader is first introduced to the term *biofeedback*, and relevant physiological and psychological processes are discussed. Techniques for coping with the stresses of daily life are suggested, and a long chapter offers an introduction to sensory awareness, since a high degree of sensory sensitivity is required for the conscious use of the body as a biofeedback instrument. Breathing is also discussed at length, because vital capacity, relaxation and invigoration, strength, and endurance may all be increased by proper breathing patterns. Next, techniques are offered for improving physical alignment, physiological processes, and psychological functioning. Exercises have been incorporated from ancient Oriental as well as from modern Western sources. Most of the exercises can be incorporated into everyday life routines and require little extra time. They have been used by students, professional performers, housewives, athletes, nurses, and others for developing physical and psychological competence and self-sufficiency through the conscious use of body and mind as their own biofeedback instruments.

The reader ought to be aware of the following: The body has a great ability to readjust and heal itself and usually reacts correctly and therapeutically if given a chance and encouragement. Increased sensory awareness and sensitivity make it possible to obtain more and better information as to the states of body and mind; good judgment will suggest what ought to be done; and willpower will insure that it is done.

1. Biofeedback

The term *feedback* is used to designate the return of part of an output or response of a system as an input or stimulus. *Information feedback* provides information about the constancy or change, the occurrence or nonoccurrence of a function and may serve at the same time as a cue, stimulus, or reinforcement to which the system will respond. Information feedback may be either intrinsic, that is, available only to the system itself, or extrinsic, that is, available to an outside observer, or both. When biofeedback instruments are used, the feedback is both. When the body is used as its own feedback instrument, the feedback is usually intrinsic only.

Information feedback may function to sustain, strengthen, direct, or eliminate an action or reaction. It may assist learning by motivating or conditioning either positively or negatively.

The body acts constantly as its own biofeedback instrument, using information feedback. Both voluntary and reflexive muscular movements are constantly monitored by means of information feedback, which enables the muscle groups involved to make necessary adjustments promptly and accurately. When the body uses up energy, stimuli from within motivate food-seeking behavior. If the sympathetic nervous system is stimulated by an exciting cue, the evoked neural and hormonal changes elicit in turn a viscious circle of sympathetic responses and/or evoke the calming counteraction of the parasympathetic nervous system. Thus, biofeedback is self-regulation in a dynamic interchange with the environment. The human body is an extremely complex and sensitive biofeedback instrument, and many of its intricate actions, reactions, and interactions are not yet known.

The commonest mechanical biofeedback instruments are feedback myographs, called also electromyogram or EMG instruments, which record changes in the electric potential of muscle; feedback thermometers, which record temperatures; feedback electroencephalographs, called also electroencephalograph or EEG instruments, which record amplitude and frequency of brain waves; galvanic skin response feedback, called GSR instruments, which measure changes in the electrical resistance of the skin and reflect emotional arousal; and instruments which record blood pressure.

Biofeedback instruments record physiological and psychological processes and are used to modify animal and human activity. The question is, how useful and necessary are instruments for either research or therapy. Much of the literature on biofeedback, especially that from commercial sources and in popular journals, is either simplistic or inordinately speculative, treating unknowns as facts and making unwarranted assumptions and generalizations.

Instrument biofeedback is necessary for monitoring certain reactions for which the body is not suitable for being used as its own biofeedback instrument. This includes brain waves, blood pressure, electric skin resistance and muscular responses too small to be preceived.

Physicians must decide whether biofeedback instruments are therapeutically more useful to elicit blood pressure changes than adequate exercise, proper diet, and medication. General relaxation of body and mind, which is frequently but not in all cases followed by lowered blood pressure, usually require no mechanical biofeedback instrument. However, for those medical and psychiatric patients who are incapable or unwilling to cooperate in doing relaxation exercises, a *Respiration Feedback* instrument, which induces a spontaneous deep physical and mental relaxation of body and mind, has been developed recently in Germany by H. Leuner, M.D.* The patient lies on a bed with closed eyes and is instructed to relax as much as possible while thinking of nothing in particular. The amplitude of the respiratory movements is indicated simultaneously by means of varying sound, heard through earphones, and the varying brightness of a lamp placed above the closed eyelids. The patient adjusts the levels of sound and light to a comfortable intensity. This results not only in spontaneous deep physical and mental relaxation, but also in a relatively deep altered state of consciousness.

On the other hand, EMG feedback instruments are absolutely necessary for retraining a patient following injury or disease, when it is necessary to observe the smallest gains in muscle function. Further, GSR instrument feedback, which appraises a psychotherapy patient of his suppressed or otherwise subconscious emotional responses, may be useful in psychotherapy.

With respect to the meaningfulness of EEG instrument feedback, not only is the interpretation of the different wavelengths of brain waves hypothetical, but the relation of psychological functions to them is extremely elusive in spite of all research; and all those pinpointing charts of alpha, beta, theta, and other brain waves indicating certain functions bring to mind butterfly collections: everything neatly pinned down and impressively labeled,

---

*Hanscarl Leuner 1977: personal communication

but with all the life gone out of it, useful primarily for classification. The human psyche still remains the Greeks' elusive butterfly, and research results should not be used as proof by commercial pseudoprofessional promoters for the efficacy of brain wave feedback therapy for relaxation and human effectiveness training.

Therapeutic claims in sales talks of biofeedback instrument company respresentatives at professional meetings are reminiscent of the panacea advertisements of quacks at country fairs fifty years ago. Following is a list of claims from printed advertisements for commercial biofeedback instruments.

EMG feedback is recommended for stress and anxiety reduction; relief of tension and migraine headaches and tension backaches; general muscular relaxation, subvocalization, and phobic desensitization; to counteract essential hypertension and bruxism, or grinding of the teeth; to relieve muscle spasms and tics; and to rehabilitate after paralysis, strokes, and operations.

Feedback thermometers are recommended for stress and anxiety reduction, autonomic nervous system relaxation, and contraception; to counteract tension and migraine headaches, tension backaches, and circulatory problems; and to treat Raynaud's disease.

Feedback EEGs are recommended for psychotherapy, stress reduction, pain reduction, and dream investigation; to counteract insomnia, reduce learning difficulties, enhance concentration, and treat alcoholism.

GSR feedback is recommended for self-awareness training, relaxation, activation, tension reduction, sleep improvement, and emotional control; to increase learning efficiency, concentration, and recall; and for pain reduction and meditation.

The price of the least expensive GSR instrument is presently about $75. Prices of EMG and EEG instruments range from about $500 to $1,000. Besides the costly equipment, drawbacks of mechanical biofeedback are that usually no more than one physiological function is fed back at one time to the subject, and that reactions must be carefully measured and monitored for the reward to be appropriately given and correctly timed.

The following purposes can be accomplished without any instruments by using the body as its own biofeedback instrument: (1) diverse muscle relaxation; (2) change of heart rate and body temperature; (3) change of breathing patterns; (4) change of behavior patterns in tics and spasms; (5) decrease of grinding the teeth; (6) decrease of stress and anxiety reactions; (7) phobic desensitization; (8) mental relaxation; (9) autonomic nervous system relaxation; (10) emotional control; (11) pain relief for tension headaches, backaches, and other aches and pains; (12) reduction of sleeping difficulties, be it insomnia or hypersomnia; (13) improved learning ability, including enhancement of concentration and recall; (14) dream investigation; and (15) meditation.

Instruments can serve only limited purposes, since body and mind are the important agents for biofeedback. The next chapter presents physiological and psychological information relevant to the use of the body and mind as their own biofeedback instruments. The remainder of the book offers practical techniques for consciously utilizing the body's biofeedback mechanisms for accomplishing most of the purposes enumerated above.

2. The Instrument: Body and Mind

Man lives in an environment of gravitational, mechanical, electrical, and magnetic forces and of thermal, chemical, electrical, and atomic energies. This environment constantly impinges upon the body's tissues and structures, and provides the mind with its sensory impressions. These determine memory, thought, imagination, and will. Further, both body and mind are influenced by needs, emotions, and other motivations.

The nervous system is the principal integrating mechanism for these complex interactions, but the hormonal system also plays an important role.

The Body

Tissues and Structures of the Body

If growth were the only property of life, the end of maturity would be but one giant cell. If a fertilized egg would mature by cell division only, a giant mass of undifferentiated cells would result. It is the differentiation of cells into diverse tissues and structures that creates the human body with its extremely intricate anatomy and functions.

The word *somatic* pertains to the body's voluntary, or striated, muscles as distinguished from *visceral*, which pertains to the inner organs and blood vessels, or viscera, with their "involuntary," or smooth muscles.

No matter whether the figure of man is scratched as an outline drawing on a cave wall; painted by Holbein as Death, the skeleton, showing only the bones; drawn as a nude by Leonardo da Vinci, showing only the skin; depicted by Vesalius as an illustration of the venous system, showing only the blood vessels; or built as a wire figure in the New York Museum of Natural History, showing only the nerves: each portrays the configuration of the human body. Many tissues are distributed throughout the body, and the feeling of being "a bundle of nerves" reflects only a heightened, but by no means complete, awareness of something which is true at all times. All tissues play their part in that most intricate biofeedback instrument—the body. Man's body with its physiological and psychological functions has not changed over thousands, perhaps millions, of years. Only technology, philosophical theories, and scientific knowledge have grown up and evolved around it.

The Nervous System

The nervous system with its various components and interactions is much more complicated than the following outline and Figure 1 indicate. It can be divided into a central and a peripheral system. The *central nervous system* (CNS) consists of brain, brain stem, and spinal cord, with the enclosed nerve cell body aggregates, fibers, and interconnections. A nerve cell with its sometimes long processes is called a *neuron*. A *nerve* consists of many processes of neurons and may extend into both the central and peripheral nervous systems. The *peripheral nervous system* (PNS) consists of the *sensory nerves*, which lead into the spinal cord and brain stem from sensory receptors and bring sensory messages, and the *motor nerves*, which issue from the spinal cord and innervate the voluntary muscles in the extremities, trunk, and head. The autonomic nervous system (ANS) has components in both the CNS and the PNS. It will be discussed later.

The Central Nervous System (CNS). Within the brain and brain stem are several areas or systems which deserve mention. See Figure 1.

The *cerebral cortex* is the much convoluted, outer layer of the brain. Its different regions are concerned with muscular functions and sensory impressions and are further instrumental in perceiving, thinking, learning, and associative functions. It also affects the interaction of functions of the sympathetic and parasympathetic parts of the ANS, and interactions between the ANS and sensory and motor somatic functions. At this highest level of the CNS are also located regulating mechanisms for cardiovascular, gastrointestinal, sexual, and other supposedly "involuntary" functions.

The *thalamus* is mainly a distribution center that relays all sensory impulses, except possibly olfaction, to the cerebral cortex and from one part of the brain to another.

The *limbic system* includes parts of the cerebral cortex as well as some lower brain structures, and it integrates emotions with motor and ANS activities.

The *hypothalamus* regulates such body functions as temperature, hunger, thirst, and blood pressure. It is also the central locus of such emotions as fear and anger, interacts with the reticular formation in the brain stem to keep the brain awake and alert, and controls the pituitary gland.

The *brain stem* influences motor functions, including posture and movement, reflexes, excitatory and inhibitory mechanisms, and activation of extensor muscles. It may alert and activate the cerebral cortex, facilitating impulses, or may block some sensory impulses. Consciousness and attentiveness are influenced by it. It also in-

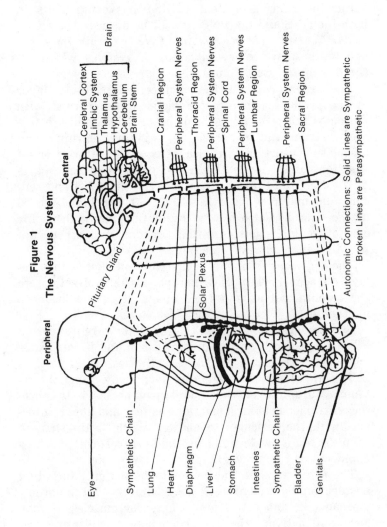

Figure 1

The Nervous System

Central

Peripheral

Brain
Cerebral Cortex
Limbic System
Thalamus
Hypothalamus
Cerebellum
Brain Stem
Cranial Region
Peripheral System Nerves
Thoracid Region
Peripheral System Nerves
Spinal Cord
Peripheral System Nerves
Lumbar Region
Peripheral System Nerves
Sacral Region

Pituitary Gland

Solar Plexus

Autonomic Connections: Solid Lines are Sympathetic
Broken Lines are Parasympathetic

Eye
Sympathetic Chain
Lung
Heart
Diaphragm
Liver
Stomach
Intestines
Sympathetic Chain
Bladder
Genitals

fluences the ANS functions of salivation, cardiac activity, blood pressure, respiration and alimentary movements. The *cerebellum* receives nerve impulses from skin, muscles, joints, tendons, eyes, ears, semicircular canals of the inner ear, and cerebral cortex. It regulates posture, balance, and coordinated movements and also influences respiration, blood pressure, and other autonomic functions. The *spinal cord* conducts and coordinates nerve impulses. It is an important location of neuron interaction, including summation, inhibition, and reflex action.

The Peripheral Nervous System (PNS). The innervation of voluntary muscles is simple. It is mediated by long processes of neurons whose cell bodies are located in the spinal cord. Smooth muscle innervation and other autonomic functions of the PNS are discussed in the section on the ANS. Sensory perception, however, requires special attention here, because of its importance for the sensory awareness training necessary for the use of the body as its own biofeedback instrument.

The *special sensory organs* are eyes, ears, nose, and tongue with specialized receptor cells. However, most important for sensory awareness training are the sensory receptors throughout the skin, mucous membranes, muscles, tendons, and joints. Sensory perception mediated by these receptors is called *somesthesis.* Temperature, touch sensations, and pain are perceived through special structures or free nerve endings in skin and mucous membranes. Tension, weight, and resistance are perceived by means of special receptors in muscles and tendons, called muscle or tendon spindles, which react to stretch. The muscle sense or perception of movement is called *kinesthesis. Proprioception* is the sensory perception of movement and of the body's orientation in space, which includes posture, equilibrium, weight, and resistances. The sensory receptors involved are in muscles, tendons, and joints as well as in the semicircular canals of the inner ear.

The Autonomic Nervous System (ANS). Other names for this system are the involuntary, vegetative, or visceral nervous system. The integrating action of the ANS is of vital importance for the constant well-being of the organism. The ANS exerts regulatory influences over the smooth muscles and glands of internal organs, skin, mucous membranes, and blood vessels, which serve such usually involuntary functions as regulation of heart rate, blood flow and pressure, metabolism, digestion, temperature maintenance, breathing, and sexual functions. Breathing and sexual functions are also partly under voluntary control. However, the ANS acts not only as an internal homeostatic mechanism, but also as a primary reactor to environmental physical and mental stimuli.

Recognition of the ANS response called the fight-or-flight reaction, which is indispensable for survival, is indeed so common and ancient that the Sumerians, in possibly the oldest writings of mankind, before the year 3000 B.C., used the figure of a human head with its hair standing on end as the symbol for the word "furious" (Majno 1975). Scientific investigation of the ANS is much more recent. Claude Bernard (1878–79) emphasized that the equilibrium of the internal environment of the organism is to a large extent controlled by the nervous system. Trömmer postulated in 1911 two mutually inhibiting systems within the ANS. Hess (1926) called these *ergotropic*, which means oriented toward work and the expenditure of energy, and *trophotropic*, which means oriented toward nourishment and the production of energy. The interaction between these two subsystems of the ANS demonstrates Cannon's (1932) concept of homeostasis. Cannon was first to describe in detail the fight-or-flight response as an emergency reaction.

The ANS has both CNS and PNS components. Within the CNS somatic and autonomic centers overlap, and there are probably no centers of purely autonomic integration. Integration of autonomic functions occurs at all levels of the CNS, but the hypothalamus with its regulatory functions of sleep, temperature, and food intake is the most important single location for this integration. Autonomic reflexes regulating blood pressure, blood vessel size and tonus, sweating, and emptying of the urinary bladder, rectum, and seminal vessels can occur, in the CNS, at as low a level as the spinal cord, without involving the brain.

The peripheral ANS components are now called respectively the sympathetic nervous system (SNS) and the parasympathetic nervous system (PSNS). They are also referred to as thoracicolumbar, since the SNS nerve processes issue from the thoracic and lumbar sections of the spine, and craniosacral, since the PSNS processes issue from the cranial and sacral sections of the spine. See Figure 1. The SNS and PSNS are inextricably connected, and their interactions are intricate. Both systems innervate practically every organ in the body, but their actions as well as their modes of action differ.

The SNS, by means of its two chains of nerve cell aggregates along the sides of the spinal column and other nerve cell aggregates and networks, usually acts in a general way. The origin of the PSNS in the peripheral nervous system as well as its actions are more discrete. It is organized for localized discharge to specific structures and systems, and not for generalized responses. In general, the SNS is concerned with the expenditure of energy, while the PSNS conserves and restores energy.

The SNS is active during the waking state, making adjustments to a constantly changing environment, the degree of activity varying from moment to moment and from organ to organ. It also helps prepare the organism for competitive, aggressive or evasive, fight-or-flight behavior. Further, sudden stresses, tension, anxiety states, and mental and physical work excite certain brain centers, which in turn influence the SNS to initiate general excitation and activate mechanisms which contribute physiologically to the production of muscular work. During rage and fright sympathetically innervated structures throughout the body are activated simultaneously. The SNS accelerates the heart rate, increases blood pressure, breathing rate, blood sugar, and general metabolism, induces the spleen to pour red blood cells into the circulation, diverts the blood from the skin and internal organs to the skeletal muscles, dilates the pupils, induces the secretion of adrenalin and noradrenalin and other hormones by the adrenal gland, stimulates other glands, among them certain sweat glands, and consequently decreases electrical skin resistance, and activates the smooth muscles at the hair roots to make the hair rise.

The PSNS promotes those bodily processes which conserve and build up energy and body tissues, mainly digestion, the building up of reserves, and relaxation. Other functions of the PSNS are the dilation of blood vessels, including the erection of penis or clitoris, and increasing salivation, nasopharyngeal secretions, mobility in the gastrointestinal tract, and lacrimation. It initiates decreases in the heart rate, tonus of the blood vessels, blood pressure, oxygen consumption, blood lactate, respiration, and general metabolism. It stimulates gastrointestinal movements and secretions, evokes lapping and similar eating movements, contracts the pupil, aids in the absorption of nutrients, induces vomiting and emptying of the urinary bladder and rectum, and increases electrical skin resistance. No useful purpose would be served if the parasympathetic nerve cells all discharged at once. In fact such general action would be harmful.

Table 1 summarizes the often antagonistic functions of the two parts of the ANS.

Those animals with the best fight-or-flight reactions have an increased chance to reproduce, and natural selection favors this response. In general, young aggressive societies and individuals seem to be primarily SNS reactors, and so seem those in cooler climates. Old, worn-out, and settled societies and individuals, and those in warmer climates are generally primarily PSNS reactors. Other factors which determine the predominance of one system over the other are culture, climate, race, individual physical differences, physical condition, mental attitude, and momentary or long-term stress, including a quiet versus noisy environment. In general, rural populations are primarily PSNS, while city populations are primarily SNS reactive; and Eastern societies predominantly PSNS reactors, while Western societies are predominantly SNS reactors. It is interesting to speculate what roles race, climate, and culture play in this.

In modern work- and excitement-oriented societies, the fight-or-flight response is frequently inappropriately initiated but then not completed. This produces unnecessary stress, and the SNS is much overworked. In addition, man has in his sheltered, civilized life been strongly conditioned to rely on external protection rather than on the innate, instinctive responses of his body. The instinctive fight-or-flight reactions have not changed, but they have now become technologically and socially inappropriate. Western man must learn to recondition his ANS. Just as the SNS responses are elicited by situations which call for hard thinking, muscular work, flight, or fight, so the PSNS responses are elicited by a quiet stream of thought, a decreased level of consciousness and muscle tone, a quiet environment, monotony, and a passive attitude. No wonder modern Western man has turned his attention to ancient Eastern methods.

Without any knowledge of the anatomy and physiology of the systems involved, ancient Eastern methods were developed to control voluntarily the actions of the ANS, and especially to induce PSNS reactions. It was long believed in Western society that autonomic functions cannot be voluntarily controlled, although they are in fact easily influenced by thinking as well as by emotions.

Table 1
Functions of the Autonomic Nervous System

Structure	Sympathetic Functions	Parasympathetic Functions
Eye	Dilation of pupil (No connection to lens)	Contraction of pupil Contraction of lens
Lacrimal glands	Vasoconstriction	Secretion, copious
Salivary glands	Secretion of scanty, thick saliva Vasoconstriction	Secretion, copious, rich in enzymes
Sweat glands	Stimulation (trunk)	Stimulation (head)
Adrenal Medulla	Secretion of adrenalin and some noradrenalin	(None apparent)
Spleen	Constriction to expel blood rich in erythrocytes	(None apparent)
Pilomotor muscles	Contraction (hair erection)	(None apparent)
Heart	Increasing rate and vigor of beat	Decreasing rate
Coronary vessels	Dilation (indirect?)	Constriction (indirect?)
Lungs	Dilation of bronchi Constriction of vessels, mild Secretion inhibited	Constriction of bronchi, weak (No effect on vessels?) Stimulation of mucous secretion
Liver	Release of glucose	(No effect?)

Table 1 (continued)

Bile ducts and gall bladder	Relaxation of bladder with inhibition of secretion	Contraction of bladder with relaxation of sphincter to expel bile
Gastrointestinal Celiac ganglion or Vagus respectively	Decreasing peristalsis, tone, and blood flow (?) in stomach, small intestine, and proximal colon Vasoconstriction in pancreas (influence on secretion?)	Increasing peristalsis and tone in esophagus, stomach, small intestine, and proximal colon Stimulating copious gastric, intestinal, and pancreatic secretion in small intestine, proximal colon, and pancreas Decreasing tone of sphincters
Gastrointestinal Superior mesenteric ganglion or Pelvic nerve respectively	Decreasing peristalsis and tone in distal colon and rectum Constricting anal sphincter	Increasing peristalsis and tone for evacuation in distal colon and rectum Decreasing tone of anal sphincter for evacuation
Kidney	Vasoconstriction Decreasing output of urine	(No effect?)
Urinary bladder	(No effect on bladder?) Constricting internal sphincter	Increasing tone to empty bladder Decreasing tone of sphincter
Genitalia	Ejaculation of semen (Uterus?)	Erection of penis or clitoris (Uterus motility?)

The Mind

The *mind* has conscious and subconscious properties. Its conscious properties include perception, memory, thinking, emotions, and will. The conscious mind is the directing agent for using the body as its own biofeedback instrument.

Even though the processes of the body seem complicated with the different nervous system and hormonal interactions, those of the mind, which are functions of the physical brain, are even more so. There is an incessant and often unconscious interaction of sensations, thought, and will with emotions, impulses, and desires, and through it all weaves the imagination. The whole becomes still more complicated since body and mind interact continually by conscious and subconscious processes.

Perception

The direct acquaintance with an object or ongoing process through the senses, that is, what is seen, heard, felt, smelled, or tasted is called *perception*. Observation, special notice, or consideration of objects or processes, with a view to action, is called *attention*. It is impossible to give attention to all that is perceived, and many protective mechanisms are built into the human system so that it will not be overloaded. Even at that, man's modern environment is constantly overstimulating and overstraining the perceptual organs and the physiological and mental processes of perceiving.

Sensory input is constantly fed into the CNS. The peripheral retinal cells alone, for example, can be activated not only by external visual stimuli, but also by internal physiological changes, the action of certain drugs, or even when they are not stimulated at all.

Minimal stimuli which occur outside the area of attention or consciousness can evoke or influence subsequent perceptions, images, and fantasies. Both perceptual and imagery phenomena are constructions of the mind. What then is perceived reality and what is imagery? A *perception* is a given sensory impression that shows adequate correlation with external objects or events. It shows considerable stability or predictable and constant changes as the relationships between it and the observer change. Decisions about reality are essentially probability decisions. An initial decision depends largely on circumstantial clues, and on the basis of these further data are processed.

Imagery may or may not originate in external reality, but is in either case modified by expectations, memories, wishes, needs, and also strangely inexplicable happenings in the mind. Imagery is discussed in a later section of this chapter.

Thinking

Critical and logical thinking is used for decision making, and one of the most important decisions in life is what and how much can be expected from or attempted with body and mind. Critical thinking should be used to learn more about body and mind in order to base decisions on facts instead of on assumptions. Learning how better to observe and identify internal sensations will ensure, for example, that excitement will not be mistaken for fear or joy, nor overtiredness for depression. This is part of sensory awareness training. Physiological knowledge which is presently available can also aid in distinguishing between some often misinterpreted reactions. For instance, lacrimation during relaxation does not necessarily mean sadness, and erection of the penis may not signify sexual arousal, but both may merely indicate that the PSNS has been aroused and is acting strongly.

Sensory awareness training also develops increased consciousness of instinctive responses, and this consciousness can be used rationally to modify further actions. This training is discussed at length in chapter 4.

Special Aspects of Memory

Memory usually implies the power, function, or act of consciously reproducing or identifying what has been learned or experienced. In using the body as a biofeedback instrument however, two other aspects of memory are important. The first is that memory often inhibits new perceptions and new learning. A trainee who learns to increase sensory awareness must consciously disregard, that is *not remember*, how things affected him in the past. And he must open-mindedly be ready to sense, feel, and experience anew. Also, new instructions are usually followed by immediate recall of something previously learned or experienced. For instance, an instruction to decrease the heart rate may evoke memories or fantasies of physical relaxation, a calmly pleasant environment, peace, and quiet. On the other hand the instruction to increase the heart rate may evoke memories or fantasies of muscular exertion, anger, aggression, tension, sexual arousal, or a noisy environment.

The second little known or recognized aspect of memory is that there are *body memories* which the mind has seemingly not registered. These body memories are located at places in the body which were related to or affected by past stressful or emotionally colored events. Somehow the body part is related to subconscious memories, and some physical or emotional stimulus may bring the memory into consciousness. Psychophysiological methods, especially those with passive approaches, are likely to bring body memories into consciousness, and trainees should be aware of this. Body memories can be very valuable for abreactions and self-analysis. These are discussed later in this chapter and in chapter 8.

Concentration and Distraction

Concentration is close mental application or exclusive attention. The power of *abstraction* is the ability to withdraw, separate, or disengage the mind or attention from something. Usually both work together toward the same purpose. They can be developed and strengthened, but the difficulties of concentration and abstraction in the face of environmental and internal interferences are known to both the schoolboy and the meditator. Distraction and laziness are the greatest obstacles to mental activity and achievement. Distraction is counteracted by concentration and abstraction, laziness by willpower. Concentration on a physical activity, such as typing, running, or following a moving target with the eyes is the easiest. Pure mental concentration, such as that required for solving arithmetical problems or playing chess, is more difficult. The most difficult is *passive expectancy*, where neither body nor mind has a definite object on which to fixate. Passive expectancy involves waiting patiently and quietly, undistractedly, unresistingly, open-mindedly, and not even actively anticipating, as also this would be too active. This procedure may lead to states similar to the nirvana and samadhi of Buddhism, and among modern methods it is advised for J. H. Schultz's Standard Autogenic Training.

Different methods are used to train the powers of concentration. Some make use of certain postures, others decrease muscle tone by physical relaxation or utilize body rhythms, as for instance observation of the slow, rhythmic breathing movements of abdomen or chest. Fixed attention on the sound or feeling of the respiratory air flow or concentrating strongly upon an object or sound in the environment also trains the powers of concentration.

The following four suggestions are useful in order to overcome environmental distractions in pursuance of an objective: first, assure strong motivation; second, complete urgent unfinished business beforehand since it interferes with concentration; third, choose a quiet environment which is free from external disturbances; and fourth, concentrate while fresh, inserting breaks, choosing a new method of approach, or changing the objective temporarily to avoid fatigue.

Internal mental distractions are more difficult to overcome than environmental interferences. The human mind is constantly active, and stopping its activity is variously known as "damming the stream of mind," "reducing internal noise," "stopping the internal gossip," or "emptying the mind." Table 2 outlines suggestions for reducing

Table 2
Suggestions for Reducing Internal Mental Distractions

1. Ignore distractions.
2. Simply say "no" to distractions when they occur.
3. Concentrate on the idea of emptiness in the mind so strongly that no distraction can interfere.
4. First acknowledge the distraction; then send it away.
5. Imagine chasing or driving distractions beneath a "cloud of forgetting" or a "cloud of not knowing."
6. Imagine blinding or deafening yourself to distractions.
7. Exhale gently and imagine that the distractions are carried from the head to a lower body part from where they can flow out.
8. Exhale gently and allow the distractions to float out of the head toward the sky.
9. Imagine collecting the distractions in one hand and throwing them away.
10. Destroy distractions by imagined fire, flood, or hurricane.
11. Utter a charm against distractions, possibly using special modulations of the sound of words.
12. Use an imagined broom to sweep the mind clear and clean, back and forth, sweeping out every cobweb from the corners.
13. Imagine wiping or washing the mind clean and clear with refreshing water.
14. Allow distractions to flow off the body as in rivulets down a mountain.
15. Imagine the mind to be a blackboard on which the distractions are recorded in chalk. Wipe it clean and clear.

16. Imagine the distractions streaming into the sides of the head from above, and releasing them through an opening in the forehead.
17. Choose a single meaningful or meaningless syllable and concentrate on it exclusively. Imagine it as a protective shield for warding off intruding distractions and as a defense weapon with which to strike down distracting thoughts.
18. Imagine a vibrating, electrically charged fence around the mind through which no distractions can enter.
19. Imagine anything that is very effective for keeping intruders out.
20. Imagine distractions to be a stream of ideas by which you are carried along. Imagine stepping out of the stream and just watching it rushing past, without paying any attention to what it carries.
21. Imagine distractions to be flocks of birds, passing overhead. Let them pass and fly away freely.
22. Perform a "symbolic strip tease" of each distraction as it occurs.

---

internal mental distractions, chosen from ancient and recently invented methods. Only one of the suggested methods should be used during a trial period since mixing the methods would defeat the purpose of clearing the mind.

Emotions

Emotions are states of consciousness involving a distinct feeling tone, often quite intense, accompanied by visceral and somatic reactions. States designated as fear, insecurity, anger, disgust, grief, joy, surprise, or yearning can be included. Strong emotions are an interference rather than an aid in using the body as a biofeedback instrument. However, sensitivity to incipient emotional reactions can be used for detecting what is going on within body and mind. Reactions can then be based on what has been detected.

An attitude of open-mindedness is essential when using

the body as its own biofeedback instrument, and fear of the unexpected or disappointment and anger caused by a seeming lack of results must be avoided.

The feeling of insecurity is an all too common aspect of human emotionality. It causes many misconceptions about reality and therefore merits discussion. An individual can be envisioned as being in the middle-of-his-life sphere as if at the center of an onion with many layers. Closest are layers of reality with facts which can be directly observed, experienced, and verified. Next come layers of assumptions which are verifiable, then layers of unverifiable assumptions, and finally the great unknown. The emotion of insecurity is both vegetative and psychic. Strangely enough, feelings of insecurity are more often lessened by unverifiable assumptions about the unknown than by verifiable facts. Transcendental, religious, and philosophical explanations have all been developed to provide a logical, causal framework for natural phenomena and random occurrences with their uncertainty and apparent lack of order. It is necessary for the human mind to order reality to be able to manage it. Ignorance of facts, fear of the unknown, and an extremely limited ability to control the course of events cause feelings of insecurity, resulting in reliance on "authorities," such as priests, physicians, psychologists, and palmists. These "authorities" often encourage belief in miracles and propagate misconceptions about nature with results which may well cause still greater feelings of insecurity.

Two kinds of unreality must be distinguished. The first, the above-mentioned unverifiable assumptions, serves as a refuge from insecurity. The other is the unreality which the brain conjures up in dreams, fantasies, and the imagination. This unreality can be useful as a tool for solving everyday problems, including that of insecurity, without recourse to "authorities." It is discussed in the next sections.

Imagination

Imagination with its associated *imagery* is the term used for the formation or synthesis of ideas, pictures, emotions, sensory perceptions, and sensations of physical activity in the mind, by free or directed associations, from memories or purely by invention. It can represent the real in its ideal or universal character and can create the unreal or novel by reevoking or recombining elements of reality and unreality. It may be vague or extremely vivid and detailed. It may synthesize, emphasize, and distort or reverse ideas, reality, and unreality.

The imagination can employ any sensory or motor memories, and it can work intellectually as well as emotionally. The more sensations, actions, and emotions are involved, the more vivid the imagination will be. Higher levels of abstraction reduce imagery. Simplest to imagine are objects, places, or feelings. Second are actions, such as walking, sitting, sleeping. However, also concepts such as "on," "under," or "but" may be easily translated into imagery by means of sign language. Sign language is based on the concept of the word, and it is basically the same in such diverse forms as ancient pictorial scripts, the sign language of the American Indians, and communication by the deaf in Germany. Words evoking the most vivid imagery produce the strongest emotional impact and are most effective in communication. The present trend toward the use of euphemisms is a great hindrance to the formation of correct perceptions and proper reactions. The word "underprivileged" is less meaningful than "poor," and "environmental control" less powerful than "save the trees from dying."

A distinction must be made between conscious, intentional imagery, making use of self-suggestions for psychological or physiological purposes, and spontaneous imagery. Spontaneous imagery is related to altered states of consciousness, which are discussed later in this chapter. If intentional imagery is used for a purpose, it should be changed if it is not effective. It should be discontinued if it arouses unnecessary anxiety. Intentional imagery differs from the imagery of free fantasy, which is not guided and serves no specific purpose.

Use of the Imagination. The imagination can be used as an aid to prethink and prestructure the form of atoms as well as architectural edifices, and can be employed by a child to scare itself in the dark or by a religious enthusiast to view heaven. However, the importance of its discussion here is that it can be extremely useful as an assistance in everyday living, if used in the right way.

The imagination should be freely employed, but in an effective and useful way. This can be done by first sensing or thinking and deciding what is desirable, and then imagining appropriate sensations or reactions. Memories of appropriate beneficial past experiences are useful in this connection. If the imagination is coordinated with appropriate actions, such as inhaling or exhaling, exertion or relaxation, even better results may be achieved.

Controlled imagery can be used to increase or decrease sensory perception, motor output, tension or relaxation, motivation, inhibition, and anxiety. It can be used to consciously direct concentration, to develop esthetic sensibility, to enhance empathy with objects and persons, for ego-building, and more. The proper use of the imagination requires that each individual must choose and devise those images which are most effective for him in achieving his purpose. It is important to make what is imagined as vivid and forceful as possible, using visual, auditory, and other sensory aspects. Further, there is a difference between imagining something like walking, and imagining *doing* something like walking, that is, becoming the performer instead of the observer. This distinction is reflected in slight muscular movements of the limbs, in the breathing rhythm, and in changes of facial expressions.

This kind of imagining is much more powerful and greatly aids in the utilization of imagery.

Much use is made of the imagination and of conscious imagery in the practical exercises in chapters 4 to 8.

Discovering the Imagination. Those who maintain they have little or no imagination usually have more than they think. For a beginning, a command is given like "Think of a house, a car, a watch, a hat, a. . . ." Then details are asked, such as "What is the color? The shape? The size? Is the owner a man or a woman?. . ." Ability to answer such questions requires the use of the imagination and establishes convincing proof of its existence. Usually those who maintain they have no imagination can answer these questions and discover thereby an ability which was denied or unrecognized.

Images and Imagery

An *image* is a CNS-aroused mental representation, not necessarily visual, of sensations or perceptions or a reproduction or reconstruction of perceptual experiences in the apparent absence of sensory stimulation. *Imagery* is the collective term for images and the operation of forming images in perception, thought, feeling, memory, and fantasy.

Imagery can occur in any sense modality. It may be externally or internally originated and may also appear to be inside or outside the body. It has been described variously as being "in the mind's eye," "before the eyes," "in the back of the head," "coming from that direction," or "out there in space." Images may occur spontaneously, be induced, or purposely changed. They may be fleeting or last for minutes, be clear or vague.

Imagery can be classified into four types: thought and memory images, perceptual images, feeling state images, and hallucinatory images. Table 3 gives examples. Hallucinatory images can be either positive or negative. Imagery that is evoked in any of the senses without a real

Table 3
Types of Imagery

Thought and Memory Images

Thought Image: A faint, subjective representation, present in waking consciousness as part of an act or thought, which can be abstract or include memory and imagination of any sensory perception.

Eidetic Image: A projected image, generally visual but sometimes auditory, of such vividness, color, clarity, and differentiation of form as to seem to the fully awake subject like a percept; it may resemble greatly enhanced thought images or greatly prolonged afterimages.

Perceptual Images

Retinal Image: The image of external objects as focused on the retina of the eye.

Icon: A visual image, seen clearly so briefly, that it is perceived but not recognized or analyzed at the moment, but may nonetheless be further processed by the brain.

Entoptic Phenomena: Visual phenomena that have their stimulus in the eyeball; they occur after pressing the eyeball, a blow on the head, etc., and may appear as luminous dots, stars, swirls, or fire; they may also be hazy spots, specks, and hair-like objects that drift across the field of vision with movements of the eyes, as if hovering in space. These are due to floating impurities, such as red blood cells, that cast shadows on the retina. Further, phosphenes, which are subjective, luminous sensations, having more or less form, produced by pressure on the eyeball, the effort of accommodation, or an electric current. They appear as moving clouds of unsaturated color, relatively static network-like patterns, dots, or flashes.

Entotic Sounds: Sound sources which ordinarily pass unnoticed, but are registered in the brain in states of lowered as well as of heightened arousal. They are due to slight shifts in the states of contraction of the muscles of the middle ear.

Physiological Afterimage: Prolongation or renewal of a sensory experience after the external stimulus has ceased to operate. They are evoked by chemical changes and nerve reactions and may reproduce the qualities of the preceding perception as a positive, negative, or complementary afterimage.

Illusion: A misinterpretation, taking the form of a sensation, which fails to represent the true character of a perceived object or objective situation.

Feeling State Imagery

Synesthesia: An actual perception of one type of sensation accompanied by the apparent sensation from another sensory modality, as in color hearing, in which sounds seem to have characteristic colors.

Body Image: The three-dimensional mental representation of the body in space, at rest or in motion, at any moment.

Dissociation: Feeling of separation from sensations, mental processes, the body image, or the environment.

Hallucinatory Images

Dream Image: Apparent sensory perceptions and motor activity, occurring in sleep, of such vividness as to appear real at the moment.

Hypnagogic Image: A suddenly appearing image, usually perceived as projected out in space, in the drowsy state just before sleep, of such vividness, clarity, and detail that it approaches sensory realism. It is usually visual, but can involve any other sense modality.

Hypnopompic Image: As the hypnagogic, but appearing after sleep in the half-waking state.

Hallucination: The experience of sensations or evocation of images with no real or external counterpart or cause. They may occur spontaneously or be induced or enhanced by certain physiological factors, chemicals, or other environmental conditions.

stimulus is called a positive hallucination. The elimination of an obviously perceptible sensation is called a negative hallucination. The different types of imagery may occur separately or combine with a fusion of their elements. Small children often experience especially vivid imagery until reality-orientation develops and image formation diminishes or even almost disappears. However, the ability to become aware of evanescent and usually ignored subjective phenomena and the evoking of imagery can be increased at any age.

Individuals differ greatly with respect to their innate capacity to evoke imagery, from very poor image formers to those able to evoke eidetic images. Also, persons who are successful in evoking one kind of imagery are not necessarily successful in evoking other kinds, and individual capabilities may vary from time to time and change due to internal and environmental factors. The experiencing of imagery is influenced also by prior knowledge of the type of phenomena that may be expected, momentary expectations, varying degrees of awareness and attentiveness, emotions, and mental attitudes. The optimal state of attention for different types of imagery varies from passive expectancy for some to extreme concentration for others.

Altered States of Consciousness (ASCs)

Altered states of consciousness range from daydreaming to hallucinations, including sleep and dreaming. Awareness of these states varies, and many which occur unnoticed for a long time may have disconcerting effects when they are noticed. Psychophysiological methods, among other things, may evoke ASCs, and a prospective trainee should be informed about their occurrence. He is probably well acquainted with some of them from everyday life without having identified them as such. Different ASCs can be purposely used for many objectives.

Many of the phenomena to be described have been disregarded by modern Western society or considered to be out of the ordinary and even pathological. They are well known in other cultures and even cherished and used for social and medical purposes. The phenomena of ASCs are by no means out of the range of the psychophysiological experience of modern Western man. For example, vivid hallucinations have been reported by radar operators, drivers on night runs and during daytime ("highway hypnosis"), jet pilots flying straight and level at high altitudes, and operators of snowcats and other vehicles in snowstorms. It is only abnormal or pathological to believe that such strange manifestations of the mind have actual existence in reality or have esoteric or transcendental meaning.

The phenomena of ASCs are as old as mankind, and behavior during stress suggests such states even in animals in the struggle for survival. A mouse, facing the danger of a stalking cat, "freezes" in an apparent ASC of tense total stillness and, thus without movement, becomes visually imperceptible to the cat. On the other hand, if the cat has caught the mouse and holds it between its teeth, the mouse may go into an apparent ASC of complete limpness, so that the cat assumes it incapable of moving and lets go, whereupon the mouse quickly becomes completely alert and escapes.

Hypnosis. Altered states of consciousness have probably been most described and publicized by the term *hypnosis*. This term was coined by a British surgeon, James Braid (1795-1860), after he experimented with mesmerism. *Mesmerism* had been developed by the Austrian physician Franz Anton Mesmer (1734-1815) as a therapeutic technique which combined suggestion, supposed "animal magnetism," and laying on of hands or "passes." Braid's *hypnosis* was a deep, sleeplike ASC for anesthetizing surgical patients at a time when neither ether nor other chemical anesthetics were known. Because mesmerism had fallen into medical disrepute at the time, Braid chose for his induced deep sleep ASC a term named after Hypnos, the god of sleep in Greek mythology. Since then much subclassification has been attempted and authors have repeatedly invented new terminology which may confuse even the experts, for example: *hypnotic, hypnoid, hypnoidal, hypnoidic, hypnagogic,* and *hypnopompic*—also called *hypnapagogic!* Milton Erickson wrote recently of the "common everyday trance" (Erickson and Rossi 1975), which amounts to nothing more nor less than having an intense interest or being absolutely attentive, popularly expressed by being "fascinated" or "spellbound." By classifying such states as well as deep trance states as hypnosis, the term becomes extremely indefinite. The operational definable term *altered state of consciousness,* by means of which specific alterations can be described more exactly, is more appropriate.

Aspects of Altered States of Consciousness. Table 4 lists some aspects of ASCs. Entries in the table may occur in various combinations for diverse ASCs. For instance, during an Autogenic Training exercise passive expectancy, relaxation, calmness, disregard of the environment, enhanced memory, and consciousness of physiological functions may all occur together. On the other hand, a political rally may evoke ASCs combining excitement, enhanced emotions, reduced critical thinking, and disregard of physiological functions. In addition feelings of satisfaction and a double awareness of an ASC and the usual self can occur in either case. Being aware of simultaneous, conflicting emotions, of which only one or neither may seem appropriate to the situation, may cause uncanny feelings. However, such contradictory or incongruous feelings are not out of the ordinary in the complicated human system. Contradictions between the whole and its parts or different parts occur in any system which functions at higher, complex levels, be it physical, physiological, or psychological.

Altered states of consciousness may be perceived or

Table 4
Aspects of Altered States of Consciousness

These may manifest themselves during extreme conditions or feelings of:

Relaxation	or	Tension
Drowsiness	or	Hyperalertness
Calmness	or	Excitement
Apathy	or	Emotion
Suggestibility	or	Spontaneity
Literalness	or	Fantasy and Symbolism
Reduced Critical Thinking	or	Enhanced Critical Thinking
Amnesia	or	Enhanced Memory
Passive Expectancy	or	Active Concentration
Disregard of Environment	or	Involvement in Environment
Disregard of Physiological Functions	or	Consciousness of Physiological Functions
Dissociation	or	Superawareness
Pleasure	or	Distress
Agelessness	or	Rejuvenation

Other factors involved:
Regressed or Archaic Modes of Thought
Access to Subconscious Material
Body Memories
Abreactions
Double Awareness of Reality and/or Altered States

pass unnoticed. Thoughts, feelings, and imagery may be vague, shadowy, and fluctuating or vivid and strong. States may last for just a fleeting moment or be prolonged for hours. They may contain mere bits of past experiences or reenact whole sequences vividly and exactly. This reenactment has been reported frequently by persons who were at the point of drowning or freezing, but were rescued. Time perception may be suspended, and phenomena of timelessness and age regression or progression be experienced. Intense "metaphysical illuminations," the kind of hallucinations which also happen during nitrous oxide (laughing gas) intoxication, may occur and scenes never before experienced, with completely new images, may take form. Visions of heaven and hell are examples.

In addition to visual, auditory, olfactory, or gustatory hallucinations, "electric" phenomena, a feeling as if a body part or system were charged with energy, may also be experienced. This is similar to the Yoga kundalini force.

Body memories of some stressful experience which was related to somatic reactions may be evoked, and manifestations of rapid heartbeat and breathing, contractions of the stomach, nausea, clammy cold hands, and pains may occur. Feelings of sinking, flying, or immobility may be evoked by sensory feedback of certain muscle tensions below the threshold of ordinary perception.

Occurrence of Altered States of Consciousness. These states may occur spontaneously or be induced. Table 5 lists factors involved in the evocation or enhancement of ASCs. The best known, most ubiquitous ASC involving imagery is dreaming while asleep. However, many ASCs occur during the waking state which are usually not recognized or identified as such. Some examples have been cited earlier in this section. Examples of states of intense attention which may evoke ASCs include watching a play, movie, television, or sporting match, or participation in the performing arts or athletics. A patient in a physician's office or a dentist's chair, a client across the desk from his lawyer, and a woman under the hair

Table 5
Factors Involved in the Evocation or Enhancement of Altered States of Consciousness

Internal Factors

Mental
   Fixation on Objects, Sounds, or Feeling States
   Intense Intellectual Involvement
   Free Fantasy
Physical
   Monotonous, Repetitious Activities
   Great Muscular Strain
   Prolonged, Intensive, Convergent Position of the Eyes
Stresses
   Anxiety or Fright
   Intense Emotional Arousal
   Great Mental Stress
Physiological
   Extremes of Body Temperatures: Fevers and Freezing
   Hyperventilation
   Great Pain
   Fatigue
   Alterations of Body Chemistry, Including Hormonal
      Factors, Hyper- and Hypoglycemia, and Poisoning
   Hypnagogic and Hypnopompic Capacities

Environmental Factors

   Fixed Postures
   Rhythmic Monotony in Any Sense Modality
   Sensory Overload or Sensory Deprivation
   Sleep Deprivation
   Sudden or Long-Term Stresses
   Awe-Inspiring Environments, Including Authority Figures
   Ingested and Inhaled Chemicals

dryer at the beautician may all be in ASCs. Modern Western society has mostly overlooked the fact that ASCs occur during religious ceremonies. Most persons, under the multiple influence of a fixed posture, awe-inspiring environment, rhythmic monotony of words or music, emotional arousal, eye closure or eye fixation on candles or sacred objects, and the influence of incense or other odors, fall without recognizing it into ASCs.

Altered states of consciousness with positive or negative hallucinations have been evoked by as diverse psychophysiological methods as Progressive Relaxation and other relaxation methods, Sensory Awareness Training, certain breathing techniques, Gestalt Therapy, Autogenic Training, and Structural Integration. Following are some examples.

During relaxation and awareness training exercises, phenomena like "floating in space," "melting into the floor," "spreading like a drop of oil on water," or "completely losing consciousness of the body in space" have been reported. In a marathon workshop of Gestalt Therapy, a middle-aged woman on the "hot seat," working out some problem related to her mother, had her first hallucination when she suddenly saw her mother's face in space before her eyes. The experience was most frightening to her, but her fright was not recognized by the workshop leader, who was himself not aware of ASCs occurring during Gestalt Therapy.

During the heaviness exercise in a Standard Autogenic Training course, a forty-year-old physician had his first hallucination, seeing his hands "mortified before my eyes in space." This was a powerful personal introduction to ASCs for him. A business executive, while participating in a preventive program for heart-attack-prone persons, reported that while he was in the sitting position on a bench, leaning his head against the wall behind him, during Standard Autogenic Training "there seemed to be nothing in this world but the back of my head against the wall, pulsating with my heartbeat. It was weird, and if I had not been told about ASCs, I would have left the program and never returned. As it is, I am intrigued to learn more." Also during Standard Autogenic Training, while doing the heart exercise, an artistically inclined business manager saw himself conducting Beethoven's Fifth Symphony. He saw the orchestra and score and heard the music "to the rhythm of my heartbeat," which was for him a happy and exciting experience.

There have been numerous reports of vivid childhood memories or of hallucinations of bright colors, lights, flashes, or scenes at painful moments during sessions of Structural Integration (Rolfing).

Finally, while working with a glass marble attached to a chain to demonstrate ideomotor movements, a subject apparently fixated the shining object strongly and saw it as an eyeball with iris and pupil painted on it.

Use of Altered States of Consciousness. Human beings seem to need to spend parts of their lives in ASCs, but modern society has greatly reduced the possibilities for doing so. Listening leisurely to fairy tales or ballads while the mind imagines; vocalizing and moving rhythmically in singing and dancing; participating in or viewing awe-inspiring ceremonies; or performing daily chores naturally in a rhythmic manner are all healthful forms of fulfilling this need. Examples are a mother rocking her infant and singing cradle songs, a peasant mowing with a scythe so automatically and rhythmically that any conscious thought would upset the smooth flow of the movement, or sailors pulling together at a rope to rhythmic chants. Also the experiences of "mystical consciousness," samadhi in Hinduism, satori in Zen Buddhism, beatific states in Christianity, or the internal peace and joy of the nature mystics serve to satisfy this need.

The examples just given illustrate the occurrences of ASCs in a lifestyle which has vanished, and in religious customs which are presently neither popular nor prevalent. Modern man must find other ways to fulfill this need, and if he can combine this with learning at the same time how to handle the stresses of modern life, so much the better.

Altered states of consciousness can be utilized to promote mental and physical relaxation, relieve discomfort, provide diversion, improve sleep, manage pain, alleviate fears and anxieties, increase emotional security, improve sensory perception or disregard stimuli at will, strengthen the ego, explore the subconscious, confront problems and solve them symbolically, and provide edification.

The exercises described in this book were not purposely designed to induce ASCs. However, certain of the exercises for increasing sensory awareness, respiration, anxiety reduction, autogenic training, and so on do spontaneously induce them, and in so far this book may also help to satisfy needs for ASCs.

Managing Altered States of Consciousness. Readers of this book should by now have an idea of what is meant by ASCs. A frequent question is how to terminate these states. This depends on the kind of ASC. In general, the opposite of what the ASC is like will induce termination. For those ASCs in which wakefulness is reduced, the simplest and most effective way is the same which the body uses every morning to arouse itself from the ASC of sleep: it stretches the muscles, inhales or yawns deeply, opens the eyes widely, and looks around until fully awake and back in reality. If necessary, this procedure must be repeated consciously. Some need more practice and willpower than others to become fully awake. Here too the body is its own biofeedback instrument: if the arousal is not satisfactory, activity should be increased by getting up and jumping or running, or by refreshing the face and neck with cold water, to arouse activity of the sympathetic nervous system. If not terminated on purpose, any deeply relaxed ASC will terminate spontaneously by "awakening" when the body is rested.

Altered states of consciousness of high physical arousal, such as dance trances or ASCs elicited by sensory bombardment or great pain must be managed differently. They too will terminate spontaneously if left alone, either in physical exhaustion, or a "peak experience," or by just fading away. They can be terminated earlier by some sensory or physical startle or shock, such as a noise, a slap, or cold water. Any ASC during which anxiety mounts should be terminated, unless it is used therapeutically under the supervision of a therapist.

Another concern may be about "losing consciousness" during ASCs. This occurs every night during sleep. It is suggested that ASCs be induced only in appropriate situations. This excludes all environments and activities requiring alert attention.

There is no harm in continuing an ASC as long as it suits the purpose and environment. However, the state should be discontinued when confusing or frightening, instead of useful and edifying, things happen. If the state is used for the purpose of analysis, unpleasant experiences should also be explored, but in general ASCs should be used to evoke useful and pleasant reactions.

Reasons for not wanting to end an ASC may be feelings of security and happy self-involvement during the state, a desire to avoid reality, or some unfinished subconscious process. In cases in which arousal from an ASC is difficult, the following procedures are helpful: First, stepwise "waking up" or alternate arousal and slipping back, each time less deeply. This procedure is especially useful when the ASC was very deep. Second, purposely prolonging the state for a short time in order to gather the strength to emerge into reality again may be helpful. And third, the state may be temporarily deepened to complete an ongoing subconscious process or to discover the reasons for not wanting to end the state. Inquiries as to the reasons for wanting to stay in the ASC can be made by means of the ideomotor responses described in chapter 3.

New glimpses into the nature of reality as well as into the depths of the mind may evoke at first reactions of fear, and only later those of wonder or edification. Apprehension of the unknown may become downright fear. The important thing in this case is to know what to expect and what to do about it. The following may happen during ASCs. Hallucinations may occur, ranging from the simplest sensory perception to apparent panoramic self-involvement in events or actions. Feelings of unreality may be experienced, ranging from sensations of the suspension of life to those of a blissful, beatific superexistence.

Also, stress reactions may be evoked by subconscious stimuli during ASCs. Such stress reactions are called *abreactions*. This term refers to the process of working off pent-up emotions or disagreeable experiences by reliving them in feelings, actions, or speech. Manifestations of abreactions may be anxiety, pain, or any ANS reaction, such as increased heart rate, sweating, or nausea. Abreactions are either indications of an overstressed or deprived body system or of subconscious mental stresses relating to past, present, or future. They are encountered most frequently during fatigue or momentary stress. Abreactions should not be feared but handled correctly. Those inexperienced with ASCs should neither intentionally evoke nor prolong abreactions, but should let them run their course and "let the mind do what it must" in the knowledge that they are nothing unusual or harmful. Anxiety can be reduced by exhaling, but if necessary the ASC should be terminated if abreactions become disturbing. Those well experienced with ASCs, and psychotherapists with their patients, may induce abreactions purposely to reduce underlying emotional pressure or to analyze past stresses.

Adverse effects of ASCs have been reported occasionally. Unstable or neurotic persons have become more neurotic; immature or imprudent persons have done foolish things; incipient physiological or psychological malfunctions have become manifest. These things occur under many circumstances of diverse stresses and were not necessarily due to the ASCs in connection with which they were reported.

Individuals who experience too overwhelming or confusing imagery during ASCs should not evoke these states purposely and should arouse themselves promptly if they slip into one spontaneously. Any use of ASCs as treatment for medical conditions should be under the supervision of a physician. However, a healthy person should need neither physician nor guru as supervisor to explore ASCs, as long as he proceeds with common sense.

Conclusion

Knowledge of the diverse actions and intricate interactions of body and mind and the resulting constant biofeedback between them is helpful for understanding some apparently spontaneous reactions, without recourse to external or transcendental explanations.

The great individual differences in the predominance of sympathetic or parasympathetic nervous system reactions, as well as in the reactions of the mind, explain many of the differences in individual responses to the stresses of life. It is remarkable how simple some of the interventions are with which beneficial changes can be made. These are discussed in the next chapter.

3. Stress and Coping with Stress

Stress is a normal occurrence in everyday life, and the body has its own systems to cope with it. The ability of the mind to cope with stress depends greatly on the imagination and on subconscious and conscious suggestion. Many methods have been devised for better coping with stress.

Stress

Stress is not, as often assumed, detrimental in itself, and the widespread notion that "stress is bad" has been fostered by the popularization of medical and research findings in experimentally overstressed animals and ill humans. H. Selye, the world authority on stress, whose research originated the work with overstressed animals, stated recently (1973), "Complete freedom from stress is death," and he advised "Live with stress and enjoy it." Many modern persons, however, lack the skills for doing this.

Physiological Facts

Stress is life and life is stress. Even any orientation

response to a new stimulus or any increased level of consciousness in order to do mental work evokes stress reactions, such as a rise in blood pressure and pulse rate, cerebral congestion, and constriction of blood capillaries in the skin of the head and the extremities, as well as other sympathetic nervous system responses.

The body has many mechanisms for counteracting stress reactions. The first is the parasympathetic nervous system, which starts acting immediately as a counterbalancing influence. Another is the hormonal system, which releases antiinflammatory or antistress hormones into the blood stream as soon as blood changes occur due to stress. A third is located in the connective tissue, where the liberation of negatively charged substances immediately counteracts the damaging effects of released histamine and other positively charged chemicals by forming ionic bonds.

Stress Makes Stronger

Not only is stress normal in everyday life, but it may strengthen body and mind. This aspect of stress has not been emphasized sufficiently in modern Western society. Ordinary and regular stressors, such as physical activity, harsh climates, and healthy emotional stimulation, increase vigor, vitality, and stamina in healthy animals and humans. Any farmer, athlete, and soldier knows this; it has been demonstrated by animal experiments (Jencks 1962) ; and history has shown that difficult rather than easy conditions produce achievements (Toynbee 1946). Strengthening due to stress has been called the Teddy Roosevelt Effect in the United States. Fredrich Nietzsche (1888) said about the perfect man, "What does not kill him, makes him stronger." Strengthening through stress is even used in medicine, when treatments of counterirritation, such as protein injections or contrast baths, are used to stimulate the general defenses of the body.

For efficient coping with stress, body and mind must

be kept in good condition by physical exercise and a positive outlook on life. Exercise can be done as recreation if everyday occupations do not provide it. For a positive outlook, self-suggestion and the imagination are indispensable. Long periods of imprisonment or illness have been successfully endured by utilizing minimal opportunities for physical exercise and by allowing the mind a wide scope of activity.

Animals and infants react to stressors much more adequately than do average adults. Adults too often allow stress reactions to occur when they are not appropriate and to continue when they are no longer useful. It is unnecessary and unhealthful to accumulate and perpetuate the effects of the stresses and strains of living. The healthy person must deal with stress at the correct time and in an adequate manner in order to be ready to meet future stress from a recovered, healthy balance. Adults can relearn many healthy, natural reactions to stressors, and most persons can repair damages caused by accumulated past stresses and become able to face everyday stresses in a more healthy manner.

Definition of Stress

The word *stress* is derived from the Latin *stringere*, to bind tightly. It first entered the vocabulary of the engineer, where it means to subject to the action of a force or forces. Everybody knows what it means "to be under stress," but the definition and description of the psychophysiological concept of stress are complicated.

Stress has been defined as: "the state manifested by the specific syndrome which consists of all the nonspecifically induced changes within a biologic system" (Selye 1950) ; "a systemic response, induced by the wave of cellular alterations identical to those which initiate inflammation" (Eyring and Dougherty 1955) ; "a process that occurs when a system is forced to react at a rate to which it is not 'geared' at the moment" (Jencks 1962) ;

"any condition that makes the body mobilize its resources and burn more energy than it normally does" (Morgan 1965) ; "the physical or mental effect of disturbance of, or interference with, any of the body's automatic biological processes" (Stephan 1971) ; "environmental conditions that require behavioral adjustment" (Benson 1974) ; and again Selye (1974) "the nonspecific response of the body for any demand made upon it."

From these definitions it can be seen, though none specifies it, that the concept of *stress* includes both the stimulus part, called *stressor*, and the response part, called *stress reaction* or *stress response.* Since stress responses to a stressor may in turn become stressors, the same physiological event may be called a stressor at one time and a stress response at another.

Stressors

Stressors act through the environment, arise from physiological functions, or are evoked psychologically. They may be pleasant as well as unpleasant, and due to overstimulation as well as to understimulation. Environmental stressors are climate and altitude, noise, change of diet or unhealthful diet, air pollution, social readjustment, overwork or lack of work, and disregard of the natural rhythms of day and night and yearly seasonal cycles. Examples of physiological stressors are illness, injury, pain, loss of blood, or restricted physical activity due to sedentary or industrial work and driving in cars. Psychological stressors are concentration, excitement, fear, anxiety, conflict, uncertainty, anger, disgust, shame, and guilt, all of which act on the human body by tightening muscles, narrowing body cavities and passages, and inhibiting healthy functioning. They are truly factors in modern life that "bind tightly." Little control is possible over environmental stressors, and most adults have been conditioned to cope inadequately with physiological and psychological stressors. However, better coping with these stressors can be learned.

The perception of stressors and the occurrence of stress responses depend on the stressor, the stressed subject, and the environment. The aspects of a stressor depend on its strength, duration, repetition, and additionally present other stressors. Additional stressors may have additive effects or counteract each other's actions. With respect to the stressed subject, his constitution, age, health, sex, and physical conditioning make a difference in what is perceived as a stressor at a certain time. Psychological conditioning, the personal value system, present morale, future goals, the present environment, the environmental value system, and the involvement of others also play a role. The same stressor may be perceived variously at different times and places.

Physiological Stress Reactions

Physiological stress responses involve cellular reactions, general physiological changes, and specific responses of the organism. The cellular reactions are a systemic response, induced by a wave of cellular alterations identical with those which initiate inflammation. Other immediate, necessary, and unavoidable reactions to stressors occur in the respiration, heartbeat, and blood pressure. Histamine, other chemicals, and hormones are released into the blood stream and body tissues, and much interaction occurs between the nervous and hormonal systems, involving practically all endocrine glands, the higher and lower parts of the brain, and the autonomic nervous system as well as the peripheral sensory and muscular systems.

Pathological Changes Caused by Overstress

H. Selye (1950, 1956) studied pathological changes in overstressed animals and sick humans. He observed nonspecific changes, which he called the General Adaptation

Syndrome, and specific responses which depended on the kind of stressor and on the part of the organism on which the stressor acted.

The General Adaptation Syndrome consists of (1) the Alarm Reaction, during which cells of the adrenal cortex discharge hormones, the fluid content of the blood decreases, the chloride level of the blood diminishes, and general tissue breakdown occurs; (2) the Period of Adjustment, also called the Stage of Resistance, in which cells of the adrenal cortex become rich in secretory granules, the fluid content of the blood increases, an excess of chloride is found in the blood, and general building up of tissues occurs, which brings the body back to normal weight. There can also occur (3) the Stage of Exhaustion. This happens when a stressor is overwhelming by being too strong or acting too long, or by other stressors being added. This stage may lead to the death of the organism.

Selye also established a Stress Index which comprises some major pathological results of overstress: enlargement of the adrenal cortex, atrophy of lymphatic tissue, and ulceration of the stomach. He further defined certain pathological consequences of long-term stress as Diseases of Adaptation. Among these he classified stomach ulcers and digestive disturbances, cardiovascular disease and high blood pressure, allergic reactions, connective tissue diseases, kidney disease, emotional disturbances, and headaches.

Psychological Reactions to Stressors

Psychological reactions to stressors or to stress producing situations differ widely. The least efficient reaction is to add anxiety and tensions by trying to block out the stressor or by general negative responses. Denial or repression, withdrawal or isolation, dissociation or overexcitement, inappropriate perseverance, and overconformity are almost always inefficient, if not damaging, ways of handling stressors.

A usual way of coping with stress is by regression, that is, by reverting to a less mature level of functioning or behaving. Such behavior has its merits as a direct reaction to stressors, but it must not become a pattern for reducing long-term anxiety. A negative attitude toward stress, as something inevitably harmful that must be avoided at all costs, can be converted into one in which stress is considered as a challenge.

Managing stress maturely brings satisfaction. This is discussed in the next section.

Coping with Stress

In some ways the body can be used very simply as its own biofeedback instrument for detecting stressors and coping with them sensibly. If the body is too heavy, slimming by reducing calorie intake is indicated. If the body is too weak, exercises for muscle strengthening are needed. If body and mind tire too easily, more rest periods must be allowed and sleeping habits improved. If the body is too stiff, stretching exercises for tendons and ligaments are indicated. If the environment is too stressful for body and mind, it must be changed or better coping must be learned. However, also "understress" must be guarded against. Constant exposure to very mild and undemanding environments weakens body and mind. No great skills are needed for adjusting many stressful situations, but much common sense and good motivation. However, there is more to coping with stress.

Sensory awareness can aid in detecting stressors and stress reactions before they become damaging. Since the processes for recuperation from stress and for repair are mainly regulated by the parasympathetic part of the autonomic nervous system, relaxation training which acquaints the trainee with the appropriate responses and enables him to evoke them at will is of utmost importance. Since both body and mind are involved, both must be retrained.

Stress situations must be assayed objectively and without anxiety; relaxation should be maintained if appropriate; sudden tensions must be released immediately; mental dissociation from the stressor should be attained, and physical removal if possible. A positive attitude toward handling stresses must be developed; self-assertion must be exercised in the face of external pressures, and appropriate and selective adaptability must be developed. Also risk taking within the limits of common sense is useful for meeting the challenges and stresses of life.

For stress prevention, relaxation of body and mind must be achieved, sufficient physical exercise and mental stimulation must be available, the mind must be used positively, self-sufficiency must be increased, and work should be performed in a manner appropriate to age, abilities, and conditions.

Suggestion

The mind is constantly exposed to more or less obvious suggestions from the environment and the imagination. Many of these suggestions elicit fears and apprehensions and unnecessarily intensify the unavoidable stresses of life. How differently may the following suggestive predictions or prayers about childbirth have influenced generations of Indian women of the American Northwest in comparison to generations of Judaeo-Christian women. In the Bible women are told "I will greatly multiply your pain in childbearing; in pain you shall bring forth children" (Genesis 3:16). Among the Thompson Indians of British Columbia on the other hand, during puberty rites, a girl would put stones into her bosom and run with them, and while they slipped down to the ground between her body and the dress, she prayed to the Dawn that, when she should be with child, she might be delivered as easily as she had been delivered of these stones (Frazer 1959).

Conscious, positive self-suggestions with intentional

imagery for inducing healthy psychological and physiological reactions are useful for ameliorating and preventing unnecessary stress.

Suggestion is the mental process by which one thought leads to another, often indirectly, through association of ideas. Suggestions arouse thoughts and desires and motivate action. Self-suggestion is the arousal of thoughts to carry out more or less indirect commands given to oneself. Success depends on the possibility of achievement, the motivation to act upon the suggestion, and the ability to carry it out.

Self-Suggestion

For effective self-suggestion one must be guide as well as subject. Concentration on giving suggestions and cooperation in following the suggestions are imperative. Self-consciousness must be avoided, but positive reactions must be acknowledged and emphasized, while negative ones must be minimized or disregarded. Suggested procedures must be changed if they do not work and better ones substituted. Avoiding self-awareness while acknowledging reactions is an example of contradictions in systems functioning at higher levels, as mentioned under *Aspects of Altered States of Consciousness.*

Suggestions are usually only effective if they are acceptable. They should agree with the value system of the person, serve the intended purpose, be built meaningfully into appropriate activities, and if possible utilize appropriate physiological states, such as the phases of the breathing and activity cycles.

Verbal suggestions should preferably be short, positive, impressive, rhythmic, and rhyme or be alliterative. Some persons work better with positive, some with negative suggestions; some find an authoritative, some a permissive form more effective. Sometimes when a strong, positive self-command does not work, compliance is achieved rather easily by clothing it in permissive terms. For instance, if for weight reduction the command "do not open refrigerator for snacks" does not work, compliance may be attained by "I can refrain from opening the refrigerator." Self-suggestions must be constructed individually for the person who is using them and must be realistic, simple, acceptable, and convincing. Examples of verbal formulas of self-suggestions for different purposes are given in appropriate places in later chapters.

Psychophysiological Effectiveness of Self-Suggestion

Conscious and subconscious thoughts evoke physiological activity resulting in movements which are correlated with the kind of thought. They are called ideomotor or ideophysiologic responses (Cheek and LeCron 1968). Thinking of running will evoke movement responses in the legs and a change in the breathing rhythm. Thinking of the taste of a lemon will evoke certain sensations and initiate salivation. Further, movement of different fingers may be designated to indicate "yes," "no," "I do not know," or "I do not want to communicate." The ideomotor responses are slow and slightly trembling or rapid and jerky. They are not smooth and obvious like conscious, voluntary movements. During ASCs, when cognitive thinking and vocalization are reduced or may even be abolished, these ideomotor responses can be used for communication during investigations or analysis. They can also be used for self-analysis and decision making.

An effective way of demonstrating the influence of the mind on unconscious movements is with Chevreul's (1786-1889) pendulum. Though it has been used for "divination" and for other "predictions" and can supposedly elicit answers from the unconscious, its "magic" is brought about by the ideomotor movements, which are nonvoluntary and imperceptible to the observer as well as to the initiator. The pendulum is a simple device, consisting of a thread or chain from which a small weight is suspended. The string or chain is held between thumb and forefinger with outstretched arm, or with the forearm supported at the elbow. At first the pendulum should be at rest. Then the person who holds it should think that it starts moving in a certain direction, either sideways, back and forth, or in circles. He must wait passively for the pendulum to start swinging while concentrating on the thought of direction. The swinging of the pendulum must not "be confused" by contradictory instructions, lack of attention, or by a conflict with respect to the instructions. Firm instructions to oneself are mandatory for all achievements with self-suggestion.

Many physiological and psychological responses can be evoked by just imagining them strongly, be the response relaxing, sleeping, or exercising. Imagining movements of the joints is especially helpful for deepening respiration. Imagining the full, soft, pink, alive lips of an infant and thinking that one's own lips become similar increase the blood flow around the mouth. Imagining athletic activities or games in all details can be used as a training period for improving accuracy, coordination, and cooperation in athletic performance. This has been called Think Training (Pulos 1969). Self-suggestion coupled with the imagination is of utmost importance for stress amelioration or stress prevention.

Advice for Coping with Stress

Following is a list of suggestions for coping with stress. Practical ways for the implementation can be found in chapters 4 to 9. With respect to using the imagery exercises for learning to cope with stress, avoidance is the least efficient way of coping unless special circumstances indicate it. Its habitual use indicates fear, overcaution, incapability, or cowardice. Confrontation should be used where courage, aggression, and daring are appropriate. Adaptation should be used when the situation calls for flexibility, endurance, or attunement. Elimination of stressors calls for strength, skill, and ingenuity. Knowledge of many ways of coping with stress allows selection of the most appropriate and efficient.

List of Suggestions for Coping with Stress

A. Immediate Responses
    1. Be reality-oriented and objective; acknowledge life's insults realistically
    2. Register the hurt, but refuse to stay feeling hurt
    3. Be elastic: relax or gather strength according to need
    4. Be self-assertive in the face of external pressure
    5. Use fast conscious abreactions: by vocalizing or movement, passing stress sensibly on to the environment, or using the aroused energy creatively
    6. Have a positive attitude toward handling the stressor
    7. Use appropriate and selective adaptability
B. Long-Term Preparation
    1. Accumulate a reservoir of strength
    2. Recondition the autonomic nervous system toward parasympathetic reactions
    3. Decondition feelings of resentment
    4. Change negative stressors and responses to positive ones
C. Imagery Exercises for Learning to Cope with Stress
    1. Avoidance
        (*a*) Hiding behind or in something
        (*b*) Fleeing by running, flying, or swimming away
        (*c*) Changing consistency by becoming permeable, liquid, soft, slippery, resilient, or hard
        (*d*) Going to sleep or into an ASC or diverting mind and body otherwise

(*e*) Playing the role of protector or imagining being protected

2. Confrontation
   (*a*) Meeting head on the fighting, biting, stinging, scratching, making skunk smell, and so on
   (*b*) Bluffing by bristling, puffing up to a large size, gesturing, and so on
   (*c*) Overcoming by outstaring, outsitting, and so on

D. Adaptation
   1. Adopting greater ranges of reactions
   2. Enlisting the stress into service
   3. Developing new capabilities

E. Elimination of Stressor
   1. Finishing unfinished business
   2. Disengaging from unnecessary or dangerous condition, situation, or position
   3. Removing the stressor

Methods for Coping with Stress

Many special psychophysiological methods have been developed in the past to increase mental and physical efficiency or to correct some defect or compensate for it. The oldest of such methods are Yoga and T'ai Chi. Since the turn of the twentieth century many psychophysiological methods have been developed also in the Western world, and since the 1950s they have vastly multiplied, especially as some students of the originators have amplified and modified earlier methods according to needs and purposes.

Methods are often invested with ideas related to the disciplines from which they derived. Authors of those developed for medical therapy may maintain that the method must be "learned from a physician." Gurus and other religious teachers imply or state specifically that proficiency cannot be achieved "without correct guidance." Such instructions arouse the expectation of miracles in some and may deter prospective healthy trainees. The aid of physicians and gurus is appropriate where the sick need medical aid or the emotionally dependent need an authority figure. The average healthy person should have no need for either, but should be able to choose a teacher and learn what he needs, keeping that which is useful and discarding what is not. The important thing is to consider the purpose to be achieved and then to learn what can be done and how to do it.

Methods are frequently named after their originator, main purpose, or some particular aspect, so that it is often difficult to know their purposes and effects without studying them in detail. Table 6 outlines the procedures and purposes of different psychophysiological methods.

Table 6
Outline of Procedures and Purposes
of Psychophysiological Methods

2000 B.C. to Present, in Approximately Historical Order

Hatha Yoga (India): Assumption of certain postures and control of breathing to increase vital capacity, flexibility and endurance, improve balance, strengthen internal organs, and induce altered states of consciousness.

T'ai Chi (China): A series of stylized movement exercises, imitating certain aspects of nature, with the spine as vertical axis and the center of gravity in the lower abdomen, for improving balance, timing, and coordination.

Kung Fu (China): Posture, breathing, and movement exercises to increase vital capacity, flexibility, muscular strength and endurance, improve balance, strengthen internal organs, and induce appropriate attitudes.

Mazdaznan (Persia): Breathing, body alignment, muscle tone, and movement exercises for the improvement of physical and mental health. (1800s)

Alexander Technique (F. M. Alexander, England): Proper alignment of head on spine to correct physical misalignments, attitudes, and behavior. (1910s)

Autanalysis (D. Bezzola, Switzerland): Attention, with closed eyes, to and verbalization of successive internal sensations to induce deep mental and physical relaxation. (1910s)

Progressive Relaxation (E. Jacobson, United States): Alternate tensing and relaxing of skeletal, respiratory, forehead, eye, and vocalizing muscles to induce physical and mental relaxation. (1920s)

Autogenic Training (J. H. Schultz, Germany): Passive expectancy with closed eyes of sensations of heaviness and warmth in limbs, heartbeat, respiration, abdominal warmth, and coolness of the forehead for inducing relaxation and an altered state of consciousness in order to recondition the autonomic nervous system. (1920s)

Self-Massage and Sport Massage (J.-E. Ruffier, France, and H. Surén, Germany): Massage for relaxation, invigoration, muscle strengthening, elimination of wastes, etc. (1920s)

Active Tonus Regulation (B. Stokvis, Netherlands): Ideomotor movements are used to prove the influence of the mind over the body; after eye-closure suggestions for relaxation of muscles, respiration, and mind are used to induce an altered state of consciousness; if necessary, a hand is laid on a tense or sore body part. (1930s)

Reichian Therapy (W. Reich, Germany): Release of chronic muscular tension, supposedly due to emotional "blocks," by breathing and psychotherapy to initiate abreactions which liberate energy and evoke memories. (1930s)

Sensory Awareness Training (E. Gindler, Germany): Paying deliberate attention to bodily functions, perceptions, and sensations, to improve reality-relatedness, calmness, composure, and self-possession in everyday life. (1930s)

Since the 1940s:

Dynamic Tension (C. Atlas, United States): A training course utilizing movement, breathing, diet, the imagination, and especially muscle tension produced by the pressure or pull of one body part against another, for building strong and healthy tissues, increasing and storing energy, and "cultivating a better self."

Table 6. (continued)

Bioenergetics (A. Lowen, United States): Body movements and verbalizations to release blocked or repressed energy and reintegrate body and mind.

Gestalt Therapy (F. Perls, United States): Use of sensory, muscular, emotional, and visceral experimentation to increase awareness of physical and mental processes.

Functional Relaxation (M. Fuchs, Germany): Slow, relaxed exhalations for differential relaxation of body parts and systems and a relaxed breathing rhythm.

Passive Movements (L. Michaux, France): Completely relaxed, unresisting cooperation while another person slowly moves joints of limbs, upper spine, and head to induce deep physical and mental relaxation.

Eutony (G. Alexander, Denmark): Repeated sensing and adjustment of muscle tensions during rest and movement to produce optimal balance of muscle tone in the body.

Awareness Through Movement (M. Feldenkrais, Israel): Movements involving limbs, breathing, facial expressions, etc. are used as bases for sensory awareness training and self-improvement.

Structural Integration (I. P. Rolf, United States): Manipulative force is applied to stretch and lengthen body connective tissue in order to align the body along its vertical axis.

Lymph Drainage Massage (E. Vodder, Denmark): Lymph drainage massage is applied along the lymph channels to remove waste deposits from the system and improve general well-being.

Respiration for Special Accomplishment (B. Jencks, United States): The exhalation and inhalation phases are coupled with the imagination to enhance respectively relaxation or invigoration, warmth or coolness, equanimity or courage, etc., for use in daily life activities and coping with stress.

Relaxation Response (H. Benson, United States): Mental, auditory, or visual fixation, an attitude of passive expectancy, a relaxed posture, and a quiet environment with optional eye closure are used to induce a relaxed state with the responses of parasympathetic nervous system dominance.

Psychogymnastics (H. Junová and F. Knobloch, **Canada):** Movement, relaxation, and an enhanced consciousness of the body's orientation in space are used for increasing sensory awareness and for spontaneous expression of a given theme in pantomime.

Terpsichoretrancetherapy (D. Akstein, **Brazil):** Aural stimulation by drums and music and vestibular stimulation by movement of the head and rotation of the body are used to induce a kinetic altered state of consciousness which results in relief of emotional tensions.

Table 7 matches methods with their intended purposes and effects and also lists additional effects. Many methods have effects which were not intended or were sometimes not even known to the originators. For instance, the frequent inadvertent induction of ASCs during Jacobson's Progressive Relaxation, Gindler's Sensory Awareness Training, Fuchs' Functional Relaxation, Perls' Gestalt Therapy, or Rolf's Structural Integration have often either been denied or not recognized.

Hypnosis and meditation methods are not listed in the tables, since hypnosis eludes definition and meditation methods are usually associated with transcendental or esoteric systems with too many vaguely described procedures.

Useful techniques from the available methods are presented in the following chapters, leaving out esoteric, transcendental, or medical overtones.

Conclusion

The term *stress* includes both stressor and stress response. Suggestions for coping with stress have been offered. However, an important but often overlooked fact is that the body and the mind under stress may develop increased stress resistance or tolerance, so that stress is not necessarily detrimental.

A high degree of sensory awareness is important for

Table 7

Comparison of Main Purposes (*) and Side Effects (+) of Selected Psychophysiological Methods

Effect	Active Tonusregulation	Alexander Technique	Autanalysis	Standard Autogenic Training	Bioenergetics	Functional Relaxation
Physical and Physiological						
Movement Abreactions	+			+	*	
Condition the ANS	*			+	*	*
Improve Respiration	+	+		+	*	*
Conserve Energy	*	+		*	*	*
Improve Sleep	+			+	*	+
Manage Pain		+		+		
Eliminate Wastes						
Improve Flexibility		+	*		*	
Improve Body Alignment		*		+	*	
Improve Balance		*			*	
Improve Posture		*			*	
Strengthen Organs					+	
Strengthen Muscles					+	
Increase Muscle Tension						
Induce Muscle Relaxation	*	*	*	*	*	*
Increase Endurance						
Invigorate the Body				*	*	
Psychological and Mental						
Invigorate the Mind				*		
Cause Dissociation	+		+	+	+	
Cause Time Distortion	+		+	+	+	
Reduce Anxiety	*	+	*	*	*	*
Reduce Perception	*		*	+	+	
Increase Sensory Awareness		+	*	+	+	*
Change the Body Image	+	+		+	*	+
Evoke ASCs	*			*	+	+
Evoke Memories	+		+	+	*	+
Improve Concentration			*	*		
Evoke Abreactions			+	+	*	+
Aid Self-Analysis						
Strengthen Self-Discipline		+				
Improve Reality Orientation		+		*		
Increase Self-Confidence	+	*	*	*	+	+
Strengthen Motivation						

Method	Ratings
Hatha Yoga	* + * + + + + * * * * * + * * * * * + + + + +
Kung Fu	* * * + + + + * * * * * + + + + * * + +
Progressive Relaxation	+ + + + + + + + * + * * * * + * * * * + +
Relaxation Response	* * * + * + + * * * * * + + * * * + +
Respiration for Special Accomplishment	* * * * + + * * * * * + + + + * * * * * * *
Sensory Awareness Training	* * * + + + * + + + + * + * * * + + + + +
Terpsichore-trancetherapy	* * + + * + + + + * + + + + + + *

If a method both increases and decreases a function, the ability to perceive, react, or disregard at will has been increased. Individuals familiar with only one method will generally assign too many purposes and effects to it; those unfamiliar, too few. Those with a knowledge of many methods will best differentiate the effects of the different methods. Since Respiration for Special Accomplishment was based on a knowledge of many other psychophysiological methods, it includes the main purposes of many.

detecting minor stresses before they accumulate and become overwhelming. Sensory awareness is treated at length in the next chapter since it is also most important for the general conscious use of biofeedback between body and mind.

4. Use of Sensory Awareness

Sensory Awareness Training

Origin and Development

Sensory awareness training originated about a hundred years ago in Europe in training methods for the performing arts. Several of the teachers immigrated earlier or later to the United States. See Table 8. Some variations of the early training methods developed into instructions for physical education and health gymnastics, others into breathing therapies and psychotherapies.

The most significant work with sensory awareness training was done by Elsa Gindler (1885–1961) in Berlin, She belonged to a group of physical education teachers who felt dissatisfied with repetitious, mechanical exercises and replaced them by working with natural, functional motion. In a battle against her severe tuberculosis, Gindler discovered that through mere awareness and readiness for change, tense muscles would relax, inhibited breathing become more free, and circulatory disturbances recover. Gindler never gave her manner of working a name, nor did she publish anything. Her extensive notes were burnt in the bombings of World War II. Speads (1944) called Gindler's work Physical Re-Education. Sel-

Table 8

Psychophysiological Methods Developed from Performing Arts and Gymnastics

E. Jaques Dalcroze
(Switzerland)
Music
"Rhythmic Gymnastics"

R. Bode
(Germany)
"Expressive Movement Gymnastics"

B. Mensendieck, M.D.
(Holland to United States)
"Gymnastics for Women"

Schools in United States,
Germany,
Holland, etc.

G. Alexander
(Denmark)
"Eutony"

C. Speads
(United States)

L. Kristeller
(Israel)

C. Selver
(United States)

R. Cohn, M.D.
(United States)

Fr. Delsarte
(France to United States)
Acting

G. Stebbin
(United States)

H. Kallmeyer
(Germany)
"Esthetic Expression"

T. Malmberg
(Germany)

M. Fuchs
(Germany)
"Functional Relaxation"

L. Ehrenfried, M.D.
(France)

S. Ludwig
(Germany)

L. Kofler
(Tirol to United States)
Music

Schlaffhorst
and
Andersen
(Germany)

E. Gindler
(Germany)
"Sensory Awareness Training"

R. Wilhelm, M.D.
(Germany)

H. Stolze, M.D.
(Germany)

F. M. Alexander
(England)
Acting
"Alexander Method"

I. Rolf
(United States)
"Structural Integration"

H. Jacoby
(Switzerland)

J. E. Meyer, M.D.
(Germany)

ver (1957) coined the term Sensory Awareness for it. Ehrenfried (1957), in France, called it Mental Equilibrium Through Educating the Body. And in Germany it has been called variously Concentrative Relaxation Exercises (Meyer 1961), Self-Experience in Movement, or Concentrative Movement Therapy (Stolze 1967, 1972).

Definition and Description

Many sensory stimuli are perceived and reacted to by the body without reaching consciousness. Sensory awareness is consciousness of sensory perceptions.

Sensory awareness training helps to develop clear and accurate perception of the messages of the body. The trainee learns to detect and feel what is appropriate, what must be changed, and how to change perceptions and responses. The body is used as its own biofeedback instrument to discover and correct malfunctioning and misalignment. The training always varies according to the needs and abilities of the trainee, and no repetitive exercises are given as in methods in which movement is used for loosening, rhythm, or role playing.

Sensory awareness training is based on the assumption that man, in the process of civilization, came more and more to disregard his body and must learn again to become more conscious of himself and the body. This opens new dimensions and improves reality-relatedness, self-understanding, and self-assurance. Sensory awareness leads from thoughts and emotions to primary sensations, from talking about attitudes to discovering their effects on feelings and motions, from passive to active participation, and from relating to the habituated past or imagined future to relating to present reality. Criticism and a search for causes do not belong in the sensory awareness method.

Increased sensory awareness leads to giving more attention to narrowed fields of consciousness and perceiving precisely and objectively the relationships between feelings and sensations and the environment. This makes it possible to experiment with and to choose the most effective and appropriate behaviors. The trainee must learn to sense with a fresh feeling, to observe neutrally without being anxious, and to beware of labeling sensations in terms of past experiences. He must become "at home" in his body, accept it as it is, and remain conscious of his feelings. He must allow biological processes to proceed without disturbing them, neither negate nor overvalue his body, and live fully in the present. He must sense himself in rest and motion and in relationship to space, ground, gravity, and objects. He must experiment with and compare relationships between body parts and the environment. He must learn to reinvest automatic actions, perceptions, and sensations with new attention and meaning; he must discover what is best for him, mentally and physically, with respect to natural breathing, posture, relaxation or tension, and appropriate muscle tonus; he must experiment with sensations, attitudes, emotions, and actions; he must learn to decide and choose anew instead of acting habitually, and must develop ways that enable him to cope more efficiently.

In particular, the trainee should become aware of and differentiate muscle tensions, pressures, temperatures, weight of body parts and objects, and the sensations of contact with objects and textures. He should become more aware of gravity in relation to misaligned posture and should consciously accept the support of a chair or the floor. He should learn to be conscious of breathing movements and pressures and their spontaneous changes without feeling compelled to interfere, and learn to be aware of the heartbeat without feeling anxious. Also vascular changes and even glandular functions, such as the secretion of saliva, perspiration, and tears, are perceived and can be used for sensory awareness biofeedback.

General Instructions

Instructions for sensory awareness training should not be direct suggestions to do something, but should evoke individual, immediate perceptions of facts, processes, and reactions. Suggestions given in the form of Ericksonian double or multiple binds (Erickson and Rossi 1975) are useful for this, since they leave the situation relatively unstructured so that the trainee can make his own discoveries. The trainee should observe in a slow, almost lazy manner, as if taking a leisurely walk through his body, and by this means also discover where improvement is necessary.

There is no correct or incorrect way to carry out sensory awareness exercises or experiments, but only the discovery and acceptance of what happens. A passive, yet attentive, attitude is essential for sensory awareness and is facilitated by words like "allow," "permit," or such questions and phrases as "What do you feel right now?" ... "What do you observe right now?" ... "What does your body tell you?" ... "Allow yourself to discover...." "Be ready to sense...." "Allow yourself to undergo...." "Bring into consciousness and stay with...." "Tell the ... to notice..." or "Let the ... feel, sense, and linger." Ellipses in exercise instructions indicate omissions, repetitions, or pauses.

Trainees must approach the exercises with a passive attitude, must become sensitive to what is happening in the body, and must allow ample time for changes to occur. Emotions and spontaneous reactions should not be allowed to interfere with attentiveness to sensory perceptions. Exercise instructions should always be given as detailed and slowly as those described in the section *Individual Sensory Awareness Training* below.

There is no prescribed sequence for sensory awareness training, but beginning with the following instructions

proved useful for beginners. Work with one's own body
and mind is the important thing, and interpersonal rela-
tions will improve concurrently with the training. Interaction in groups is superfluous for sensory awareness
training.

Trainees' reports are added at ends of sections to illustrate the variety and individuality of possible responses.

Exercises for Increasing Sensory Awareness

Individual Sensory Awareness Training

The following instructions are guidelines for individual
work with a trainee or a patient. It is not necessary to
give the whole sequence at one time or in the order presented here. Ample time must be allowed after each question for reactions and answers. The trainee should sit
on a chair or stool while the instructor stands next to
him and says slowly:

"Permit me to put my hand lightly on your shoulder.
Can you feel my hand on your shoulder? Can you feel
your shoulder under my hand? I am now going to take
my hand away gently. Can you feel your shoulder? Keep
your mind on your shoulder; sense your shoulder; feel
your shoulder; linger at that place. I am putting my hand
there again. Can you feel my hand? Can you feel your
shoulder under my hand? Now again, keep your mind on
that shoulder while I take away my hand. Keep your
mind on that shoulder while you feel it, sense it, linger
there. Compare it with the other shoulder. Can you feel
the difference?

"Now I will put my hand heavily on your shoulder.
How does my hand feel now? How does my hand feel
when it is lifted to the position where it touches your
shoulder only lightly? How does it feel, if held just above
your shoulder, where it loses touch but is close enough
that you can feel its warmth? Which one of the three
positions is the most comfortable for you?"

Then the trainee is told to lie down, and the instructor says: "How do you feel lying there? Where do you feel comfortable, and where are you not comfortable? Would you like a pillow? What about your arms, your neck, and your lower jaw? What about your back, your legs, your knees?

"Now, permit yourself to close your eyes, and while you exhale, feel yourself sinking down, slowly and deeply. And now tell me how that feels."

The instructor can evaluate the natural tendency of a trainee to slip spontaneously into an ASC from the reactions to these directions. If the trainee reports sensations of floating or changes in his body image, an ASC has been induced. In this case thorough invigoration by stretching or inhaling is required before sensory awareness of a consciously awake state can be resumed.

"And now, start thinking of the shoulder with which we worked a moment ago. Can you feel that shoulder now? How does it feel? Can you describe it? You may feel it as being more relaxed, more sensitive, or just different from the other shoulder."

If the trainee closed his eyes spontaneously during the sensing, it should be pointed out that he should learn in time to sense, feel, and experience without having to close the eyes, and that closing the eyes may enhance the tendency to slip into ASCs.

Increasing Sensory Awareness During Movement

These exercises draw attention to muscular and sensory awareness during movement in order to discover inadequacies in walking and to observe how moods, such as tiredness, timidity, or eagerness, are reflected in postures and movements.

Tired Walk. Walk through the room as if you were extremely tired. Feel any tensions in your body while walking. Feel also any heaviness, any letting go, any holding back, any oppression. Observe your mood. Note the associations you make with the tired walk. Take your time. Do not hurry. Now walk in your normal way and compare it with the tired walk.

Active "Eager Beaver" Walk. Walk very actively, as if you were hurrying to an appointment or rushing in a big town during the rush hour. Imagine this "eager beaver" walk were a habit of yours. Feel any tensions in the body. Check face and neck, chest and abdomen, arms and legs for tensions. Compare the back and the front of your body. Observe your mood. Note associations you make with this walk. Remember, you are in a hurry. Allow yourself to bump into people. What is your reaction? Then walk in your normal way. Compare the normal walk with the "eager beaver" walk.

Timid Walk. Walk timidly. Imagine that you are afraid to look at people and that you have almost no right to exist in this world. Feel any tensions in your body while you are walking. Notice your breathing. Check what you are doing with your eyes, the mouth, the stomach region. Observe your mood. Note the associations you make with the timid walk. What is your reaction if an "eager beaver" charges into you? Remember, in this walk you are afraid to go ahead. Now walk in your normal way and compare it with the timid walk.

The Trainee's Ideal Walk. Walk your ideal walk. Imagine that you are growing straight upward an inch or so. Note the position of the head, shoulders, hips. Ascertain whether this feels good or whether you are putting a strain on yourself. Let the breath flow. Check any tensions, any relaxation. Observe your mood. Note the associations you make with your ideal walk. Remember, this is your ideal; you have not yet achieved it in everyday life. Walk now in your normal way. Compare the normal walk with the ideal walk.

Trainees' Reports. ("In the tired walk my shoulders sagged and I tended to buckle in the middle. My arms were fairly relaxed, but I lacked support within. I tended to buckle and collapse." "As 'eager beaver' there was a great deal of tension in my arms and legs and around the eyes. I was leaning forward from the waist, my steps were longer, my mouth was set." "With the timid walk I held my chest in tightly, so that my breathing almost stopped. I had a tense jaw and tight lips and felt as if I did not dare look around."

Enhancing Sensory Awareness While Lying Very Still

These exercises draw attention to both normal and unnecessary tensions in the resting body. They show how increased sensory awareness makes it possible to feel consciously the alternation of tension and relaxation which accompany the normal respiratory cycle, and they help to discover unnecessary tensions. Relaxed exhaling and passive inhaling are practiced by means of mental images.

Movement and Stillness. Lie on the floor; arms and legs in a comfortable position; eyes open or closed. Imagine that you are melting into the floor, or that you are spreading like a drop of oil on water. Lie very still. Is everything really still? Feel where there is movement in the body. Feel where there is stillness in the body. Sense it, feel it, linger over it. Observe what moves. Observe the normal movements of the body while you are lying very still. Are there places where normal movements are inhibited due to tensions? Check the chest, the head, the limbs. Feel again where there is stillness and where there is movement in your body.

Detecting Tensions. Feel any tensions in the body while you are lying very still. Sense them, linger over them. Do tensions remain in the same place or do they wander? Become aware of your limbs, one after the other. Could tension keep you from feeling your tensions? Might you be able to feel more if there were no tensions? Release with a deep sigh any tensions which you can locate. Check again your whole body, the eyes, the mouth, the jaw, the shoulders, the arms, the hips, the legs. Where is tension, where is relaxation?

Changes of Tension During Respiration. Notice your breathing. Do not change it purposely. Just observe. Feel where the breathing results in movement. Feel where the breathing seems to be blocked. Feel when the breathing brings relaxation. Feel when the breathing results in tension. Sense it, feel it, linger over it.

Balloon. Imagine during exhalation a shriveling balloon. Feel where the shriveling occurs in your body. Sense it, feel it, linger over it. Do not imagine the shriveling for more than two to three successive exhalations. The respiratory rhythm should never be consciously interfered with for a prolonged period. During the following two to three exhalations, permit yourself to sense and to feel what is happening in consequence of imagining the shriveling.

Ribcage. Lie comfortably on your back; relax while exhaling deeply; then let the respiration take over in its own rhythm. Feel the movement of the breastbone. Feel what it is doing during exhalations. Feel the movement of the ribs during exhalations in comparison with the movement of the breastbone.

Lake. Lie on your back and imagine a lake in the lower abdomen. Feel the water in that lake. Are there waves? Are the waves related to the respiration? Do not change anything. Just feel. Then, if there are no waves, make waves with inhalations and exhalations. Do not use abdominal breathing intentionally. Do not be disturbed by noises from the intestines. Do not tighten up to reduce them, just relax and allow them to occur. Feel the quiet waves from the respiration. Feel how the crest becomes the trough and the trough the crest. Feel the waves going through the whole body.

Pause for Feeling: The Creative Pause. Exhale and feel the arms become heavy and relaxed. Now become very quiet, turn all attention inward, and listen. Become aware of what it feels like to be alive. Listen to your body. Sense any movement, hear any sounds, be very relaxed. Relax deeper with an exhalation, but stay very aware. Feel the three phases of breathing: Inspiration lifts. Allow this to be followed immediately by a relaxing exhalation. Then follows a pause. Wait patiently during the pause and spend it in quiet expectancy. Let the inspiration rise by itself out of this quiet pause. Feel exhalations as satisfaction, equanimity, or the desire to give. Feel the pause as a time for patient lingering, self-adjustments, and restful endurance. Feel inhalations as invigoration, inspiration, happiness, and courage.

Passive Observance of Respiration. Sit or lie in a comfortable position, limbs relaxed and well aligned. Observe the respiration alternately through several sensory systems. Not all have to be tried at the same time. Listen to the sound of air moving through the nasal passages and windpipe. Feel the breath move in and out of the nostrils. Feel the increase and release of pressure in the chest.

Respiration may also be perceived by watching an object, such as a piece of paper, move up and down with each breath as it lies on abdomen or chest. Similar procedures are used in some Oriental methods for carrying a trainee into deep relaxation and meditation.

Passive Observance of Heartbeat. Become very still. Disregard the breathing and become conscious only of another rhythm, which originates from the heart region but goes through the entire body. While being very still, little oxygen is needed. The respiration can become very quiet and slow. It may at times even seem as if breathing stops. Don't worry, breathing takes over by itself when the body needs oxygen. Allow the breathing and the metabolism to rest. If you have anxious or other thoughts, you are not concentrating on the rhythm of the heart. It does not really matter whether you feel it exactly or not, but think of the rhythm of the heart, which keeps you going all the time, day and night, whether you keep track of it or not. Sometimes it goes faster, sometimes slower, and sometimes it skips. That is quite normal. Stay with the thought of your heart for a while and say "thank you" that it does such a good and faithful job for you. And if the thought is pleasant to you, think of the monks on mount Athos, who pray to the rhythm of their heartbeats. — *Trainees' Reports.* "As the drop of oil, I became very flat, as if I went on into eternity. And I seemed to be pleasantly one with the floor." "I did not like the lying still on that hard floor. It pressed, and I became very nervous, and everything started to bother me." "I felt first very heavy and relaxed. Then, suddenly, the floor became very soft. And then I became very light and started floating. That was a strange sequence!"

With the Ribcage exercise: "The breastbone drops in, as if the chest is caving in!" "The sternum moves inward and downward, toward the pit of my stomach." "The ribs seem to stretch and move outward and downward from the sinking breastbone." "I feel a broadening of my ribcage at the sides which feels really good." "My ribs seemed attached with elastic to the breastbone, and then the elastic just 'gave' during exhalation, and on inhalation it pulled tight again."

With the shriveling Balloon exercise: "It was as if the chest collapsed when the balloon shriveled; everything collapsed in. At the same time the tensions in my body seemed to ooze away through the limbs." "I got the image of an umbrella tent, and taking the tent-pole away during exhalation made the tent fold down, and then it went up again, and down again."

"Oh that Lake! I remembered being on a big ocean liner, observing the horizon. And I was the ship which went gently up and down on those long, slow waves."

"I could feel my respiration like a child's toy top. During inhalation it would wind up, and during exhalation it would unwind, just spinning out." "Inhalation made my

chest feel congested. Exhalation opened and relaxed it."
"I had to start yawning, and I yawned and yawned.
But then, during the Pause for Feeling, suddenly everything became very quiet, and I could deeply relax. That
felt good." "I cannot get that Creative Pause. I always
want to inhale immediately. I feel that something could
happen if I'm not on top of my breathing. I guess I am
just not that patient. I liked the other exercises, but I
just don't get that Pause for Feeling."
"Hmm ... that Observance of Heartbeat. At first I
was afraid. You know, my mother died of a heart attack,
and I think I will too. But your sentence about not worry-
ing when the breathing seems to stop, that did it. Suddenly I was not afraid any more, and suddenly I felt my
heartbeat, sound and strong. It was almost a weird
feeling, so healthy and strong."

Detection and Release of Muscular Tensions

Tensions can be produced by tensing voluntary muscles, by holding joints stiffly, by inhaling, and by holding
the breath. Release of tension at the joints makes time
consuming progressive relaxation of voluntary muscles
unnecessary. The imagination, coupled with exhalations,
is the best technique for reducing tensions.

Exercise Instructions. The trainee should repeat an
exercise two or three times within the breathing rhythm,
and for the next two or three exhalations he should sense,
feel, and allow his mind to linger at the place in his body
where he worked. For example, to loosen tension in the
jaw, he may think "let go" during three consecutive exhalations, disregarding the inhalations or allowing the
air to stream in passively. Then, during the next two or
three exhalations, he should allow the Pause for Feeling,
in which aftereffects take their course and during which
he passively observes what is happening or has happened
in the jaw region. The pause for feeling and the passive
observance are extremely important for allowing physio-

logical effects to occur and by that achieving the desired results.

Only small, subtle, careful stimuli bring the results which these exercises are designed to achieve. Gross changes may set up new blocks in the respiratory system or may initiate new inappropriate habits. Thus, just thinking during exhalation "relax the shoulder joint," and allowing the response to the self-suggestion to occur, brings more precise and effective relaxation than physical vibration and relaxation exercises or the tedious repetitions of Jacobson's (1938) Progressive Relaxation.

The relaxation exercises may result in spontaneous reactions related to the respiration, such as sighing, yawning, coughing, or to movements of air in the intestines. The trainee must not interfere with such reactions, but allow them to occur and take their course.

The eyes may be closed or kept open during the exercises. Closing the eyes promotes slipping into ASCs. The trainee should in time become able to do the exercises with open eyes at any place and in any situation.

Since many trainees observe tensions in head, neck, and shoulder regions, the first exercises are for these.

Head and Neck Region. Close the eyes and pay attention to head and face. Observe whether the teeth are merely touching or are clenched. Feel whether the jaw is set or loose. Feel how the eyes feel and the skin of the scalp. Feel if there are any tensions in the neck. Attend passively to any tensions. Do they remain? Do they wander about? Do they disappear?

Increase tension in the head by clenching the teeth. Feel what happens in the temples, to the forehead, to the eyes, around the ears, in the throat, to the tongue, to the space within the mouth, and to the neck. Gently release the tension which you created with a soft sigh. Feel the mouth and lips becoming soft. Purse or tighten the lips as if pondering, or being anxious or angry. Feel whether this creates tension in face, mouth, throat, or anywhere else. Release the tensions gently with repeated exhalations and feel release and softness around mouth and eyes.

Next work at the jaw. Move it and feel during exhalations where the joints are. Release the jaw while thinking "let go" during two or three exhalations. Then sense, feel, and linger during the next two or three exhalations in the area around the jaw. Sense the letting go, the relaxing, and all the sensations which follow in the wake of relaxing the jaw. Imagine the relaxed jaw being a dish and put the tongue down into this dish during an exhalation. Feel whether the tongue is relaxed or whether tightness remains at its root. (Additional exercises for loosening the root of the tongue and the palate are given in chapter 8.)

Stiffen the neck. Feel where this creates tension in head and torso. Relax the neck during a deep exhalation. Feel the release of tensions. Tense the shoulder joints. Feel where this creates tension in head and torso. Relax the shoulders during a deep exhalation. Allow them to let go, to soften, to sag, to hang heavily.

Inhale and hold the breath for a moment. Feel where this creates tensions in torso and head. Release the evoked tensions one by one during successive exhalations. Disregard the inhalations or allow the air to flow in passively. Feel again whether and where there is tension in the neck. Release the tension by thinking "let go" and making very small releasing or nodding movements during two or three consecutive exhalations. During the next two to three exhalations just sense, feel, and passively observe the area where tension was released.

Relaxation of Neck. Let the chin sink gently to the chest during an exhalation. Then slowly and gently, but stretching as far as possible, raise the chin to one shoulder during the next inhalation. Exhale slowly and allow the

chin to return to the chest and the head to hang relaxedly. Repeat to the other side, and also backwards to
both sides.

Complete Neck Roll. Work very slowly, leisurely, and
relaxedly. Imagine the head being a bowling ball on a
cord. Let it sink forward during an exhalation. Inhale
and roll the head up and around to the back. Exhale and
bring it around and down the other side until the chin
rests again on the chest. Repeat this two or three times,
then reverse the direction.

Warm Shower. To counteract tension in the shoulder
and neck region, imagine water from a warm shower
streaming pleasantly over the back of the head, shoulders,
and neck. Feel the massage the single droplets give the
skin. Feel the flow of warmth and relaxation during
exhalations.

Trainees' Reports. "When I clenched my teeth, my
tongue moved upward and pressure developed in my
throat. With relaxation my jaw dropped, warmth
streamed in my mouth, and the tenseness in my neck
relaxed." "Putting the tongue down into the jaw as into
a dish was very relaxing. My throat and even my eyes
relaxed with it." "At first I did not seem to have any
results with the nodding. But when I kept the movements
really small, all the tension in my neck just drained
away."

Shoulders, Arms, and Hands. Relax the joints of shoulders, elbows, and wrists one by one while standing or
sitting. Be very conscious of the joints and think of them
as living connections. Start thinking of one shoulder. It
has a ball and socket joint, held by tendons. Lengthen the
tendons while you breathe out, and repeat this during the
next two exhalations. Then, during the following three
consecutive exhalations, feel, sense, and allow the mind
to linger in the area of the shoulder joint.

Then do the same with the elbow. Lengthen the space
in the joint while exhaling. Allow the lungs to fill with

air passively, and then lengthen again during exhalation. Then, during consecutive exhalations, feel, sense, and linger again where you worked. Do the same for the wrist joint, but see to it that the lower arm is well supported for this.

Tensions in arms and hands can also be relieved by feeling the warmth of the blood in comparison to the room temperature, or by feeling heaviness in arms and hands, when voluntary muscles are relaxed and the arms hang loosely from the shoulders, like plumb lines.

For relaxing the fingers, make or imagine making miniature movements with the fingers while exhaling. Relax the whole arm, but especially the wrist while doing this. Repeat. This exercise is difficult for persons with tensions in the hands. Take ample time for sensing and feeling the aftereffects during the next exhalations.

Trainees' Reports. "Relaxation flowed down my arms, so that they became very heavy." "After doing it with my right arm joint by joint, I could relax the left arm all at once." "My arms feel really relaxed and alive now." "Those finger movements make my fingers warm and alive." "I just imagined putting a drop of oil into each finger joint, and they relaxed so much that I wanted to pop them, and they then popped very easily."

Hips, Pelvic Area, and Legs. Sit on a chair and cup one knee with a hand. During exhalations push the knee gently forward into the hand, keeping the buttocks stationary, thus stretching the hip joint. Repeat during three consecutive exhalations. Then feel the difference between the two hip joints. Repeat for the other side.

Be conscious of the joints in hips, knees, and ankles. Lengthen or stretch them one after the other during exhalations as was done with the arm joints.

For leg relaxation, feel the pressure of the chair against the thighs. Exhale, allow the legs to go limp, and take advantage of the supporting environment, see below. Feel the support which the floor gives legs and feet. Exhale and allow it to support the legs. Feel the legs resting securely and heavily. Feel free to adjust your position to a more comfortable one during exhalations. Then again allow the legs to go limp and heavy while exhaling. Imagine relaxation "draining down" into the legs while exhaling, or imagine something flowing in them. Be passive and allow the flowing to proceed by itself.

Trainees' Reports. "With the hipjoint exercise the tension in my lower back melted away. I have much more freedom in that area now." "Before the hipjoint exercise I had considerable pain in my lower back. I have only a little pain there now." "The whole area of pelvis and lower back feels much warmer and soft." "It not only released my pelvic area and lower back, but also my whole back." "Since those leg exercises last week, I have been able to take long walks again. Before, my legs always started hurting after a short while." "I was never able to get warmth in my legs during Autogenic Training exercises. Since I learned to relax my legs with these exercises, the warmth in the legs comes easy also in Autogenic Training."

Spine. Sit on a chair and think of your spine. Straighten the spine during an exhalation. Then start at either the uppermost or the lowest joint of the spine, and release and relax joint after joint while thinking during exhalations "let go," "relax," or "soften," while allowing relaxation to occur at the joint at which you work. Work at as many joints as you can imagine. It does not matter at how many places you imagine joints. Do it where you think there ought to be freedom of movement. Some trainees imagine only three or four joints in the whole spine, while others imagine more than there are anatomically. Then, for the next three successive exhalations, feel the area where you worked, sense it, linger there. Repeat the same procedure down or up the spine, joint by joint, as long as it feels comfortable. Inhale and stretch intermittently if you get drowsy. Detect the areas

along the spine where the sensations are not so noticeable. These areas need special work.

This exercise should also be done lying on the side,
back, or stomach. One can also imagine making minimal
movements at each vertebra forward and backward, sideways, gyrating, or undulating. This is especially good for
the small of the back.

Feel and sense the effect of working thus on the spine.
Feel and sense the relaxation of the back muscles, the
freedom of movement, the possible change in length of
the spine. The sensing and feeling are the important
aspects, not the physical movement.

Trainees' Reports. "I can feel my whole spine. It seems
a unit made up of bumps. I was never as conscious of it.
It feels very alive." "My spine has an elongated feeling.
I had to move forward on my chair to accommodate this
longer spine. It feels very long and thin." "I could en-
vision a hand going up and down my spine, articulating
the joints. I know that feeling from when we have done
that in reality with other relaxation methods." "My spine
had a liquid feeling to it—it was wonderful! I could imagine bending in any direction." "Those undulating movements made me feel as if I were flying. I sometimes
dream that I can fly, and it was the same feeling of
being able to glide freely through the air."

Sensations of Temperature and Moisture

The sensations of warmth and coolness, moisture and
dryness, are closely related to blood flow and glandular
secretions, and changes are brought about mainly through
the autonomic nervous system and through certain reflexes. These innervating mechanisms are usually thought
of as acting automatically. However, the imagination is
a powerful agent with which to influence blood flow and
glandular secretions, especially if it is coupled with the
appropriate phase of the respiratory cycle.

A healthy circulatory system keeps the tissues of the

body well supplied with needed substances and carries away waste products. Many glandular functions have similar functions and contribute much to the well-being and comfort of the body. Obvious examples are saliva, sweat, and tears. Relaxation of contracted muscles around blood vessels allows the blood to flow more freely, and the skin reddens and expands as the blood vessels dilate in response to warmth and pleasure, but also to irritation. Skin and mucous membranes pale as blood vessels contract due to tension, cold, or anxiety.

Skin sensations can vary from hot to cold, dry to moist, tense to loose, or itchy to comfortable. The perception of skin sensations can be changed by becoming aware of temperature gradients between the body and the environment with its air currents and by using these in coordination with the breathing rhythm for changing perceptions.

Trainees learn with the help of the following exercises not only how to become more aware of autonomic functions of the body, but also how to use the imagination to evoke beneficial physiological changes, and how to influence sensations of dryness or moisture, coolness or warmth. Before one begins these exercises, tensions should be released in the respective body regions.

Warmth in Extremities. Cold extremities can be made warmer and more comfortable by imagining flowing warmth in the skin during exhalations. Thinking "warm" during exhalations and "cool" during inhalations may bring the effect of a contrast bath. Cold hands and feet can be warmed by small, fast, imagined movements of fingers and toes during exhalations. Imagining the soles resting on a hot pad and feeling light vibrations in them during exhalations will bring a sensation of tingling. This may then travel up the legs, bringing the sensation of warmth. Some trainees imagined during the inhalations "charging the battery for powering the hot pad."

Also imagining "somebody's warm hand under the sole

of my foot," "a warm rabbit fur blanket over my arthritic knees," or "bathing that bad elbow in warm water" have been effective thoughts used by trainees to change perceptions of temperatures. Often the differential gradient of the real temperature of body versus environment can be enlisted for changing perceptions. Thus, thinking of the cooler air of the room on a bare forearm, versus thinking of the warmer blood within that forearm, allows two different perceptions at almost the identical place.

Coolness of the Forehead. Coolness of the forehead in conjunction with a relaxed, warm body is conducive to mental work. Inhale while thinking "coolness of the forehead," and exhale while thinking "relaxation and warmth in the lower body." Allow relaxation of the jaw during the exhalations. Repeat the thinking of temperatures for three breathing cycles, and for the next three just feel, sense, and linger at the place of coolness or warmth respectively.

Counteracting Blushing and Heat. Imagine coolness in the face during inhalations and warmth in the legs and feet during exhalations. This counteracts blushing and hot flashes and makes work under hot spotlights easier. Better circulation in the legs will also draw warmth away from the upper body. See the exercises for relaxation of hips, pelvic area, and legs, etc.

Desert Driving. While you are driving through the hot desert without air conditioning, imagine "cool" during inhalations and "relaxed" during exhalations. Allow the relaxation to occur wherever tension develops due to long driving. Exercises during driving should be especially brief in order to avoid slipping into an ASC. However, they may be repeated after a short while as necessary.

Altitude and Climate. To become accustomed to living and working at higher altitudes, inhale more deeply for increased air and energy. If the climate is too wet, think "dry" during inhalations; if too dry, think "moist" during exhalations; if too hot, think "cool" during inhalations and relax during exhalations; if too cool, think "warm and comfortable" during exhalations.

Cave of Mouth. Imagine during exhalations that the mouth is a dark, moist, warm cave. Disregard the inhalations.

Lake in Mouth. Imagine that the Cave of Mouth has a lake at the bottom. Allow the moisture to increase during exhalations. Dry it up during inhalations.

Boat on Lake. Imagine during exhalations that the tongue is a boat which floats on a lake. Feel during exhalations whether moisture is noticeable in the mouth. Feel whether this moisture is cool or warm, comfortable or excessive. If the moisture becomes excessive, think "cool and dry" during inhalations in order to reduce it.

Food. Imagine a steak or something you relish to eat. Notice what happens to the sides of the mouth, to the roof, to the tongue, to the position of the jaw, to the nostrils, to the mucous membranes in the nose, to the throat. For comparison imagine bitter or sour foods.

Infant's Lips. Imagine the full, pink, soft, alive lips of an infant. Imagine that your lips become like an infant's lips. Permit them to become soft, warm, and well supplied with blood during exhalations.

Gate. Swallow hard and feel the place in the throat where the constriction during swallowing occurs. Imagine at that place a gate which can be opened and closed at will. Feel the gate closing when swallowing. Allow the gate to open wide during an exhalation. Imagine again the Lake in Mouth, and then imagine during exhalations opening a water gate at the place where you imagined the gate. Feel during exhalations the water from the imagined lake stream downward through the throat. Feel how far down into the chest it may flow during consecutive exhalations.

Shower or Waterfall in Throat. Imagine a warm waterfall or shower running down inside the wide open throat during exhalations, or just think "warmth and moisture are flowing down." This is good for soothing sore or dry throats.

Nose and Sinuses. Relax the jaw, throat, and tongue. Think of the mucous membranes of the nose and sinuses during exhalations. Feel the air stream out. Disregard the inhalations for the present. Feel the spaces become wider during exhalations; feel them become moist; feel them warming.

Compare the effect of exhalations versus inhalations in the nose and sinuses. Feel the warmth and moisture during exhalations; feel the coolness and drying effect during inhalations. Feel widening, softening, and relaxation in the whole mouth-nose-eye area during exhalations. Feel constriction during inhalations.

For a running nose think "cool and dry" during inhalations and "calm" during exhalations, or disregard the exhalations. For a stuffy or dry nose think "warm, wide, and moist" during exhalations and "light" or "opening up" during inhalations, or disregard the inhalations.

A cough or a tickle in the throat may be controlled by using both exhalations and inhalations. Thoughts like "calm," "warm," "moist," "comfortable," or "relaxed" should accompany exhalations, and "fresh," "cool," or "very still," inhalations.

Eye Comfort. Close the eyes and note how they feel. Are they tense? Dry? Burning? Is there movement? Think of the hollows which surround the eyes. Are the eyes comfortable in their sockets? Consider what might do the eyes good in their present condition and choose from the following. For removing tensions, think "let go," or "loose" during exhalations. Also the following should be thought or imagined during exhalations. To counteract dryness, imagine the eyeball swimming in a warm saline bath. For calming disturbing movements, think "calm and still," "a calming palm cups my eye," or "dark and comfortable." During inhalations, on the other hand, think "cool air streams through my eyelids," or "light and cool," or use both phases of the breathing rhythm by thinking for burning eyes "moist" during exhalations and "cool" during inhalations, or imagine the eyes "floating . . ." during exhalations, and add ". . . in cool water" during inhalations. (More exercises for the eyes are given in chapter 8.)

Skin. Think of the skin in the neck and shoulder region. Feel it and sense it. Then relax the tendons which hold the neck and imagine, during exhalations, the skin being draped loosely over shoulders and neck. Try the same for other skin areas.

Imagine the skin on the back of one hand becoming cool during inhalations, and the skin of the other hand becoming warm during exhalations. This may take some practice before results are noticeable, but it is a very good training procedure for learning to change blood flow.

Itching. Itching may be controlled by imagining breathing through the afflicted skin area with the thoughts of "cool" or "still" during inhalations and "calm" or "relaxed" during exhalations. This has worked for heat rashes and certain allergic conditions. It may take considerable concentration to control bad allergic reactions in this manner. An additional aid is to involve the imagination generally for counteracting a skin condition, as for instance by thinking "I am (exhalation) resting in a (inhalation) cool and refreshing, yet (exhalation) relaxing and comforting, (inhalation) relieving bath." Also thoughts of floating in the ocean, or even diving into cool water in a diving bell, were useful images evoked by trainees for reducing itching of skin areas.

Trainees' Reports. "I never knew how much tension there was around my mouth until I did that Infant's Lips exercise." "I have always cold hands and feet, and I can get my hands warm with Autogenic Training, but not the feet. But that vibrating hot pad—gee, that really worked. My feet are really warm in no time now."

"That boat works well. It opens up all my throat." "I had a tremendous amount of saliva while I imagined the boat, but with the 'cool and dry' during inhalations it seemed to dry up." "The gate opened very well, and there seemed to flow a tremendous amount of saliva, and air seemed to flow down through my throat into my shoulder blades and my chest." "With the Gate I had the image of a great rubber funnel, which went from the throat through the chest into the abdominal cavity. And it closed off at the top while I was swallowing, but with a 'let go' the air flowed all the way down." "I had a tickle in the throat the other day in the theatre, and I did not want to cough. Just thinking 'warm and moist' two or three times during exhalations eased it, so that I did not have to cough. And it went away and did not come back." "Ah, that gate! That was beautiful. The picture of a black tulip came to me, and my throat seemed all relaxed, and wide, and moist from dew."

"I have more difficulty feeling moisture in my nose than in my mouth and throat. But if I first get the mouth moist, I seem to be able to 'evaporate' the moisture from there into my upper nose." "I got the widening and the narrowing and the dryness, but not the moisture." "My nose was running, and I could really get it dry with inhaling coolness and forgetting about exhaling."

"My eyes feel much cooler after those eye exercises. And they feel more liquid than solid." "My eyes became cool, moist, and relaxed." "There was flittering like electricity in my eyes, like impulses. And the coolness worked, but the 'calm' did not. I removed a good deal of my discomfort, but there was still tension, like a block. And then, upon thinking 'the block dissolves' it felt as if a block were dissolving, and my eyes were more open and eased."

Gravity and the Supporting Environment

It is a good habit to take advantage of all possible physical support from the environment. This not only relieves tensions and economizes energy, but it reduces anxiety. The trainee must learn to experience the pull of gravity on separate limbs as well as on the whole body, and the support of floor, bed, or chair while lying, sitting, or walking.

Heaviness. Lie on the floor on your back. Lift one arm a little and then just let it drop heavily while you breathe out. Let it rest there a moment. Now lift it again, but very little, just enough to feel its heaviness, and then allow it to drop again. And now imagine lifting the arm, but don't lift it in reality, just imagine lifting it enough to feel its heaviness. And imagine dropping it while breathing out. Let it rest there, supported by the floor. Allow the body to adjust itself and release any tensions during exhalations. Repeat the exercise for the other arm and each leg. Become aware if all limbs react similarly, or if one has more difficulty in relaxing than another. Practice mainly with those limbs which have difficulties.

Gravity. Sit or lie down and sense the weight of every part of the body. Permit yourself to feel how the earth attracts every ounce of body weight, wherever it is distributed, not only the limbs, but the trunk and every structure in it. Feel also the comfort of having this weight resting comfortably on floor, chair, or bed. Learn to trust in gravity and in the feeling of the heaviness of the body. Feel the security, the steadiness. Sense, with these feelings in mind, real rest and relaxation.

Floor. Lie on the floor and feel your body. Feel especially those parts which have a relationship to the floor. Feel, sense, and linger. Are all parts in contact with the floor? Which parts might make better contact? Check with one hand under the neck, the small of the back, the knees. Do the Loosening Joints exercise in chapter 5, and then do Floor again. Feel whether now more places make closer contact with the floor.

Sitting. Sit on a chair. Sense and feel with which parts of your body you are sitting. Where is your weight? Where do chair and floor support you? Where is your center of gravity? Are there any unnecessary tensions? Check your shoulders, neck, jaw, eyes, throat. Check the arms and legs. Redistribute your weight and adjust your center of gravity so that you expend the least energy to stay centered within yourself while sitting.

Feel how much weight you let the chair and floor support. Allow all your weight to be supported adequately. Raise one foot and feel the redistribution of weight. Do the same with the other foot. Then allow the floor to support the whole weight of both legs, and allow the seat and back of the chair to support your upper body. Feel, during exhalations, how the chair securely supports the weight of the body. Use this way of sitting for reducing tensions and anxiety.

Now experiment with sitting. Lean against the back of the chair. Then sit without resting against the chair. Are you sitting in the chair? ... on the chair? ... hanging? ... leaning? Experiment sitting up straight, then slump. Do it again slowly and feel how the center of gravity and tensions change. How do the two postures differ? Where are too many tensions? What about relaxation? Now sit upright but easily. Take all possible support from the back of the chair, the seat, the armrests. Keep the feet securely and comfortably on the floor. If necessary support feet and lower arms by raising them with a footstool or pillow. Let tensions flow down and out of the body into the chair during exhalations. Feel the support from the chair.

Now move away from the back of the chair and sit vertically. Almost leave the seat a little and then allow gravity to take over just enough to lower your bones onto the seat. Let it support the smallest body area on which you can sit. Feel where the body meets the seat. Explore your sitting structures. Raise one buttock and slip one hand under it, palm down. Gently raise the other buttock and slip the other hand under it. Where is hardness, where is softness? Distribute your weight on both hands. Make small movements with the hips, as if walking or rotating. Feel the lowest parts of the pelvis, the "sitting bones." Notice the unnecessary padding. Sit simply supported by the architectural alignment of the bones. Allow freedom of legs and spine. Notice your posture. (See Figure 3).

Once more explore the reality of sitting: the stool or chair, the pull of gravity, the structure of the skeleton, tension or relaxation in different muscles, aliveness and changeability, contact, and support.

Experiment in a similar manner sitting on the floor in any position or squatting.

Center of Rest. Sit on the edge of a straight chair or a bench, your lower legs vertical like two columns, about two fists apart. Imagine the spine being elongated vertically through the chair to the floor, so that your legs and spine form a tripod on which you sit. Sway gently and explore your balance. Straighten the spine during exhalation. Sit with easy grace. Feel yourself as a center of rest around which everything else moves and from which you can move, act, and exert force.

Standing and Walking. Stand without shoes, feet securely on the ground. Feel the supporting floor during exhalations. Sway gently and establish your balance. Continue feeling the support from the floor. Imagine during exhalations that tensions are flowing out of you into the floor. Feel again the support of the floor. Feel the feet squarely on the supporting floor or earth. Inhale in order to increase strength and power. Then walk a few steps, exhale, and feel the support of the ground.

Stand, sense, and feel which position requires the least energy to counterbalance the pull of gravity. Experiment with the smallest changes in weight distribution, unbalancing, and rebalancing. Dare to give up a habitual position or posture. Discover the constant flux around your center of gravity. Al'ow the changes from moment to moment. Come to be really in touch with the ground. Stay in touch with the ground. Move your feet so that they can stay in touch with the ground. Become sens:tive to the fact that you are standing: inside your middle, in your skin, with your breathing. Are your fingertips aware of your standing? Your shoulders? Your legs? Your head? Let them cooperate. Notice the tonus of the muscles of the legs, pelvis, and back. Tell them to allow easy standing.

Third Leg. Stand, and again straighten the spine during exhalation. Imagine the spine extended to the floor like a third leg. Imagine that the extended spine and your legs are a rather high, three-legged stool on which you can gently lean, or one of those British hunting sticks on which you can "sit while standing." Do so by relaxing the buttocks minimally during exhalations. This should release tension from the back of the legs and the lower back. If tension results in the thighs, the movement was too great or you are doing something else wrong.

Tail. Imagine the spine continuing in a tail which just barely reaches the floor, or wearing a dress with a train. Drop the tail or allow the train to trail while you breathe out shortly, and feel what this does to the hips, pelvis, and lower back. Walk slowly, and imagine being supported by the Third Leg or feel the Tail drag slightly on the floor. Notice how this walk will loosen the hip joints and take the pressure off the legs.

A variation of this is the "dinosaur" (Todd 1937) : "imagine a dinosaur tail dragging from the end of your spine, and your legs trying to run away from it."

Walking. Stand without shoes and be consciously in touch with the floor with your feet. Shift your balance very slowly and sense every movement of making a step forward. Do the same for a step or two backward. Feel the shifting weight, the positions of the bones, the movements of the joints, the changes in touching the supporting ground. Mobilize only precisely the energy necessary to counterbalance gravity. Do not waste energy. Do not overactivate body structures or systems.

Stick. Gindler's famous "broomstick exercise" requires

total relaxation, complete absence of anxiety, and giving oneself up to gravity and the supporting environment. It is not often practiced these days.

The basic prerequisite for this exercise is that the trainee be thoroughly familiar with and experienced in the above described exercises—Heaviness, Gravity, and Floor. Lie down on the floor completely relaxed, with every limb and every part of the body supported by the floor. While remaining as relaxed as possible, slide a round stick, like a broomstick, under the spine, so that all vertebrae and the back of the head are lying on the stick. The important thing is that the stick is rolled under the body with the least expension of energy and that conscious contact is kept every moment during the movement with the feeling of gravity and relaxation. If the exercise is done in this manner, the stick is not experienced as torture, but the spine seems to align itself along this hard and straight support, and this is sensed as pleasant. If, on the other hand, the spine is ill aligned and the back muscles tensed, this posture becomes torture. The trainee must allow himself to accept the stick and the sensations it brings, feel how complete relaxation changes perceptions and sensations along the straight, well aligned spine, and feel what sensations remain after all anxiety has left.

Trainees' Reports. "With that Heaviness exercise I just felt like a giant rag doll! I have never been so relaxed in my life." "Sitting with the slump I felt squeezed inside, and I could not breathe." "Gee, putting those palms under my sitting bones—I never knew I was sitting on so little and could balance so well!" "Moving away from the back of my chair, my center of gravity seemed to move up, and I had more freedom of the thorax in this position." "Moving away from the back of the chair was less comfortable since it required more effort." "The ground under me seemed alive in standing. And yet I seemed anchored to it, just like a tree with its living roots."

"I felt tension released in the small of my back. Letting the tail hang down gave me the feeling of aliveness in the back and the pelvic area." "I know what I did wrong at first. I went too far. It just takes the smallest movement to relax the lower back and pelvic region." "The Third Leg and Tail would not work at first. Then I tried it with one leg after the other and it worked. And now I can do it with both at once." "My legs feel much more comfortable since imagining letting my tail hang down. That releases the tensions in the backs of my legs." "Lying on the stick I felt as if I was two parts, right and left. And then afterwards, without the stick, I felt like one broad mass."

Relaxation Through Attending to Internal Sensations

In this simple technique, the body serves as its own excellent feedback instrument. It was first described by Bezzola (1907, 1918) in Switzerland and was used to calm excited patients or to teach them how to preserve nervous energy rather than expend it unnecessarily. The procedure is simple.

Sit or lie down comfortably; close the eyes, and pay attention passively to anything which goes on in the body. Describe aloud whatever happens. Do not analyze; do not intellectualize; just pay attention and report what is sensed. Scan the body and feel more clearly what is happening in different places. For example: "Pressure in stomach ... eyes flutter ... right ear rings ... throat tight ... left foot itches. ..." Omit all unnecessary words and all personal pronouns and articles, such as "I ..., my ..., and. ... " Just observe and describe locations and sensations felt. The verbalization, even if only in whispers, is an important aspect of the technique, and it must be adhered to for private use or in therapy. Gradually this procedure quiets restlessness and clears the mind. After a few minutes, sensations become fewer and a calm state, possibly sleep, follows.

Emotion as Motion

Behavior is habitually emotional, and a reaction to feelings. It is rarely rational. The body records the emotional thinking, and for every thought supported by feeling, there is a muscle change which can be seen or felt by the sensitive observer.

A trainee should in time learn to perceive, observe, and distinguish. He must, for instance, identify excitement as different from fear or joy, and overtiredness as different from depression.

Sensations usually arise in the framework of past experiences, but a trainee must dare to be conscious of his feelings in a new way, without constantly referring to past sensations, actions, and reactions.

Movement is freely used as one of the healthy manifestations through which pleasure and displeasure are expressed. Children and animals do this much more freely than adults. Much adult anxiety results from restriction or inhibition of the motions of emotions. A trainee must learn to notice where he holds back, in order to let go; where he suppresses, in order to explode or allow other means of decompression; where he narrows, in order to allow widening; and where he hardens, in order to allow softening. The restrictive action of anxiety and techniques for coping with it are discussed in chapter 8.

Sensing the Simple and Spontaneous

Teachers of sensory awareness often refer to the simple and spontaneous behavior of animals and infants. Usual examples are: ease of movement, exploring "gravity," alignment of body, spontaneity of action, and "animal comfort." The ultimate purpose of special exercises is to help adults regain such behavior and sensations. In the course of doing the exercises, the trainee discovers physical and mental blocks and learns to allow them to dissolve or disappear, or to remove them. The exercises are useful for self-analysis or for use in analytical psychotherapy.

Animal Behavior

Snail. Imagine being a snail. Do you carry a shell in which you live or are you naked?... Ask yourself, are you stiff, inhibited, or lazy from the cold of the night or even immobilized by winter, or are you moving and nibbling fresh greens on a spring morning?... Are you feeling, sensing, thinking as a snail? Are you soft, very pliable, and possibly so slippery that the human hand that wants to grasp you has no hold? Experiment... sense... feel... linger....

Dog and Cat. Imagine alternately being a dog and a cat. Imagine alternately making their respective noises. Mew, bark, growl, hiss, or purr.... Which suits you best presently? Imagine confronting different persons or being in different situations. What doglike or catlike communication or other behavior would you use?

Cow. Imagine being a cow. Feel the tough leather hide, the satisfaction of complacently chewing the cud in a meadow. Sense, feel, experiment with the imagined environment around you. Do you feel useful? Satisfied? Bored? Or what else are your sensations and thoughts?

Bird. Imagine being a bird. What time of year is it? What kind of a bird are you? Are you fluttering... singing... chasing another bird in anger, play, or love? Are you sitting on a branch... gliding high above the earth? Feel the freedom, see how small and distant the earth lies below you... how small and insignificant the abodes of man seem from your height.

Horse. Imagine being a horse. Are you fenced in in a pasture... ranging free... in a stable... or elsewhere? Are you a work or pleasure horse, or a wild one? In which century are you living, now, when horses were used by knights and peasants, or before man encumbered the animal kingdom? Are you alone, or what other animals are around you?

Fish. Imagine being a fish. Are you gliding freely through the ocean, in a river, or in a fishbowl? Is clear water around you, muddy water, salt water, or fresh water? Are there plants and stones to hide behind from an enemy? Feel the support of the water and the freedom of movement as you swim.

Bear. Imagine being a bear. Feel your posture on your four feet. Imagine rearing up, a little awkwardly. Are you loveable, threatening, or something else? Feel yourself lying in the sun . . . or in your den. . . . Feel your soft fur. Allow your skin to be draped loosely around you . . . loosely and softly. . . . Look around you, are there other bears in sight? Any cubs? Is the environment to your liking, or where would you rather be? Feel . . . experiment . . . sense.

Awake Cat. Imagine being a very awake cat, intensely awake, so that you can feel it in the tips of the hair of your fur. What is it that makes you so awake? . . . Pleasure or apprehension? Allow yourself to feel intensely awake and aware. What are you doing with your breath? Your limbs? Your eyes and ears? Look for some goal. . . . Are you approaching it stealthily or getting at it in one big jump? Feel your alertness, your agility, your strength. . . .

Resting Cat. Imagine being a purring cat, just about to go to sleep, lying comfortably in a sphinx position. You are breathing deeply and quietly, the haunches moving up and down, slowly and regularly with every breath. Imagine feeling or watching these movements. . . . Feel as if there were nothing in the world but these relaxed, rhythmic movements. Imagine that the air you breathe is moving in and out through the skin where you perceive the movement.

Stretching Cat. For this exercise, actually carry out the movements in the phases of the breathing rhythm. Imagine that you are a cat who just wakes up from sleep.

Stretch during an exhalation, and then arch your back during an inhalation. Feel how stretching during an inhalation differs from stretching during an exhalation. Repeat this, and then relax completely during an exhalation while imagining going back to sleep in the most comfortable position possible, and actually "purr" softly.

Snake. Imagine being a snake, uncoiling and rearing. Stretch during exhalations when and where you feel resistance in the spine. Be very straight with your upper body in the air and look around keenly during an inhalation. Then coil down again and settle back to sleep in the sun.

Oyster. Imagine being an oyster. What do you feel, the hard shell . . . the softness inside . . . the water around you . . . or is it sand? . . . Is everything soft inside you or is there something hard? Could it be a concretion, maybe a real pearl? . . . Where in your body is the hardness? . . . Feel . . . sense . . . explore.

Spider. Imagine being a spider, very agile, very long legged. A hand wants to catch you. . . . What do you do? Do you run away? Bite? Let yourself down on a thread . . . or something else? Do you dare to hang free from the ceiling, suspended in the air, with possibly an idea of how long your thread is, but no knowledge how far to the ground? . . . How do you feel dangling there, moved by a breeze, hanging by but a thread? . . . Then find your way back to the ceiling or down to the ground and start walking . . . walk up a wall . . . walk upside down on the ceiling . . . feel . . . sense . . . experiment.

Animal Comfort. End any longer series of exercises by just relaxing in a position most comfortable to you, and feel the "animal comfort" which comes with healthy relaxation.

Trainees' Reports. "I was such a happy snail in my house—all well protected, only ever so often I put out my feelers to see what was going on in the big world." "When I was angry, I would be a dog and bite and bark at persons, but with people I liked I was a cat and just lay there and purred." "The cow I did not like at all. It was too passive. I am just an eager beaver by nature. And also that leathery skin does not appeal to me—but I loved being the bear with the cuddly fur coat!" "I was a sea gull, just sailing over the Salt Lake valley, and it looked like when the pioneers came, and I was one of those who saved the crops from the crickets. And then suddenly I saw the valley as it is now, all houses and developed, and I could not even find a field to feed on, and that made me sad." "I was a Kodiak bear, so big! And I just lorded over everybody and everything!"

Infant Behavior and "Growing Up"

These exercises allow insight into movements, momentum, and the experience of gravity, and they provide situations in which "growing up" and becoming self-sufficient can be practiced.

Exploring Infant Movements. Lie on the floor in any desired position. Imagine being an infant which does not know how to sit up. Begin to experiment with movements of the head, hands, and feet and later the larger limbs. Allow yourself the surprise of making an unexpected movement. . . . Let the movements be as random as possible. Do not allow them to fall into a repetitive pattern for long. Rest when they become a chore, and allow movements to start spontaneously when lying still becomes boring. Imagine being very calm and somewhat sleepy . . . then, being happily excited . . . then being angry. . . . Sense, feel, explore how these feelings become movements. . . . Now begin to push or pull the body away from the ground . . . at first just the head, a hand, or a foot. . . . Push with an elbow or try to roll over. . . . What parts of your body seem to be in the way? Just explore. . . . Do not use any previous knowledge of movement or momentum, but learn by just experimenting. Explore how difficult

it is to move larger limbs lazily, but the relative ease when the excitement of anger or joy "motivates" them.
Learning to Stand on One's Own Feet. Lie on the floor and imagine that your motor apparatus is maturing: the supporting structures of bones and tendons become stronger, the muscles start to contract and relax at will and begin to move the supporting structures, and coordination develops, allowing useful movements. Start to defy gravity by pushing and pulling against it.

Have some solid furniture at hand to grasp or lean upon and move from lying on the floor to a sitting position. ... Slide or drop down again, and move from a lying position to a crawling position. ... Crawl at first by exploring more or less random movements, then become more and more agile "on four legs." Allow yourself again to change from lying to sitting or from lying to crawling and back to lying with complete awareness. Be awake to changes, be adjustable. ... Repeat the process with closed eyes for better sensing the functions of your proprioceptive system. ... Find your own way to move, to get into a position, to hold it through constant small adjustments.

In learning to stand and walk, a child must explore the action of gravity on his body, and he must repeatedly let himself glide or fall to the ground, and must make efforts to get up again. The falling is dispersing energy, and reaching relaxation and entropy. The getting up uses energy and brings structure, order, and growth. It requires examples, repetitions, and patience to achieve this.

Learning to Walk Alone. This means first to be able to stand on your own feet, remaining upright, and daring to be without support. Sense, feel, explore this posture as if it were an absolutely new sensation. ... Do you long for security and protection? ... Do you feel like exploring new possibilities, but also new dangers? Can you go far enough ... but not too far ... ? Stand and then sense and explore the process of walking slowly forward

... backward ... sideward. ... Leave your base of support on two feet, sense the changes of equilibrium ... return to equilibrium and secure support from the floor. Sense the space traveled with one or more steps.

Does knowing how to walk give you new self-assurance? ... Do you sense new possibilities? ... Do you have new aims? ... Where and what are the new dangers?

Practice the new function: the stop and go ... stumbling and catching yourself ... falling and getting up ... surprise and possible pain ... courage to try again. Feel the joy and satisfaction of a new achievement. Appreciate the fact that you can walk!

Playing Gravity. Drop something. ... See it lying there ... and pick it up. ... Sense, feel, explore the movements. Defy your old habits and experience the unaccustomed. Allow new, meaningful movement to develop.

Body Image and Body Language

Sensing the Body. Stand, sense, and explore different parts of your body. Feel the length of your arms. Feel the size of your hands. Feel the length of the torso from the bottom of the pelvis to the top of the neck. How much space is between your shoulders and the floor? ... between shoulders and knees? ... between feet and the top of the head?

Feel the separation between torso and head. ... How long is the neck from the shoulders to where the skull starts at the back of the head? ... Lengthen the neck straight upward during an exhalation. Allow the head to rise during an inhalation. Allow the arms to hang like plumb lines during an exhalation. ... Tell the shoulders to let go of the neck. ... Tell the neck to let go of the head .... How long does the neck feel now?

Feel the connection between head and body: the bones, the tendons, the skin, the passages, the nerves. Allow small movements. ... Then sense again. ... Feel the width, the depth, the coordination of skeletal structure, the tissue masses.... Detect some organic functioning. ... Feel the blood, the warmth, the streaming, the pulsating.... Feel the coverings of the body, the hairs on the skin, the moisture at mucous membranes. Sit upright and bring your hands easily and gently to the top of your head. Let them rest there lightly. Assay the space between your hands and your sitting bones. Think of all the structures and functions inside you in that space.... Allow them ample room.... Be aware of the space.... Make any necessary readjustments in posture during exhalations.... Feel aliveness during inhalations. Allow the hands to return and rest on the thighs. Allow the feeling of the inside space to remain. Sit with eyes open, very sensitive to yourself, very alive.

Become aware of the shoulder-neck-head region.... Allow the head to be carried by the whole spine, not only by the neck. The neck-shoulder region is the crossing point of the vertical and horizontal axes of the body. It is related to many necessary and to many more unnecessary tensions. Allow this area to be a fulcrum, a central, pivotal point around which everything can rotate easily.

Changing the Body Image. The body image can change spontaneously in many ways, as indicated by certain remarks in the Trainees' Reports. Following are diverse instructions for changing the body image on purpose. Such changes may be initiated for experimentation, for reducing certain stresses, or for therapeutic purposes.

Hand Pressing. Support both hands lightly on a table. Then, keeping the shoulders as even as possible, press one of the hands as hard as possible on the table to the count of fifty, or approximately one minute. Keep the other hand as relaxed as possible. Then relax, sense and feel, and notice not only what happens to the two hands, but in the two halves of your body.

Excursion. Make an exploratory trip through either the right or left half of your body, but stay on one side only. Imagine that you see and touch as you move through all the different tissues and spaces: the bones, the blood vessels, the connective tissue, the special organs, and especially the spaces between them. Go up and down the long marrow cavities in the long bones and through the thickness of muscles. Go along blood vessels and explore organs. Turn your whole attention to them. Then sense and feel how the perception of the side of the body to which you paid attention differs from the other side. Allow the sides to equalize by imagining what ought to be done, utilizing inhalations and exhalations, as described in the next chapter.

Directed Breathing. Choose one side of the chest and work only with that side. Imagine at first that all the air you breathe flows into the tip of your lung, way up at the shoulder, while you breathe in deeply. Disregard the exhalations. Breathe slowly, so that you do not overbreathe, for four to six breathing cycles. Then imagine that all the air you breathe in flows way down, to the bottom of that lung, down at the waistline. Repeat again for about four to six breathing cycles. Then do the same, imagining that all the air you inhale flows only to the middle of that lung, between the places at which you worked first. Then feel how the side of the body into which you breathed differs from the other side. Check not only the chest, but face, arms, legs, and the whole body image. Be sure to equalize the two body sides by again imagining what needs to be done and incorporating inhalations and exhalations, unless you want to experiment purposely with feeling how long the aftereffect of the exercise remains.

Skin Changes. Imagine your skin as a hard shell, like that of a turtle. Then imagine changing it into a cowhide, leathery and tough. Now change it into something very soft and cuddly, like a furry animal or a fur coat. Imagine it again becoming hard or tough during an inhalation. Change it to soft and loose during exhalations. Experiment with imagining yourself in different situations, and "try on" which kind of skin is the most appropriate.

Toad. In order to change your body image on purpose for a stressful situation in which you feel too small and powerless to cope, imagine that you are a toad. Inhale and blow yourself up to an enormous, imposing size. Stay this size in your imagination, but relax while you exhale.

Body Language. The interactions of body and mind are incessant, and the term *body language* has been used in at least two ways. One is that body movements, positions, gestures, and facial expressions denote what a person feels or thinks, though his words may contradict this. An example is the person who, while sitting on a straight chair, stretches his legs far out, almost to a lying position and yawns, saying at the same time aloud "No, I am not tired and bored!" Such body communication is used much in Perls (1969) Gestalt Therapy and related psychotherapies. The other kind of body language are body-related expressions in speech. These are usually much more adequate to convey true meaning than all the modern euphemisms. For instance, the obsolete "having an alvine call," from the Latin *alvus*, meaning belly, is much closer to fact, with respect to the message being sent from the body and received by the mind, than the expression "needing a bathroom," or worse yet, "searching for the powder room."

The oldest recorded body language known is over 5,000 years old and was mentioned in chapter 2. It is the human head with its hair standing on end as the symbol for the word "furious." Many examples could be given, as "to put the finger on," "to be broken hearted," "to take heart," or "to keep in touch"; also "to get a kick," "get off my back!" or "to get a leg up." The important aspect of body language with respect to sensory awareness training is that practicing such verbal expressions in the imagination and expressing them in body movements can be very useful for changing sensations and behavior, as for instance, "keeping the chin up," "getting more backbone," or "having guts." Any trainee should be able to develop the exercises he needs for himself after sensing his deficiencies and deciding what ought to be done about them. In the following section a method is described in which sensory awareness of physiological processes is used for inducing a relaxed, altered state of consciousness.

Schultz's Standard Autogenic Training

Schultz's Standard Autogenic Training (Schultz 1932, Schultz and Luthe 1969, Jencks 1973) was experimentally developed from investigations started in German medical hypnosis around 1900. The method is based on the development of sensory awareness of ongoing physiological processes, mainly muscle relaxation, body warmth, and the rhythms of heartbeat and respiration. In addition the temperature gradient between the body and the environment is sensed on the forehead.

A summary of Schultz's training procedure is given in Table 9. The method has proved especially effective for long-term reconditioning of upset autonomic nervous systems. The changes brought about by the practice of Standard Autogenic Training are diametrically opposed to those evoked by stress, and many stress-induced symptoms can be counteracted successfully by autogenic training. The method is also useful for improving self-command and self-sufficiency. For its use in medicine and psychotherapy, the reader should consult W. Luthe's volumes on Autogenic Therapy (Luthe 1969-1973).

Jencks (1975) designed a program for children, called

Table 9
Training Procedure for J. H. Schultz's Standard Autogenic Training Exercises

Exercises are practiced three times daily. During each practice session the sequence of formulas and the procedure for ending the exercises is repeated three times. The standard formulas are repeated only after the trainee is in his training posture, has closed his eyes, and, if desired, has carried out a preliminary relaxation. Each formula should be repeated four to seven times. Heaviness is practiced for at least one week before the other five formulas are added successively at approximately weekly intervals, the training periods becoming longer and longer.

A minimum of six weeks should be allowed for learning the six standard exercises since a shorter time does not allow sufficient time for conditioning. As training progresses, and after all six formulas have been added successively and mastered, they may be shortened. After several months of training the trainee should be able to achieve the induced altered state of consciousness by simply thinking: Heaviness—warmth—heartbeat and respiration—solar plexus—forehead.

The Standard Formulas

1. Heaviness: "My right arm is comfortably heavy." If, with practice, the feeling of heaviness in the right arm is achieved regularly, becomes more pronounced, and generalizes to other limbs, the formula is extended to include the other limbs: "My left arm..., both arms..., my right leg..., my left leg..., both legs..., arms and legs...."
2. Warmth: "My right arm is comfortably warm." The same progressive procedure as with heaviness is used for the warmth formula.
3. Heartbeat: "Heartbeat calm and regular," or just passively observing the heartbeat.
4. Respiration: "Respiration regular—it breathes me," or passively observing the breathing rhythm.
5. Internal Warmth: "Solar plexus comfortably warm."
6. Coolness of the Forehead: "Forehead pleasantly cool."

Procedure for Ending the Exercises

After the standard formulas have been repeated four to seven times in the sequence given, the altered state of consciousness is ended in a manner similar to awakening from a deep sleep. For this the trainee repeats to himself and acts out:

"Flex and stretch arms! Inhale or yawn deeply! Open eyes!"

the Autogenic Rag Doll, in which all aspects of Schultz's autogenic training are included, but which works through imagery instead of with Schultz's precise, intellectual formulas. Sensory awareness is aroused through images, for which suggestions are made in the form of Erickson's (Erickson and Rossi 1975) therapeutic double binds. The program is useful for children, as it can be assigned as an exercise. It has also proved valuable for relaxation in the elderly and in the procedures for natural childbirth.

Following is the approximate wording of the Autogenic Rag Doll. Wording, imagery, and length of repetitions should be changed according to need. Inappropriate, unpleasant, or useless phrases should be disregarded and those suggestions repeated which work best.

The exercises should be done in a quiet place and at a comfortable temperature, if possible. A blanket should be used if the room is cool. The body should be comfortably supported in a symmetrical lying or sitting position. Tight clothing should be loosened. For the first few days, Heaviness of the Limbs alone should be practiced. Then, one by one, always after a few days of practice, the other exercises can be added. If the total series becomes too long, Heaviness of the Limbs and Warmth of the Limbs can be abbreviated.

Since the subject closes the eyes for the program and may relax fairly deeply, a good "waking up" from the state of altered consciousness is needed to end the relaxation. The simplest procedure is to "wake up" like a healthy person after a good night's sleep: to *stretch the arms* and maybe also the legs, to *yawn* and *inhale* deeply and refreshingly, and to *open the eyes* and feel refreshed and full of vigor. This procedure should be followed after every practice session, unless the exercises are used to induce sleep in the evening. In that case also the Coolness of the Forehead may be omitted. Frequently the exercises are restricted to heaviness and warmth. These produce by themselves a deep relaxation.

The Autogenic Rag Doll

Heaviness of the Limbs. Make yourself comfortable and allow your eyes to close. Then lift one arm a little, and just let it drop. Let it drop heavily, as if it were the arm of a Raggedy Ann doll, one of those floppy dolls or animals. Choose one in your imagination. Choose a doll, an old beloved soft teddybear, a velveteen rabbit, a bean bag toy, or even a pillow or a blanket. Choose anything soft which you like. Lift the arm again a little and drop it, and let it rest there a moment. . . .

Now think of your arm again, but don't lift it in reality, just in the imagination. Lift it in the imagination and think that you are dropping it again, and do this while you breathe out. Let the arm go limp like a rag while you breathe out. . . .

And now work with the other arm. Use either your imagination or really lift it at first. It does not matter. But do not lift it too high, just enough to feel its heaviness, and let it drop, but gently and relaxedly. Learn to do it more and more in the imagination only. And when you breathe out again, drop it, let it go soft, let it go limp and relaxed. . . .

Next lift both arms together, and allow them to drop, simply relax them, allow them to be limp and soft. . . .

Then lift one leg. Lift it only a little, just enough that you can feel its heaviness, and allow it to drop, limp and relaxed, limp and soft. . . . Do this always when you breathe out. Don't lift the leg too high, so that it does not hit too hard. Or better yet, lift it only in the imagination. Do this a few times in your imagination only, and just let it become heavy and relaxed. . . .

Now do the same with the other leg. Lift it a little, and while you breathe out let it relax. Let it go soft like a rag. Let it drop like the leg of a giant rag doll. . . .

Feel free to move your legs or any part of your body to a more comfortable position any time you want to do so.

And now both legs together, lift them in your imagination, and let them relax, limp and soft, like a rag or a bean bag. . . .

And finally all limbs together, both arms and both legs, breathe out and allow them to be limp and relaxed, heavy and comfortable, like a giant rag doll, well supported by the chair, the sofa, or the floor.

Warmth of the Limbs. Next imagine that you put your rag doll into the sun. Let it be warmed by the sun. The giant rag doll is lying very relaxedly. Feel how the sun is shining on it. Feel it on one arm first, and then on the other. See to it that the head of the rag doll is in the shade and kept cool, but all the limbs are sprawled out in the sun. Feel your arm, warm, soft, and relaxed. . . . And then feel the other arm, warm, soft, and relaxed. . . . And then let one leg be nicely warmed by the sun. . . . And then the other leg, nicely warmed, soft, and relaxed. . . . Remember, you are the giant rag doll, and you are lying in the sun; all your limbs are nice and warm, but your head is lying in the shade and is comfortably cool. . . .

Heartbeat. And now that you are such a nicely relaxed rag doll, imagine you have within yourself something that is like a little motor, which makes you go all the time, and that is your heart. It just keeps you going all the time, day and night, whether you keep track of it or not. And just as you walk or run, sometimes a little faster, sometimes slower, sometimes skip along, just so that little motor in you sometimes goes a little faster, sometimes slower, and sometimes skips. That is quite normal. And now just feel, if you can, the rhythm of your heart. It does not really matter whether you can feel it or only imagine it, but think of your heart and say "thank you" to it. This organ works all the time for you, whether you think of it or not. So now just stay with it for a while, and say "thank you." . . . Thank your heart that it does such a good job for you. . . .

Respiration. Next, for a moment, pay attention to your

breathing. The breathing rhythm, just like the heart, sometimes goes fast and sometimes goes slow. Allow it to go as slow or as fast, as shallow or as deep as it wants to. If you have to sigh, that is fine. If you want to inhale deeply, that is fine. Just follow the breathing.... And then, for a moment, just imagine that the air which you breathe streams in at the fingers while you breathe in, up your arms, and into your shoulders and chest; and then, while you breathe out, down into your abdomen, down into your legs, and out at your toes. And repeat this for two or three breaths.... Then imagine that you are floating, floating on an air mattress on the ocean, a big river, or a swimming pool. Let slow and gentle waves carry you up and down in the rhythm of your breathing.

Internal Warmth. Now breathe into the palm of your hand and feel the warmth of your breath. Such warmth is within you all the time. Repeat it, and then put the hand down again and imagine. Imagine that you breathe this same kind of warmth into your own inside.... While you breathe out, imagine that you breathe that warmth down into your throat, down into your chest, down into your abdomen.... Just become nicely warm inside.... Or you may imagine that you are drinking something which really warms you nicely inside, or even that something like a warmly glowing ball is rolling around within you. Allow it to warm your inside, so that it becomes all soft and relaxed.

Coolness of the Forehead. Bring one hand to the mouth and lick two fingers. Then stroke the moist fingers over your forehead. Just stroke your forehead and feel the coolness of the moisture. If you want to moisten the forehead again, feel free to do so.... And then, while you breathe in, feel the refreshing coolness of your forehead, and imagine again that giant rag doll or rag animal, lying with its head in the cool shade....

Now just lie there and relax completely for a while, and think of the rag doll with its body warmed comfortably, relaxed in the sun. Feel again the gentle cradling of the waves of the breathing rhythm. And while breathing in feel the cool shade, the coolness on your forehead, and while breathing out feel your comfortably relaxed body.

Ending the Altered State of Consciousness. In time, become more and more aware of being refreshed during inhalations. And when you decide it is time to end the state in which you are now, yawn and breathe in deeply and refreshingly while you stretch and flex arms and legs. And then open your eyes, look around and breathe in once more. If you were lying down, sit up by supporting yourself with the arms while you breathe out. This keeps the body relaxed and prevents dizziness after the deep relaxation.

Conclusion

A large number and variety of exercises for increasing and using sensory awareness have been presented since individual differences and diversity of needs require a wide choice of techniques. However, there is no hard and fast rule to which sensory awareness exercises must conform, many more may be devised as occasion demands, and those in this chapter may be varied according to needs.

Schultz's Autogenic Training has been included in this chapter because this technique of conditioning the autonomic nervous system toward its parasympathetic functions is based largely on the sensory awareness of psychophysiological responses during an altered state of consciousness. Respiration is discussed at length in the next chapter since it is the most useful and versatile of the bodily functions which can be used as biofeedback instruments.

5. Breathing for Special Purposes

Man's breathing rhythm is closely related to his intellect and his emotions, and the Greeks had observed this when they used the same expression, *phren*, to denote the diaphragm as well as the mind. The physical and physiological interactions between the diaphragm and the mind are more easily felt than explained. But just this feeling and experiencing of the interdependence between the breathing rhythm and the mind is important.

Breathing Mechanisms

Breathing is under both voluntary and involuntary control, and it may involve all muscles of the trunk. It can, first, be diaphragmatic or abdominal, involving the diaphragm and the muscles of the abdomen and flanks; second, chest breathing, involving the muscles of the chest and the ribs; and third, high breathing, involving movement and tension in shoulders, arms, and head. The first is the most useful and natural, and relaxed breathing is practically done by the diaphragm alone.

The Diaphragm. The diaphragm is a dome-shaped, musculomembranous wall, which separates the abdomen from the thoracic cavity. It contracts with each inhalation, flattening downward, and relaxes with each exhalation, returning to its domed shape. As the diaphragm contracts, it acts like a piston which moves downward and forward. At the same time the chest muscles contract and draw the ribs up and outward. Thus the space in the chest cavity is increased, creating negative pressure. Due to this, the atmospheric air rushes through the respiratory passages into the air sacs of the lungs, expanding them. When the diaphragm relaxes, the ribs and sternum lower by their own weight, the air sacs collapse, and the air is expelled. Thus, breathing proceeds practically without effort.

Second to the heart, the diaphragm is the most continuously active of all body structures. It does not become fatigued, partly because, like the heart, its rest periods are longer than its working periods. That is, the phase of relaxation is longer than that of contraction, and there is a slight pause after exhalation.

The diaphragm affects many things besides breathing. Its wide swing acts like a kind of "inner massage" on heart and abdomen. Its vertical movements elongate the heart and promote a better circulation in its walls. During inhalations it compresses the abdominal viscera and during exhalations allows them to expand. This stimulates peristalsis and affects digestive rhythms and excretion through physical action on the stomach, liver, intestines, and kidneys. Further, the diaphragm affects the skeletal musculature through nerve reflexes.

Phases of the Breathing Rhythm. The phases of a relaxed breathing rhythm are a tension-reducing, long, slow exhalation, followed by a patient pause of relaxed relative emptiness until the need for oxygen finally prompts a passive inhalation.

The phases of a tense breathing rhythm are a forced inhalation which usually employs the chest muscles maximally, followed by a tense pause of retention, until too much or too long tension forces an exhalation.

In addition to the breathing phases, also the length of respirations, repetitive rhythms, real or imagined breathing pathways, and "locks" or tense contractions at certain places in the body may play roles in the use of breathing.

Exhalation is largely a passive occurrence related to relaxation: the chest muscles and diaphragm relax, the ribs drop back close together, the lungs recoil, and air is expelled quietly. An exhalation should be experienced as a "giving" of breath and as a "letting go" of the tension which developed spontaneously during inhalation. Although the air stream moves upward during an exhalation, a downward movement can be felt. This is due to the wave of muscle relaxation associated with exhaling.

Inhalation has an invigorating, strengthening, exhilarating effect. However, it also produces tension. In general, attention to the inhalation phase should be minimized because of the tension-evoking effect. Care should be taken that inhalations for invigoration do not result in hyperventilation. Active or passive movements of the limbs and neck produce deeper inhalations reflexively. The impulses for such reflexive breathing arise apparently from nerve receptor cell endings in or around the joints. Deeper breathing and reflexive sighing or yawning increase the mobility of the diaphragm.

Deep inhalations aid the venous circulation, but in high breathing the strain in the muscles near the collarbone and top ribs interferes with the circulatory structures at the important top area of the heart.

Nature takes care of breathing, and the lungs need not be "filled." The muscles of the body should be as relaxed as a task allows for the best kind of breathing. The virtue of "full" breathing has been highly overestimated. Relaxed diaphragmatic breathing is the important thing. The amount of residual air in the lungs is sufficient to keep the oxygen balance. When more oxygen is needed for the body cells, as during great activity, breathing is faster and deeper. This deep breathing in response to physical or chemical needs of oxygen is primarily vertical breathing, involving the movements of the diaphragm.

The Personal Breathing Rhythm

The normal breathing rhythm varies according to the demands of a situation, and the healthy and self-reliant usually achieve spontaneously a comfortable interaction between mental, physiological, and emotional states and the breathing rhythm. They usually need no additional skills, unless they must learn to utilize their breathing for special purposes as athletes, singers, dancers, or actors.

Those who do not have a healthy, spontaneous interaction of body and mind do not automatically achieve a comfortable interaction between the breathing rhythm and emotional, mental, or physical activities. They can greatly profit from improving breathing skills. The best way of breathing is to allow the diaphragm to swing freely. The infant's body, not yet inhibited by habitual reactions to stress, does this spontaneously. Most adults, and especially psychosomatics and neurotics, must learn again to allow the diaphragm to swing freely.

Prolonged disturbed rhythms are a sign of dysfunction and disorder, unless they are consciously evoked to achieve a special effect, as by performing artists or during Yoga and athletic exercises.

Work with the personal respiratory rhythm proceeds on the border between the conscious and the subconscious, and subconscious rhythms should not be rudely interfered with nor modified continuously.

The personal respiratory rhythm must be searched for patiently by allowing the body to find, through sensory awareness, a more adequate and healthy rhythm by itself. Careful retraining of the breathing rhythm is promoted by work with the imagination and movements of joints. Necessary and unnecessary stress reactions evoke the following breathing changes.

Unintentional Breathing Changes

When one is gasping during a shock, air is inhaled while the ribs lift and become rounded and rigid. Lesser, but noticeable changes are evoked by sudden fright, fear, anxiety, irresolution, awe, shyness, joy, or cogitation. All inhibit the relaxed swinging of the diaphragm. Also movements, like bending, getting up from the bed or a chair, climbing, or even writing and reading can disturb the natural, relaxed rhythm. The breath is often held unnecessarily, and inhalations are shallow and tense. This tenses the muscles of back and abdomen and narrows alimentary and respiratory passages, especially stomach and throat. Such tensions can by themselves produce a state of anxiety and will greatly add to the stresses of life, if they become habitual. Irregularities in the normal breathing rhythm can be observed by anybody even during small stresses. Immediate relaxation by means of the following exhalations will greatly reduce the stress factor and prevent inadequate breathing habits.

The imagination, indirectly, greatly influences the action of the diaphragm. Suggestion works through the imagination. The accepted suggestion of sleep results in a breathing rhythm similar to that during sleep. The accepted suggestion of imagined exercise initiates faster, deeper breathing. The suggestion of stress or fright may halt the breathing rhythm or make it irregular. Susceptible persons react to the suggestion of a depressive situation by reducing the frequency and depth of breathing. Hostile and angry persons may, when a conflict is suggested, react with increased rapidity of breathing. The imagination is an important tool for working with the respiration and vice versa.

Observation and Intentional Alteration of Breathing

Breathing exercises are often designed to initiate "good breathing." The question is, what is good for whom? This varies widely according to needs, physical condition, mental attitude, and so on. Superimposed, structured, conscious exercises do not necessarily help to improve inadequate breathing and bring about "good" breathing habits.

Different breathing techniques, depending on the purpose, use different combinations of the following possible interventions with breathing: attention to pathways and locations of movements or sensations of breathing; retention of inhalations with or without additional tensing of muscles or tapping and beating of body areas for a vibrating effect; counting the breaths and using certain prescribed breathing rhythms of inhalation-exhalation ratios; using "locks" or body tensions at certain places in the body during breathing; pumping the breath; and using imagined verbalizations or real sounds of humming, whistling, or singing with the breathing.

Most Westerners, with overexcited nervous systems and too much tension and intention, must be guided to a relaxed breathing rhythm. Most Eastern breathing exercises on the other hand, as from Yoga, T'ai Chi, Kung Fu, Zen, and Mazdaznan, were developed for well relaxed or even lax systems in order to evoke tension and stamina. These exercises are good for the healthy, strong, and overrelaxed, but they are often too exerting for the average Westerner in the long run, though he may initially like them.

Even for the Eastern exercises it is advised that conscious modifications of breathing should in no case exceed five minutes in the course of five hours. Attention to the breathing for relaxation must even be shorter, unless it is used to induce altered states of consciousness.

Relaxed breathing must be mastered before the following exercises for intentional breathing changes are attempted.

Yogic Breathing

In Yoga there are many kinds of breath control exercises, just as there are many positions in Hatha Yoga.

Yogic breathing is strenuous for most Westerners, and especially the advanced exercises should be practiced only under the guidance of an experienced teacher.

Yogic breathing purposely encompasses the entire breathing apparatus and uses abdominal, chest, and high breathing. In abdominal breathing the muscles of the abdomen, flanks, and diaphragm are utilized; in chest breathing those of the ribs; and in high breathing those which raise the shoulders and collarbones.

Breathing Capacity Test. The efficiency of the three different kinds of breathing may be tested in the following manner. (1) Abdominal breathing: Sit erect, the feet well supported. Look at a watch with a second hand or be prepared to count and note the time of your inhalations. Exhale deeply and start counting the time from the beginning to the end of the inhalation. Do not count during pauses before or after the inhalations. Breathe in as deeply and slowly as possible by pushing the abdominal wall and the flanks gently out as wide as possible and, so to speak, sucking the air into the vacuum created in the abdominal cavity. Allow the diaphragm to descend, but keep shoulders and chest as motionless as possible during this inhalation. Note the time the inhalation lasted; allow the inhaled air to stream out; and breathe normally for a minute or two. Then repeat the procedure two more times and figure your average abdominal inhalation time. (2) Chest breathing: Repeat the above instructions, but inhale as deeply and slowly as possible by only expanding the chest. Keep diaphragm and abdomen as motionless as possible and do not allow the shoulders to rise. (3) High breathing: Repeat the instructions of (1), but inhale deeply and slowly allowing only the shoulders and collarbones to rise, while keeping the ribs motionless and contracting the abdomen and holding it against the diaphragm. Then compare the average times of the three tests. Also note the relative amounts of energy used for the inhalations, any occurring pressures, and possible lightheadedness. Decide which kind of breathing is the most efficient for getting the most air with the least effort. For the healthy with a relaxed breathing rhythm, it is the abdominal breathing.

In yogic breathing, abdominal, chest, and high breathing are used successively during the same breath, and long exhalations are made, with the ratio of inhalation to exhalation time being 1 : 2. Later a retention pause of four times the inhalation time is inserted after the inhalation, so that the ratio of inhalation, retention, and exhalation is 1 : 4 : 2. It should be noted that the yogic pause for retention at the end of the inhalation is just the opposite of the Pause for Feeling at the end of a relaxed exhalation, described in chapter 4.

There is an endless number of yogic breathing exercises with varying durations of the complete breathing cycle and varying ratios of inhalations, exhalations, and pauses (Vishnudevananda 1960).

Much attention is paid in yogic breathing also to the real pathways of the air, such as the nostrils, sinuses, mouth, throat, and lungs. Further, attention is paid to assumed places to which the "breath power" goes, as, for instance, certain locations along the spine and the solar plexus. Finally, yogic breathing makes use of "locks" or tense contractions at the chin, anus, and upper abdomen.

Yogic breathing can induce much tension either purposely or unintentionally and may lead to hyperventilation and the induction of altered states of consciousness. Yogic breathing is useful for improving the ability and capacity of the healthy and strong, but it is not a therapeutic tool for patients with impaired breathing functions. Students of Yoga have repeatedly found Jencks' (1974) respiration exercises useful for enhancing their success with yogic breathing.

Kung Fu Deep Breathing

The exercises described here and the Riding Horse Position, described in chapter 6, are probably not the most spectacular and widely popularized of the Kung Fu exercises, but since they are extremely powerful and useful, they are described in detail.

Sit in a well-aligned posture, rather straight. Notice any unnecessary tensions in the body and release them with successive exhalations. When a relaxed state is attained, start the following breathing patterns.

First, breathe by only expanding the abdomen during inhalations and contracting it during exhalations. Do not move the shoulders, but keep them relaxed. Breathe deeply, allowing the air to stream freely in and out through the nose. During this procedure the diaphragm flattens during inhalations, while the abdomen expands; and it relaxes during exhalations into a dome shape, while the abdomen contracts. Become aware during exhalations of the simultaneously contracting abdominal muscles and the relaxing diaphragm.

Second, inhale through the nose and feel the air stream through the nasal passages, down through the throat, and into the lungs. Imagine filling the whole lungs, from the bottom to the top, as if filling a reservoir. Exhale through slightly opened lips, the tongue curled back against the roof of the mouth to break the air stream. Allow the air to stream out audibly past the tongue, through teeth and lips, while the imagined reservoir is being emptied from the top to the bottom. Repeat this several times and learn to allow the whole process to occur as one smooth, continuous flow. Learn the correct timing and pacing, so that no shortness of breath results at the end of the complete exhalation.

Third, add the following pattern. During inhalations imagine the air streaming in through the nose to the back of the head, and then all the way down along the spine, to its base. Imagine during a pause between inhalation and exhalation that the inhaled air flows through the pelvic area to the front of the body. Then, during exhalation, imagine the air flowing easily up inside the front of the body and out around the curled tongue between the teeth. Then begin another inhalation through the nose to the back of the head and repeat the smooth, uninterrupted, rhythmical cycle. Do not continue if strain or lightheadedness develops or if the cycle cannot be performed smoothly. In these cases practice only the first and second patterns again. When the third pattern is added correctly, a strange feeling of two opposite processes going on at the same time may be experienced, namely, during inhalation the feeling of the air moving down along the spine, while at the same time the reservoir fills from bottom to top; and during exhalation the feeling of the air streaming upwards in front, while at the same time the reservoir empties from top to bottom.

Through the close attention to repeated rhythms, the practitioner is usually in a state of altered consciousness by the time the third pattern is added.

A Japanese Zen Breath Concentration Exercise

Sit straight, yet relaxed. Inhale through the nose; feel the air flowing down through the throat and into the lungs, and imagine that the breath continues to flow through the diaphragm into the middle of the lower abdomen.

During the following slow exhalation count "one" and imagine that the exhalation places the "one" in the abdomen.

Allow the next inhalation to flow in by itself, while you think about nothing but the "one" in the abdomen. During the next slow exhalation, put a "two" next to the "one" in the abdomen. While the next inhalation streams in by itself, think of nothing but the "one" and "two" together in the abdomen.

Repeat this up to ten numbers together in the abdomen. If necessary, start then with "one" again and repeat the series until "the whole mind seems to have descended into the abdomen." If repeated to that state, a fairly deep state of altered consciousness has been induced.

Mazdaznan Exercises

The following exercises (Hanish 1914) have their origin in the Middle East. They have been known in the United States only for the last hundred years.

Prelude Breath. Begin by taking short breaths: in—out, in—out . . . six or more times. Then empty the lungs with a long exhalation. This must be done before every Mazdaznan exercise, but it is also by itself a method to relieve shortness of breath. In the latter case it is followed by a few deep, relaxed breathing cycles.

Individual Breath. Sit well aligned on a stool, facing away from the light. Put the hands on the upper legs, the thumbs apart from the other fingers. If the stool is too low or too high, put a book on the stool or under the feet, so that the position is comfortable. Separate the heels one to two inches and the toes five to seven inches. The lips should be closed lightly, the teeth separated, the tongue resting relaxedly in the lower part of the mouth, the tip gently curled down against the lower teeth. The chin should be drawn in, the spinal column erect, but all muscles relaxed. Everything following should be done easily, gracefully, and with perfect tranquility.

Concentrate on a small, dull object or a spot at eye level, four to seven feet away. Empty the lungs by exhaling all air possible without effort. Do not strain. Then inhale through the nose for seven seconds, gently, slowly, fully, as regularly as possible. Fill first the upper lobes of the lungs as much as possible without effort. Then fill the remainder of the lungs to the utmost. Exhale for the next seven seconds in the same relaxed manner. Sense the current of the breath as it enters the nostrils, goes up the nose and down the air passages into the chest. Sense the reverse current during exhalations. Repeat this even, regular breathing for three minutes at a time, three times per day, but not within half an hour after meals.

When this pattern becomes easy, use it also in walking

by taking seven steps during the inhalation, holding the breath for a few steps, seven steps during the exhalation, and several steps while pausing after the exhalation before repeating the cycle.

Full Breath. Stand erect; head thrown back; chest raised and forward; shoulder blades back and down; hands open as if ready to grasp objects too low for them to reach; muscles of face perfectly relaxed; and mouth closed.

Inhale through the nose as long as possible without effort or any strain on any part of the body. To release tenseness in the sides or chest, make the spinal column as vertical as possible with its weight resting on the lowest vertebrae. Allow the knees to relax and bend very slightly.

After filling the lungs to full capacity, raise the arms in an arc as high as is easily possible, and while holding the breath, move the tongue as if masticating, smack the lips, and swallow the saliva which has accumulated in the mouth. Bring the arms down and, throwing them backwards, begin to exhale slowly. Empty the lungs as much as possible. Repeat the exercise seven or more times.

Counteracting Uncertainty. Doubt and uncertainty interrupt the relaxed breathing rhythm and create tensions. Otoman, Prince of Adusht, suggested in *Mazdaznan Health and Breath Culture* (Hanish 1914, p. xiii) : "Whenever in the least dubious, remember and breathe out upon one breath the words of the Rubaiyat: Predestination, paradise and hell/I sought to find beyond the skies, pell-mell, / When to me spoke the still small Voice: 'My friend, / In thee dwell fortune, paradise and hell.' " Repeating these lines during one exhalation allows for a good opportunity to let off steam, to exercise patience, to reinstate equanimity, and to practice lengthening the exhalation!

Awakening. Stretch each limb thoroughly during consecutive deep inhalations. Then stretch all limbs together during the next deep inhalation and relax suddenly with a thorough exhalation.

Other Eastern Exercises

Chinese Health Breathing. Sit quietly and fixate one big toe. During inhalations think "relaxed"; while holding the breath think "quiet"; during exhalations think "let go." Repeat as long as comfortable. Let the quiet holding pause get longer and longer.

Breathing Movements. Pay attention only to the breathing movements. Watch the abdomen, chest, or navel move; feel the movement of the air stream, the breathing muscles, or of a feather on the lips; or listen to the movement of air in nose and throat. However, do only one of these during any single exercise.

Gatekeeper. Pay attention only to the nostrils, as if you were a gatekeeper there, and watch the incoming and outgoing breath. Pay full attention to the air as it passes the nostrils. Do not pay any attention to where the breath goes or comes from. Be like a gatekeeper who does not supervise the movements of people outside or inside the gate, but only those that pass.

Counting Breaths. Attend completely to the breathing and to nothing else. Count each breath, either during exhalation, inhalation, or the full cycle. The full cycle is the most difficult, since it needs a longer attention span. Any time extraneous thoughts interrupt the counting, begin again at one. If the complete concentration can be kept on the counts, start at one again after reaching ten. Higher numbers are supposed to distract.

Inducing Stillness. Count during an exhalation. Become stiller and stiller and count again during the next exhalations. As the breathing slows down, the counts will become longer and longer. Finally the breathing should slow down to only two or three respirations per minute.

Relaxation Through Attention. Be very conscious of only the breathing rhythm and any body part or function that should be relaxed, calmed, or influenced. Think: "I exhale while attending to and calming my. . . . I inhale while attending to and calming my. . . . " Add any suggestions during both exhalations and inhalations and keep repeating them.

Breath Meditation with Acoustic Images. Repeat a sound, word, or short thought in the imagination once with every breath or divide them in rhythm with exhalations and inhalations. A variation of this is to say each word of a sentence or prayer during consecutive exhalations.

The Beetle-Droning-Breath. In this yogic breathing exercise, the fingers are placed on the head in the following manner: the ears are closed with the thumbs, the eyes covered by the index fingers, the nostrils with the second fingers, and the upper and lower lips with the third and little fingers respectively. The tongue touches the front teeth, the lips are pursed, and the breath is expelled very, very slowly with a droning sound.

The droning should be continued during a single exhalation for as long as possible. With practice, it may be extended for two to three minutes. As soon as the lungs seem entirely empty, they are refilled and the droning begun anew. The instructions are that the exercise must be continued for at least half an hour to produce the right effect, and practiced every day for at least a month.

Breathing and Movement

Exhalations have a naturally relaxing effect and promote ease of movement, while inhalations naturally produce tensions and retard movement. These natural effects may be incorporated purposely with movement. Exhalations facilitate real or imagined downward, outward, and forward movement of the limbs and the whole body. Inhalations facilitate real or imagined inward and backward movement of the whole body, upward movement of the limbs, and upon occasion upward movement of the whole body. Ease of movement while holding the breath depends on the amount of air in the lungs. With filled lungs, strong, jerky, or stiff movement may be produced, but movement may also be unsure due to tension. When the lungs are relatively empty and the diaphragm is relaxed, holding the breath may allow very relaxed, quiet, and sure movement. Exhaling while stretching will facilitate and lengthen a stretch, while inhalation will retard and shorten it. Exhalations can help an arthritic to reach and tie shoelaces which were out of reach while holding the breath because of stiffness or for fear of pain. Inhalations during muscle-tensing exercises, whether these are executed in reality or only imagined, have an especially invigorating effect.

Counterbreathing. This term has been coined for this book, since there seems to be no other expression for the procedure to be described. The body follows this procedure naturally during a refreshing stretch, and it is used in the described Mazdaznan Awakening exercise, and in Hatha Yoga exercises. It is useful for increasing the efficiency of calisthenic exercises. See chapter 6.

Counterbreathing purposely reverses the natural relaxing or tensing effects of breathing on movements. Inhalation during stretching produces extra tension, but it also invigorates and increases the physiological effect of the stretch, making any stretching exercise more effective. Inhalation during stretching may also seem to increase energy in the spine and limbs. This invigorating, energizing effect of inhalations during a stretch or an outward movement is just the opposite of the natural muscle relaxation with exhalations during outward movements.

Counterbreathing can also be used for slowing down forward or downward movement. For instance, putting a phonograph needle on a record during a slow inhalation retards the speed of the lowering hand and may prevent a too strong impact and scratching the record.

Another example of counterbreathing is its use in mov-

ing the whole body against gravity. Inhalations aid the
lifting of the limbs. However, this does not usually apply
when the whole body weight must move against gravity.
This contradiction is explained below. It can easily be tested
by the following procedure.

Movement Against Gravity. Sit on a chair and stretch
one arm horizontally forward. Allow the arm to follow
the breathing. It will rise with inhalations and lower during exhalations just due to the respiratory movements.

Then test lifting the body against gravity. That is, rise
from sitting to standing three times, each time breathing
differently. First, rise while holding the breath. Second,
rise during an inhalation. Third, inhale while sitting, and
rise with the ensuing exhalation. Notice the differences.
The facilitating effect of the exhalation on rising is generally immediately felt. It is especially perceptible to those
who have keen sensory awareness and to those who do
not have much energy to spare. If it becomes habitual,
much energy can be conserved, and it is mandatory for
those who have difficulty remaining relaxed while rising
to give a speech before an audience.

Exhalations similarly facilitate raising the body from
a lying to a sitting position or climbing stairs. Disabled
persons, who were not able to manage stairs due to asthma
or heart trouble, have been able to do so again by climbing during the exhalation phase and halting on a step
during the inhalation phase of the breathing rhythm.

The muscle tensions produced by inhalations facilitate
raising the limbs. These same muscle tensions act as an
inhibiting factor when the whole body weight must be
moved upward, since they restrict relaxed movement and
waste energy. Relaxing exhalations during rising or climbing reduce unnecessary energy wasting body tensions and
thus facilitate moving the body against gravity. The young
and strong can demonstrate this if they compare dashing
up consecutive flights of stairs during exhalations to doing the same during inhalations.

Triple Time Breathing. Triple time or triple measure is a measure of three beats, the first or last being accented. For triple time breathing, exhalation proceeds during the first two beats, or counts, and inhalation on the accented third. Each count should last about a second. Exhalations should flow out audibly between teeth and lips, and inhalations be short and easy through the nose. This results in the rhythm out-out-in, out-out-in. ...

Because of the extended exhalations, triple time breathing results in reducing the residual air in the lungs, and it allows more fresh air to stream in. It should be used during movement exercises, during shortness of breath, or when energy is expended. Otherwise it leads to hyperventilation.

The inhalation of triple time breathing is counterbreathing with respect to the stretched side in bending exercises. More air streams into the stretched side, since the lung on that side expands much more than the one on the nonstretched side. Since the stretch during inhalations alternates from side to side, both sides of the lungs get the benefit of deep inhalations.

Using the Breath for Increasing Strength and Rigidity

It is quite natural to first pump the breath into the upper chest and then hold it during the effort of lifting a heavy weight or giving a hard push or pull. This kind of breathing is used by weight lifters. On occasion, the pumped breath is held only until the time of exertion, and at that time expelled suddenly with an explosion at the moment of the effort, with or without a yell. At other times the held breath may be expelled slowly in a controlled manner, resulting in a rhythm of short, deep inhalations and prolonged rhythmic exhalations. This is the type of breathing done by work gangs to old chants. Pumping and holding the breath is also used therapeutically. Exercises are described later in this chapter.

The use of special breathing patterns for producing

muscular rigidity is less known and practiced. It can occasionally be observed in children during a tantrum. Otherwise, in the Western world, it is used in stage performances of the "human plank." This can be performed on command with or without induction of an altered state of consciousness. Actually, it is not difficult to purposely produce muscular rigidity, and the "human plank" feat needs only a strong body and motivation. It has been shown experimentally (Collins 1961, Barber 1970) that no altered state of consciousness is necessary to produce such rigidity. However, the concentration required and the strong contraction of almost every body muscle, or imagining being a wooden plank, may of themselves induce an altered state of consciousness in susceptible subjects.

Human Plank. The attainment of complete body rigidity usually requires shallow, high breathing. The diaphragm as well as the peripheral muscles are tensed, and when a heavy weight is supported in the suspended rigid position, the breath is usually held. For learning to increase muscular strength and hold body tension, the position should first be practiced on the floor. The upper and lower half of the body are tensed separately at first, and a feeling of weightlessness of the tensed body parts should be developed. Buttocks and kneecaps should be well drawn in. The toes may be pointed or held vertical. Holding the position is facilitated by stretching the arms over the head in the plane of the body, with the fingers interlaced and the palms outward. This exercise improves control over muscles not often used in daily life, and it invigorates. The effect of muscle contraction on lifting against gravity can easily be tested in a relaxed position by tensing one half of the body while leaving the other half relaxed.

After one practices on the floor, books, hard cushions, or the ends of a sofa can be used for support. There are two positions for support. In one, the support is placed under the body at the calves and shoulders. In this position it is very easy to support much weight on the stomach region. In the other position the support is under ankles or heels and under the neck or the back of the head. This position is more difficult. Young, strong persons, who are not overweight, should have no difficulties with these positions.

Besides its use in stage performances, complete body tension with tensed diaphragm is sometimes used in the Hatha Yoga "corpse" exercise. Here it is usually followed immediately by complete body relaxation. In the Mazdaznan Egyptian positions, total body tension is held for a prolonged period of time with feet and head supported by "two earthenware vessels as the Egyptians used them" (Hanish 1914).

Direct Versus Indirect Breathing Changes

Most Eastern exercises alter breathing directly by involving the will, activating the chest area, creating tension, and inducing an "upward pull." They compensate for cultural habits that emphasize quiet and relaxation, and place the idea of the center of man in the lower abdominal region.

Western man, in a head and chest oriented culture with habitual tense breathing patterns and much will and self-imposed stress, generally needs compensating exercises which relax and "lead down" toward the abdominal region. Nevertheless, most therapeutic breathing methods use the will and conscious alterations of breathing, such as structured diaphragmatic breathing exercises, intentionally extended exhalations, or intentional slowing of the air stream. Since conscious thought by itself produces inhibitory tensions, this is not the best way to induce relaxation in general and especially not in upset respiratory systems.

Respiration functions at the borderline between the conscious and the subconscious, and it should never be observed or purposely changed for long if either tension or an altered state of consciousness is to be avoided. Changes should be evoked as if a pendulum were set in motion and then left to swing freely at its own period. The respiration is best and most easily influenced by recourse to circuitous imagery.

M. Fuchs (Fuchs 1949/50, 1974; Jencks 1970a,b,c,d, 1971, 1972) developed a therapy that attempts to minimize conscious intervention while retraining too tense, restrained, or obstructed breathing rhythms. The development of B. Jencks' (1974) respiration exercises was much influenced by Fuchs' therapeutic method. In Jencks' exercises the imagination and suggestion are often utilized, so that physical and mental reactions are evoked indirectly. The exercises can be used at any time and place and are meant for the healthy in everyday stress.

Fuchs' Functional Relaxation Therapy

Fuchs searched long for a name for her method: Breathing Therapy and Relaxing Body Work (1949/50), Breathing Therapy or Rhythmicizing Relaxation Therapy (1959), Self-Rhythm Through Relaxation and Breathing Without Hypnosis (1964), Breathrhythmicizing Relaxation Therapy (1971), and finally, Functional Relaxation (1974). Jencks (1970) called Fuchs' therapy in English Self-Rhythmization.

Fuchs' method was designed to aid patients to find a healthy, personal rhythm. Special attention is given to joints, body openings, skin, and voice. Tension and pressure changes in the body are sensed; fixated, inhibited, or obstructed functions are contacted mentally; and relaxation is induced locally by long, relaxed exhalations, evoked by directed but circuitous images. These include, for improving posture: "the inner scaffold," "deeply rooted tree," "building and furnishing a house," and "spine as a third leg"; for relaxing: "to flow like a river," "to melt like snow in the sun," "to let the elevator descend," and "a bottomless ribcage or pelvis"; for work with the spine: "a chain instead of a stick," "moving like a snake in every possible way," and "letting the head have free play in any direction on top of the spine"; for the voice: "purring like a cat," "copying the Metro-Goldwyn lion," "chewing and smacking the tongue," and "laughing down into oneself." This use of the imagination is an excellent means for circumventing conscious thinking to evoke desired reactions.

In Functional Relaxation, the therapist observes the breathing of the patient closely, and gently uses his hand to detect inhibiting tensions. Later the patient may use his own hand as an aid in detecting and relaxing tensions. The smallest and subtlest changes are suggested, and humming is used for extending relaxing exhalations. Nothing is suggested and repeated for more than two or three breathing rhythms to prevent the patient's slipping into an altered state of consciousness. Each time after changes or suggestions are made, a "creative pause" during which changes can occur and be sensed is intercalated for two to three respirations.

Functional Relaxation is strictly a therapy, requiring a therapist's guidance and "helping hand," added explanations, rationalizations, practice of negative factors like halting or tensing, and physical movements like stretching and bending.

Jencks' Respiration Exercises

During work with Fuchs' therapy it became apparent that long, deep exhalations are very effective and important for relaxation and the reduction of anxiety in psychosomatic and psychotherapy patients. However, for students, actors, athletes, businessmen, and diverse other professionals, invigoration and strengthening exercises were often indicated. Therefore a manual was prepared (Jencks 1974), which included a mixture of Eastern and Western exercises, using the respiration for the most diverse purposes.

In practice it was found that trainees "discovered" or "invented" similar images and exercises over and over again, often exactly what had been only recently "invented" or what had been written ages ago in obscure exercise instructions. The fact is, that all psychophysiologically oriented methods which have been developed experientially work with one and the same material: man's body and mind, which has not changed basically in milleniums. Thus, nothing really new is described in the following, but much of what is available is presented in an organized and practical manner, with thanks "due to those who first broke the way to knowledge and left only to their successors the task of smoothing it" (Samuel Johnson 1903).

Jencks' exercises are designed for self-training or group instruction courses for professionals. However, they can very easily be adapted by therapists for use in physical therapy as well as in psychotherapy.

Much use is made of the imagination, stimulated by multiple suggestions. The imagination works immediately, and no theory or extensive practice of the exercises is necessary. It is left to the discretion of the trainee whether a state of altered consciousness is induced purposely, or whether exercises are kept short for use during daily life situations like driving a car or attending a business meeting.

For training purposes, acquaintance with at least some of every group of exercises is suggested. Much can be done to relax or invigorate, to preserve or increase strength, etc., by utilizing the breathing in conjunction with the imagination. For practical use, the question should be asked: What do I want to change? And then diverse exercises, using the imagination and the breathing rhythm, are designed and tested for effectiveness. Useful imagery exercises must always be designed according to individual needs of the moment. For general use of the methods described in this book, see chapter 9.

Breathing Skills

Most persons, even those with experience in breath control like actors, musicians, athletes, and dancers, have not learned to fully utilize the breathing apparatus. Usually they have not even considered all the possibilities by which breathing techniques can be improved to reduce effort and to facilitate controlled actions.

Breathing can be felt as being relaxing, invigorating, oppressive, strengthening, and so on. The sensations related to breathing depend on the phase of the breathing rhythm, the relative length and strength of inhalation and exhalation, the inserted pauses, and the body parts or areas involved in breathing.

Real and Imagined Breathing Pathways. The imagination can be employed for directing the attention away from the usual breathing movements and pathways. Numbers one to five in Figure 2 show body areas and movements which are actually used in breathing, and numbers six to twenty those which may be involved through use of the imagination. Imagining breathing through the latter pathways will generally have the following effects: up or down through the arms and legs will lengthen and deepen the respiration; through the hips and the small of the back diverts the attention from the actual pathways which are often oversensitive during breathing difficulties, and it allows the respiration to ease and deepen; through the back of the neck releases muscular tension in that area; through two holes under the chin may open up congested sinuses; through the crown of the head, the temples, the forehead, or the back of the head may relieve tension headaches; through the armpits will loosen tension there, as it will do in any body part or area. Filling an imagined abdominal reservoir or letting the air stream "through the diaphragm as through a sieve" eases tension in the diaphragmatic region and deepens and lengthens the respiration; and vertical breathing as if up

Figure 2

Real and Imagined Breathing Pathways and Movements

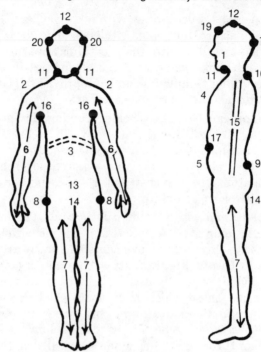

1. Through nose, mouth, and throat
2. Raising the shoulders
3. Raising and lowering the diaphragm
4. Expanding and contracting the ribcage
5. Expanding and pulling in the abdomen
6. Through the arms
7. Through the legs
8. Through the hips
9. Through the small of the back
10. Through the back of the lower neck
11. Through two holes under the chin, to the right and left
   of the throat
12. Through the crown of the head
13. Filling an abdominal reservoir
14. By means of a pump at the anus or crotch
15. Up and down a tube from the throat to the pelvis
16. Through the armpits
17. Through the navel
18. Through the back of the head
19. Through the forehead
20. Through the temples

and down a vertical tube in the middle of the body or by means of a pump from the anus is very useful if, for some reason, ribcage movements are restricted. In general, the more different ways of breathing that are used under different conditions, the deeper and more relaxed breathing will become.

Feelings, Images, and Actions Related to the Breathing Rhythm. In general, long, slow, deep exhalations are conducive to relaxation with the accompanying sensations of sinking, widening, opening up, and softening; feelings of comfort, heaviness, warmth, and moisture; and moods of patience, satisfaction, and equanimity. Inhalations evoke invigoration, tension, or levitation; feelings of lightness, coolness, and dryness; and moods of courage, determination, and exhilaration. A feeling of oppression may be experienced with short, choppy, restricted breathing movements. Self-suggestion during breathing phases can help to change spontaneous feelings and moods to more appropriate ones, as, for instance, tension to exhilaration, lightness, or coolness, and boredom to contemplation, comfort, or equanimity. Certain movements of the limbs or the whole body are facilitated when they are executed during exhalation, others during inhalation: forward and outward movements during exhalation, pulling or swinging back and light lifting during inhalation. For heavy lifting the breath is held, or pumped and then held. Table 10 lists feelings, actions, and images which are predominantly related to different breathing phases. This table (Jencks 1974) has been constructed on the basis of the experiences of most of the students and patients who used Jencks' exercises. Often feelings elicited by inhalations are diametrically opposite to those connected with exhalations, as, for instance, tension with inhalation and relaxation with exhalation, or the feeling of warmth with exhalation and the feeling of coolness with inhalation. However, the entries on the same lines of the table are not necessarily opposites, and not everybody experiences all sensations.

Table 10
Feelings, Actions, and Images Related to
the Breathing Phases

	Exhalation	Inhalation	Holding the Breath
Physical and Physiological	Relaxation	Increase of Tension	Maintenance or Increase of Tension
	Heaviness	Lightness	Unstable Equilibrium
	Calmness	Stimulation	Restlessness
	Warmth	Coolness	Variability
	Darkness	Brightness	Variability
	Softness	Hardness	Rigidity
	Moisture	Dryness	
	Weakness, Weariness	Strength, Invigoration, Refreshment	Momentary Conservation of Strength
Psychological	Patience, Endurance	Speed, Being Startled	Anxiety, Oppression
	Contemplation	Ready Attention	Strained Attention
	Equanimity	Courage	Cowardice
	Deep Thought, Concentration	Openmindedness, Creativity	Closed-mindedness
	Introversion	Extroversion	
	Boredom	Excitement	Keen Interest
	Satisfaction	Curiosity	Uncertainty
	Depression	Cheerfulness	Nervous Tension
	Comfort	Exhilaration	Uneasiness
	Generosity	Greed	Stinginess

Actions	Relax, Release, Let Go, Loosen	Tense, Bind, Tighten, Grasp	Hold On
	Release Pressure, Stream or Flow Out	Increase Pressure, Stream or Flow In	Maintain or Increase Pressure
	Liquefy	Solidify	Maintain Consistency
	Expand, Widen, Open	Contract, Narrow, Close	Dimension Unchanged or Congestion
	Sink, Descend, Fall Asleep	Ascend, Levitate, Rise, Wake Up	Maintain Level
	Lengthen	Shorten	Maintain Length
	Move or Swing Forward, Strike, Kick, Punch, Reach Out	Move, Draw, Pull or Swing Backward, Haul In	Stop, Stand or Hold Still
	Send, Give, Help, Offer	Receive, Take, Demand	Keep, Interrupt
	Laugh, Sigh, Giggle	Sob, Gasp	Smile, Frown
	Soothe	Irritate	

Coupling the appropriate breathing phases with the imagination is extremely effective, and ingenuity can be used for designing exercises utilizing the appropriate breathing phases in conjunction with the imagination to achieve desired results. Special formulas may be constructed which utilize both breathing phases alternately. If, for example, the effect to be attained is "cool and moist," suggestions can be timed to coincide respectively with inhalations and exhalations. Table 11 gives examples of self-suggestion formulas for use with the breathing phases.

Suggestions made during inappropriate breathing phases may counteract the suggested responses. Subjects can be

Table 11
Self-Suggestion Formulas for Use with the Breathing Rhythm

For Relaxation:
Body relaxed (EX), mind alert (IN)
Relaxed (EX) and easy (IN)

To Ease the Respiration:
Breath streams calm and free (EX), limbs are light (IN)
Breath streams into small of back (IN), slowly out through legs (EX)

For Concentration:
Concentrated on task (IN), yet relaxed and steady (EX)

For Motivation:
When the going gets tough (IN), the tough get going (EX)
(Note: some athletes like reverse breathing phases for this.)

For Invigoration:
Awake and aware (IN), I blow away all tiredness (EX)
Sweep out slag (EX), fresh air in (IN)!
Exhilarated and excited (IN), but body steady (EX)

For Strength and Endurance:
I am a mountain (IN) of endurance (EX)
Endless endurance (EX), solid strength (IN)

For Competition:
Compete intensely (IN) with relaxed control of body (EX)
Compete calm (EX), cool (IN), collected (EX) and competitive (IN)!

To Reduce Anxiety:
Fear flows out (EX), courage comes in (IN)

To Reduce Eye Discomfort:
Eyes cool (IN) and relaxed (EX)
Eyelids light (IN) and soft (EX)
Moisture on eyeballs (EX), eyelids float (IN)

To Ease a Sore Throat:
Throat wide and moist (EX), coolness on forehead (IN)

(EX means during exhalations, IN means during inhalations)

made quite confused by having suggestions for the induction of deep relaxation timed to coincide with inhalation phases only, while they are instructed to let their minds "go blank" during the exhalation phases. Reported responses were the inability to cooperate in spite of good will, hyperventilation, tension, and anxiety. When, on the other hand, suggestions for the induction of relaxation are timed to coincide with the exhalation phases of the subjects, they invariably induce deeper relaxation.

Instructions

While you are trying out or practicing many of the following exercises, keep in mind the effects listed in Table 10. The instructions for the exercises should be modified by experimentation according to personal needs. For such experimentation the following instructions are helpful: (1) Do or imagine something only two or three times during consecutive breathing rhythms; (2) Use minimal real stimulation, but maximal involvement of the imagination; (3) Observe a pause-for-feeling, or "creative pause," to allow time for the imagination to work and the body to react.

Experimentation should not be continued when the desired results are not obtained after a few trials. In this case other images should be substituted. However it should be kept in mind that different exercises and images may be effective at different times or under different circumstances.

Many of the following exercises were developed by Jencks and her students, and most involve the breathing rhythm. The exceptions were included because of their great usefulness.

Facilitating Respiration and Increasing the Breathing Capacity

Relaxed Breathing
Long Breath. Imagine inhaling through the fingertips, up the arms into the shoulders, and then exhaling down

the trunk into the abdomen and legs, and leisurely out at the toes. Repeat, and feel how this slow, deep breathing affects the whole body, the abdomen, the flanks, and the chest. Do not move the shoulders while doing the Long Breath.

Stone into Well. Imagine a deep well in your abdomen. Then imagine that you are dropping a stone into this well during a relaxed exhalation. Follow its fall. How long did the fall last? How deep did it fall? Where did it come to rest? Repeat.

Bellows. Breathe as if the flanks were bellows which are drawing in and pushing out. Inhale while the bellows are drawing in the air, exhale while the bellows contract and expel the air. Imagine that the air streams through the flanks freely.

Hole in Small of Back. Sit or lie comfortably and breathe normally and relaxedly. Disregard the chest and throat completely for a moment and imagine a hole in the small of the back, through which the breathed air flows in and out comfortably. Breathe deeply and relaxedly through the hole for three or four breathing cycles. Then just close the eyes for a moment, let the mind drift, and enjoy the feeling of deep relaxation.

Swing. Lie on the back and imagine a swing swinging with your respiration. Push the swing during one exhalation. Let it swing in its own rhythm. Do not push the swing all the time. Permit it to swing by itself. Feel tensions swinging out during exhalation. Feel energy streaming in during inhalation.

Pendulum. Inhale and halt the breath momentarily. Exhale and imagine that this sets a pendulum in motion. Permit the breathing to find its own rhythm. Allow it to swing or flow as it wants to do.

Waves or Tides. Lie on the back and imagine ocean waves or tides flowing with your respiration. Allow them to flow out passively. Allow them to return passively. Do not push. They flow by themselves. Feel the passive flowing in and out of the waves or tides. Observe where you feel movement. Feel to where the waves are flowing. Feel from where the waves return. Do not prolong this exercise beyond two to three respiratory cycles. Then feel what happened in the body during the next two to three cycles. Get up from the lying position first to a sitting and then to a standing position during consecutive exhalations. This preserves the relaxation and prevents dizziness after deep relaxation.

Stand relaxedly, arms hanging easily at the sides, inhale and feel what is set in motion by the rising wave of inhaling. Then allow the wave of the breath to decline and fade, as if into a great distance. Repeat, and allow the arms to move easily with the breathing waves.

Imagined Drug. Imagine that you are inhaling a bronchodilator agent, which relaxes and widens the walls of the air passages in bronchi and lungs. Allow them to become soft like rags and relaxed, collapsing during the exhalations, and allow them to become widely expanded during the inhalations, while the air streams in easily.

Breathing Through the Skin. Concentrate on the forehead or any other body surface area and imagine inhaling and exhaling through the skin there. Exhale and feel something going out. Inhale and feel something coming in. Exhale through the skin and permit it to relax. Inhale through the skin and feel it refreshed and invigorated.

Relaxing the Diaphragm. The release of tensions will result spontaneously and unconsciously in slower, deeper exhalations. Such relaxed breathing is similar to that during sleep and during the waking state may be felt as "being breathed" rather than active breathing. The respiration is deepened when the tendons of the neck and shoulders are relaxed, the mouth-throat junction is felt as a wide open space, and exhalations are felt throughout the whole trunk, especially in the flanks and in the small of the back. Also imagining making movements with the joints, as in calisthenics, or using the vocal mechanism by humming, chanting, sighing, or growling will relax the diaphragm.

Loosening Joints. Work on the joints is especially effective for relaxing the diaphragm, since nerve cells which deepen the breathing rhythm reflexively are located around and in the joints. Allow any yawning, sighing, or changes in the breathing rhythm to occur naturally during joint exercises.

The following exercise is similar to F. M. Alexander's technique, and it is especially effective for the head-neck-shoulder region, which was the location with which he worked.

Sit in an armchair with a high back to rest the head, the arms well supported, the feet squarely on the floor with knees bent at right angles, or lie on the floor on the back, with the legs drawn up, the feet on the floor. Then think each of the following phrases during an exhalation, disregarding the inhalations, or letting the air stream passively into the lungs as if a vacuum were filling gently. Use any or all and repeat as needed: Tell the shoulders to let go of the neck. . . . Tell the neck to let go of the head . . . . Tell the head to let go of the jaw. . . . Tell the throat to let go of the tongue. . . . Tell the eye sockets to let go of the eyes. . . . Tell the shoulders to let go of the upper arms. . . . Tell the elbows to let go of the lower arms. . . . Tell the wrists to let go of the hands. . . . Tell the hands to let go of the fingers. . . . Tell the spine and sternum to let go of the ribs. . . . Tell the lower back to let go of the pelvis. . . . Tell the hipjoints to let go of the upper legs. . . . Tell the knees to let go of the lower legs. . . . Tell the ankles to let go of the feet. . . . Tell the feet to let go of the toes. . . .

Similar to this are some instructions in A. D. Read's (1944) relaxation method for natural childbirth. The practitioner is instructed to imagine, for instance, that the shoulders "open to the outside," the arms fall "out of the shoulder sockets," the back "sinks through the couch to the floor," the legs, knees, and feet "fall by their own weight to the outside," the head "makes an indentation in the pillow," the face "hangs from the cheekbones," and the jaw "hangs loosely." All of these involve the loosening of joints and are effective, especially if done during relaxing exhalations.

Filling and Emptying the Bottle. This is a German version, taught to actors and singers, of a yogic exercise to relax and deepen breathing. Remember that, when liquid is poured into a bottle, the bottom fills before the middle and the top. When the liquid is poured out, the bottom will empty before the top. Imagine that the trunk is a bottle. Fill it with inhaled air, first the bottom and then higher and higher. During exhalation imagine the bottle tipped and the breath flowing out, emptying first the lower abdomen, then the upper, and finally the chest. Repeat, but no more than three times consecutively. Then resume normal breathing.

Facilitating Inhalations

Rubber Ball. Imagine during exhalation squeezing the air out of a hollow rubber ball with the thumb. Imagine releasing the pressure on the rubber ball and permit it to refill passively and recover its form while the air streams in by itself. Squeeze the air out again during exhalation. Then allow it to refill once more, and with the next exhalation relax completely and resume the normal breathing.

Breathing Pathways. Imagine any of the breathing pathways described above and pictured in Figure 2. Breathe in and out through any of these or any other place you choose. This diverts the attention from strained respiratory passages and much eases inhalations.

Fragrant Flower. Imagine finding the first fragrant flower of spring. Gently inhale its odor and let it linger in your mind during repeated gentle inhalations. Imagine all the beauty, all the gentleness, and all the new life of springtime.

Detecting a Scent. Imagine being an animal that has detected some scent on the wind and is testing it, deliberating whether the smell means danger or something attractive.

Perfume. Imagine that you are testing the very delicate fragrance of a perfume or of the bouquet of a precious wine. Allow the inhaled air to be perceived by the sense of smell. Imagine it to flow upward and backward to the brain, then along the inside of the skull to the back of the head, and from there down the spine, and at the level of the middle of the back into the lungs. Repeat, but no more than two or three times in order to prevent hyperventilation.

Eiderdown or Clouds. Breathe in so lightly that the air rests in the lungs like eiderdown feathers. Breathe in gently, so that the feathers are not disturbed. Relax during exhalations. Then, during inhalation, imagine again the bed of light, fluffy feathers, or imagine a "featherbed of clouds," as it can be seen from above from an airplane, resting on nothing but light air. Feel the air in the lungs rest with such lightness and ease.

(*Managing Real and Apparent Breathing Restrictions*)

Work with the imagination is especially important for easing restricted breathing. Imagining anything that will remove a barrier or block, make something impenetrable permeable, soften a hard resistance, or change the direction of a movement may work. Greatest success is attained if the exercise is constructed according to the previous question "what does the restriction feel like, and what, just in your imagination, could counteract this particular kind of restriction?" Success is highly individual, and a person who does not succeed in "breathing through the small of the back" according to Figure 2 may have great success with the Resting Cat.

Sieve. The diaphragm may be imagined as being permeable, so that whatever can be imagined to flow through it can do so. The movement during a relaxing "letting go" of the breath during exhalation may be felt as a streaming or flowing downward into the lower abdomen or down and out of the body. It can be felt while lying down, sitting, or walking and will always have a very relaxing effect. Just imagine the diaphragm to be a sieve. Feel during exhalations that something streams downward and outward or downward and inward. Relax deeply with the streaming and allow the abdomen to stay relaxed during the following passive inhalation.

(*Tennis Court.* If there is a feeling that not enough air can be inhaled, this exercise is helpful. Imagine that if the surface space of all air sacs of the lungs were spread out, it would cover an area approximately as large as a tennis court. Breathe, and imagine doing it "with the whole tennis court.")

Vertical Breathing. This exercise works especially well for real physical restrictions, such as body casts or corsets, but also for being very still and calm for a longer period of time as is necessary for an actor on stage when he plays being dead. Breathe very slowly and relaxedly while imagining that the breath moves up and down a vertical tube inside you. This tube can be between throat and pelvis, extend from the crown of the head to the toes, or even extend along the vertical axis of the body out into space.

Relieving Shortness of Breath. For relieving shortness of breath or the feeling of suffocating, press firmly under the nostrils with two fingertips. Breathe through the nose while moving the pressing fingers outwards toward the cheekbones.

Trap Door. To relieve a restricted feeling in the region of the diaphragm at the end of an exhalation, give the diaphragm a little push with the last breath, and imagine that the bottom were dropping out of the diaphragm, or that it were opening up like a lowering trap door to a room below.

Slowing the Exhalation

Steam Whistle. Imagine being the leaking lid of an almost boiling whistling teakettle or the leaking lock of a pressure cooker. Exhale very slowly, allowing the air to stream out through slightly parted teeth and lips, making a hissing sound as long as the breath lasts. Time yourself by counting and try in time to extend the exhalation longer and longer.

Purse and Puff. Purse the lips while the tongue is curled up loosely or held against the roof of the mouth. Breathe out very slowly, allowing the cheeks to puff up slightly, while letting the loose lips say "popopo . . . ," "papapa . . . ," or "pupupu . . . ," in little puffs for as long as possible.

Hum. Curl the tongue back along the roof of the mouth and hold it there while making a long, slow hum, letting the air stream out very slowly through the nose, allowing the roof of the mouth to vibrate.

Strengthening Breathing Muscles

The following exercises should be mastered consecutively. The first one is so simple that it should be used routinely by those suffering from asthma or emphysema. The last two are among the most difficult yogic breathing exercises. The In-Up-Back is a simple adaptation for Westerners of a yogic exercise.

Extinguishing the Candle. Point the lips and blow out shortly, sharply, and strongly while pulling the abdomen in tightly, as if blowing out a candle. Then let the abdomen fall or sink downward and forward, allowing the air to stream into the lungs passively. Repeat three to five times, not more.

In-Up-Back. This exercise may be done any time and place, sitting, standing, or lying down, but it should be avoided after meals. It reduces the waistline and strengthens the abdominal muscles. Exhale, then pull the abdomen in as strongly as possible on "in," then, without inhaling, up on "up," and once more in on "back." Hold it in that position as long as possible while resuming breathing with chest and shoulders. Ever so often repeat the in-up-back movement when the abdomen sags.

Creeping Air. Inhale until the diaphragm seems tensed, but continue inhaling and feel the air "creep up the back, filling the area at the shoulder blades and upper tips of the lungs." This brings much tension. Release any unnecessary tension by consciously dropping the shoulders. Keep the lungs fully expanded as long as possible, but keep the muscles of the limbs and face as relaxed as possible. When you cannot hold the full breath any more, let it flow out slowly and resume normal breathing.

Yogic Abdominal Contraction (Uddiyana Bandha). This exercise should be attempted only if the previous ones can be performed comfortably. It is practiced sitting or standing, but should be practiced only on an empty stomach, that is, at least three to four hours after the last meal.

Exhale, inhale deeply, and then exhale forcibly while drawing the stomach in and up. Contract the abdominal muscles strongly to make as large a hollow as possible under the ribs, expelling the last remains of breath. Maintain the completely exhaled contraction as long as possible. When it cannot be held any longer, allow the abdominal muscles to relax suddenly and "fall" downward and forward while the air streams into the lungs passively. Resume relaxed breathing.

Stomach Flapping. Exhale, inhale deeply, and then exhale forcibly while pulling in the abdomen. Without inhaling start flapping the stomach out and in. Practice until in time twenty-five contractions can be made without inhaling.

Utilizing Sounds

Making sound vibrations not only serves communication, but it is extremely healthful by itself. Animals will make sounds without obvious reasons, and the old customs of singing with small children, while hiking, during work, or church hymns are beneficial, since the singing releases excess energy, raises the spirits, induces relaxation, and lengthens the attention span or diverts the mind from physical strain. The Bible admonishes "Make a joyful noise... sing...." (Psalm 66: 1-2), and advice is given in Mazdaznan (Hanish 1914) to sing, hum, and whistle as much as possible and to perform the Egyptian posture and movement exercises "with song on the breath."

The breath, streaming past the vocal cords, produces the sound vibrations on which all language is based, but movement of vocal cords is also induced by merely thinking of sounds. Thinking the holy syllable OM of the Hindus, the silent prayers of all religions, and the "mental device" (Benson, Beary, and Carol 1974) of a sound, word, or phrase being repeated silently in Transcendental Meditation or Benson's Relaxation Response all produce sound vibrations.

Different sounds are felt in different parts of the body: the slow, low frequency vibrations of the syllable OM are usually felt in the abdomen or chest, while the high frequency vibrations are usually felt in the throat or head.

Animal Sounds. Purr like a cat and then spit like a cat. Feel the difference. End with purring. Roar like a lion, howl like a wolf, bark like a dog, and feel how these sounds affect different parts of the body.

Feeling Vibrations. Make a vocal sound and feel the vibrations in the different body cavities of mouth, throat, chest, and abdomen, one after the other. Change the size of body cavities by alternately tensing and relaxing their walls and notice the different feelings and sounds of the vibrations.

Vibrating Spaces. Make a steady hum and vibrate the front of the throat, the cheeks, the chest, the abdomen, or even the forehead by shaking or lightly tapping them. Change the frequency of the hum from low to high and from high to low and feel the differences in the cavity reverberations.

Vowels. Form different vowel sounds by changing the lips and mouth position: for a as in *a*sk, the mouth, throat, and chest should be or feel wide open; for ā, as in *a*le, the mouth is pulled broad; for ē, as in *e*ve, it is pulled very broad and narrow; for oo, as in f*oo*d, the mouth becomes round; for o, as in g*o*, it is very small and round; for the German ü, which is also the correct pronounciation of the French "u," the mouth is very small and very pointed. Vibrate the different cavities while trying out different sounds.

Lip Movements. Make small, vibrating movements during exhalations, or say softly but very fast "bribribribri-brrribrrrriiii-mamamamamaaa-mimimamamimimamaa," and so on. Feel the vibrations. Increase the accuracy of pronunciation and speed of the movements.

Flowing Speech. Read or recite a passage or poem and let the words "speak themselves." Let them make their own vibrations, disregarding the speaker as well as the hearer.

Sound Meditation. Concentrate on an imagined sound, a word, or a phrase, either mono- or multisyllable, high or low frequency. Experiment with different sounds at different times. The low ones will be relaxing, the high ones invigorating or exciting. Search for adequate sounds or sound combinations for different purposes.

Conclusion

Exercises in this chapter include those useful for the healthy in everyday life, for patients with breathing difficulties, and the rather advanced and difficult ones for expanding the breathing capacity of athletes and performing artists. Breathing therapists must choose exercises according to the special needs of their patients and must remember that the use of the imagination is especially important for circumventing self-consciousness, which may interfere with the usually subconscious process of breathing. Often when one exercise does not achieve a purpose, another one, which suits the imagination better, will do so.

The imagination also plays an important role in the posture and movement exercises in the next chapter.

6. Body Balance and Movement

Physical and emotional trauma upset the balance of body and mind, so that much energy is wasted in muscular tensions, bringing on unnecessary tiredness and exhaustion. If stress reactions (see chapter 3) become habit patterns, muscles and tendons shorten and thicken, and excessive connective tissue is deposited, causing a general consolidation of tissues. This in turn increases the difficulty of handling the stresses of life and so produces a viscious circle. The physical limitations involved may also cause less sensitive perceptions and under- or overreactions, resulting in an even more upset mental and physical balance.

Well-developed sensory awareness (see chapter 4) is an excellent feedback indicator for detecting tight tendons, stiff muscles, creaking joints, poorly aligned posture, interfering fat, and physical imbalance. It provides the information necessary for conscious recognition of the need for flexibility, better muscle tone, increased circulation, a better sense of balance and movement, and weight control. Correct adjustment of these will not only economize energy and improve physical well-being, but also reduce anxiety, increase self-sufficiency, and lead to healthy, mature psychological reactions.

Most modern physical work and recreation are not sufficient and not performed in a manner for keeping body and mind in good condition. Self-discipline and perseverance are necessary for incorporating appropriate physical and mental exercises into such everyday activities as walking, sitting at a job or in a car, house or garden work, and recreation. However, everyday activities offer all the information and opportunities necessary for corrections of body alignment, flexibility, muscle tone, and balanced movement.

The purpose of the exercises in this chapter is to increase awareness of and improve the alignment of spine, limbs, and head; the flexibility of joints and tendons; the balance of muscle tone; and the equilibrium at rest and in motion.

Body Alignment

Infants sit naturally. Adults often slump. Figures 3a and 3d show good body alignment. The spine is straight, the angles between the spine and ribs approach 90 degrees, and the pelvic bone is oriented in a straight line with the spine. Figures 3b and 3c show poor body alignment. The spine is rounded, the ribs are pressed together, and the pelvic is tilted. This causes strain on muscles, joints, and nerves; obstructs breathing; displaces internal organs and many cause them to function poorly; interferes with proper circulation; disturbs body equilibrium and free motion; and causes unnecessary fatigue. In general, poor body alignment indicates a lack of physical and mental fitness. Good body symmetry and easy carriage are necessary for good health.

Body alignment follows the general laws of mechanics. There will be strain to the degree to which alignment deviates from the optimal configuration for the counteraction of gravitational pulls. The force of gravity acts

Figure 3
Body Alignment

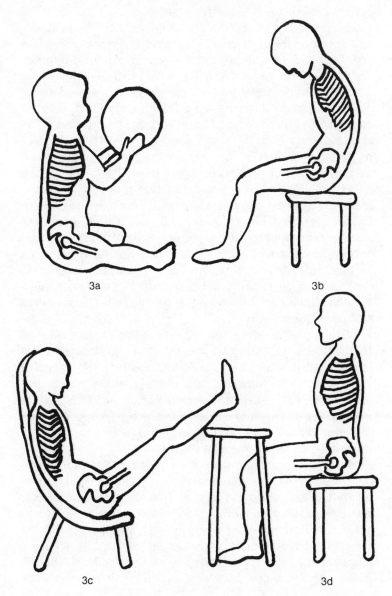

3a

3b

3c

3d

at right angles to the earth, and the body should also be perpendicular to the earth to support and balance the head, spine, thorax, pelvis, and legs with the least strain and expenditure of energy. The erect body should be like a stable stack of well-aligned blocks. There is an interdependence of all parts from the feet to the head and, as with a building, a sound structure requires a good foundation. To make improvements and repairs and prevent damage, the laws of mechanics must be applied. The structure of the body must be well-aligned from the feet up. At the base this depends on the contact of the feet with the ground and their relation to the bones of the lower legs. The ankles cannot function properly when the toes point out. Knee and ankle must both be aligned to function as true hinge joints. Only on well-aligned feet and legs can the hip joints and pelvis be well aligned, and only on such a well-aligned base can the spine serve as vertical axis. Asymmetry of a leg or the upper body may, especially when the force of momentum acts, easily damage the alignment of the spine, resulting in pinched nerves and consequent pain.

With a well-aligned body, a new relationship of head to shoulders to spine becomes possible, and the rotation of the head is not accomplished by the superficial muscles attached to shoulders and collarbones, but by the deeper ones which are nearer the spinal vertebrae. This results in a feeling of freedom and ease in the head-neck-shoulder region and makes movement more easy and graceful and improves appearance and well-being.

Much can be done in simple ways at any age to improve body alignment. The connective tissue, of which the above-mentioned anatomical structures for alignment are made, has an amazing capability for renewal when conditions are right. Consciousness of poor body alignment with its resulting detrimental effects should constantly act as a stimulus for improvement to arouse the desire to correct it. Choose from the following exercises those which are most appealing or invent new ones, and keep doing them! Remember always that exercises which contain imagery must have personal appeal. One exercise from M. E. Todd's (1937) excellent book *The Thinking Body* may have appealed to trainees of the 1920s and 1930s, but it has been utterly disliked by Jencks' trainees of the 1970s. In it is suggested, for straightening the spine, to imagine the head reaching up toward a hook in the sky and "like Bluebeard's wives, you are hanging by the hair."

Review also the section on Detection and Release of Muscular Tensions, and Gravity and the Supporting Environment. See chapter 4.

Alignment Exercises

Spine. For erectness straighten the spine during exhalation and feel it supported from below. Imagine inhaling up along the spine, and exhale while allowing the body tissues in front to become soft and relaxed. Inhale for strength and straightness, and for "getting more backbone." Exhale thinking of the support from the solid base of chair or floor.

String Puppet. During inhalations imagine being a string puppet or marionette, suspended by a string through the crown of the head. Strings attached to the limbs raise them during inhalations and lower them during exhalations.

Link Chain. Imagine the spine being a large link chain. Straighten it during exhalation.

Slinky. Imagine the spine were a "slinky" toy, that is, a springy coil which can move freely. Imagine moving all parts of the spine in all directions. Remember, this toy works best if it is moved slowly and rhythmically.

Stack of Blocks. Imagine the spine being a stack of building blocks and the head a ball. Imagine a shallow dish on top of the stack of blocks in which the ball can roll around. Let the stack of blocks sway gently in a circular motion while the imagined ball is rolling around in the dish atop. Relax the shoulders. After a moment reverse the direction. Do not repeat this exercise for too long.

Freedom of Head. Hold the head erect and turn it lightly back and forth. Feel the smallest plane on which it balances. Feel the head being moved and balanced only by the deep muscles closest to that plane, and not by those attached to neck and shoulders. Try your voice and test if it becomes freer by carrying the head in this manner. Look at your neck in a mirror and see if it becomes slimmer by carrying the head in this manner. Feel the better blood supply to the head.

Plumb Lines. Stand up, feel the vertical support of the spine, straighten it during exhalation, and let the arms hang like plumb lines from the shoulder joints. Imagine two other plumb lines hanging down from the ears.

Horizontal Axes. While you are sitting or standing, establish the vertical support to the floor by straightening the spine during exhalation. Now imagine a crossbar between the shoulders along the shoulder blades. This bar makes an "upper cross" or "upper fulcrum" with the supporting spine. Feel the crossbar. While standing, also feel the "lower cross" or "lower fulcrum" between the hip joints or a little higher across the lower back. Explore how moveable the upper and lower fulcrums are by gently moving them during exhalation. Move sideways like an old balance scale which can be weighted at either end. Bend slightly forward and backward. Make small gyrating movements. Remember that joints are structures which connect different parts and that they should be freely moveable. Imagine energy streaming outward and/or downward from the spine through the upper and lower cross.

Clothes Hanger. Imagine the head-neck line together with a line along the shoulder blades forming a clothes hanger which is somewhat stiff but very supporting. Imagine draping the tissues of the shoulder and neck region loosely over this support during exhalation. Feel whether the neck remains relaxed and relax any tension by exhaling. Walk a few steps and imagine getting your whole support from the clothes hanger. Imagine a cord through the crown of the head, held from above. Let the clothes hanger hang from this cord. Add Plumb Lines during exhalation.

Pulling Cord. Imagine the Clothes Hanger with the cord which pulls up through the crown of the head. Imagine the pull during inhalation. Imagine some superior force holding you upright by that cord, so that you can stay so without effort. Let the muscles and skin of the shoulder region relax loosely over the hanger during exhalation. Repeat this two or three times and feel invigorated while the cord pulls up during inhalation. End the exercise with an invigorating inhalation.

Water Jar or Book. Imagine balancing a heavy water jar on the head. Walk about in this posture. Sit on a chair and get up again, still balancing the jar. If you have difficulty with this exercise, do it with a real book. Balance the book on the head while walking, sitting down, getting up, and straightening the head with the balanced book toward the ceiling. Feel the position and movement of the spine. Keep the body relaxed with exhalations during the exercise.

No-Slouch. Imagine wearing a "no-slouch halter." This consists of shoulder straps, a strap across the chest below the bust line, and two broad, crossed, elastic straps across the back. The tension from the back straps gives lift and straightens the back. First imagine the tension across the back straightening you, then, during exhalation, relax comfortably inside the outer straight shell. Keep breathing relaxedly and normally while imagining wearing the halter.

Sliding Door. While you are standing or sitting, straighten the spine during exhalation. Imagine the shoulder blades being sliding doors which slide together toward the middle during exhalation. Feel them sliding shut during

exhalation. Feel them opening gently during inhalation.
Wings. Imagine wings attached to the shoulder blades.
Spread them wide during inhalation, and fold them gently
during exhalation. Relax and let the normal breathing
rhythm take over. Breathing helps walking erect without
effort. While walking, inhale for lightness, then feel the
solid ground under foot during exhalation. Walk with the
"wings" opening and closing and permit yourself to be
carried effortlessly.

Alive Good Posture. Stand up in the consciously "good
posture" portrayed in some books, that is, the back to the
wall, the spine straight and stiff like a stick, the abdomen
pulled in, and the chest out. Then become alive. Imagine
the spine being the Link Chain. Let the Clothes Hanger
take care of the upper cross and walk back and forth in
this new, good posture. Then let the spine become stiff
and dead like a stick and walk with the stiff spine. Alternate between "dead" and "alive" good postures. Notice
developing tensions, and release them with exhalations.

Fountain. This exercise is advanced and should be attempted only after practicing some of the previous ones.
Sit on a straight chair, stand, or walk while imagining
the spine to be a jet of water, a fountain which is fed and
carried from below. Exhale and feel how a surge of water,
a surge of energy comes from below. Feel free to change
your position any time. Remember the Clothes Hanger
and permit the tissues of the shoulder region to hang
loosely over that imagined clothes hanger, so that the
neck and shoulder region becomes very free. Imagine again
the fountain which straightens the spine from below. Then
imagine the head being a ball that plays on top of the fountain. Permit it to play freely, play gently, play lightly up
there. Let the ball lift during inhalation. Allow it to relax
onto the water during exhalation. Allow it to rise again
or be thrown higher during inhalation.

Imagine a gentle wind from the right or left, which
makes the jet stream of the fountain move very slightly.

Counterbalance the wind. Keep the shoulders loose, and let the ball on top of the fountain play, dance, roll, and move freely. Ever so often imagine a new surge of energy from below. Allow freedom and ease in the head, neck, and shoulder region. Allow straightness, liquid cohesiveness, fluidity, and mobility in the spine. And then, after a moment, stretch and flex the arms and end the exercise with a refreshing inhalation.

A trainee, for whom none of the exercises for straightening the spine worked, finally succeeded upon the following suggestion: "Imagine again the fountain. Put your hands on the hips, palms down. During an exhalation press down on the hips and feel the water of the fountain spurt up inside you along the spine." Upon imagining this, he spontaneously straightened the upper spine for the first time, got the feeling of that position, and was then able to repeat the straightening at will.

Flexibility

Limberness of the body is extremely important. It aids the circulation and helps prevent nerves from being squeezed or pressed as well as the tearing of muscles, the spraining of joints, and the breaking of bones. It also economizes energy since it requires less effort to move a flexible body.

Flexibility is improved by yogic and Kung Fu positions, calisthenics, stretching massages, passive movements, and Structural Integration, see Table 6 and Table 7 in chapter 3. Structural Integration is a treatment performed by a trained specialist and cannot easily be self-administered (Rolf 1958).

Review the following exercises and also the chapter on Self-Massage and Sport Massage and choose from them whatever is most appealing and/or necessary.

Lengthening Leg Tendons. Stand on a stair step or any place where the heels can be dropped. Hold on to something and lower the heels, first alternately and then together, leaving them a few seconds in the stretched, lowered position. Stretch the tendons to the upmost during exhalation while keeping the rest of the body as relaxed as possible. This exercise is especially important for those who shortened the leg tendons by wearing high heels and for those with lower back pain. Lengthening tendons in this manner accomplishes the same as wearing "earth shoes."

Stretching the Tendons Inside the Thighs. Sit crosslegged, elbows resting on knees, hands dangling over feet. Press one knee down with the elbow during exhalation, stretching the tendons inside the thigh. Rest in that position until the urge to inhale is felt. Then straighten during inhalation. Repeat with the other leg. Repeat exercise four to eight times.

Forward Circles. Make a slow forward circle with the head by stretching the neck as far as possible first downward and forward, then upward, then backward and return to the starting position. Do not turn the head sideways. Inhale while lowering the chin, exhale while raising it. Do this first in reality, then just imagine it with the described breathing. Repeat the exercise, making the circle with the whole upper body: move neck and spine downward and forward during inhalation and up and back to the starting position during exhalation. This exercise is done with counterbreathing, see chapter 5, for a stronger stretching effect.

Rubber Joints. Flexibility is enhanced by exhalations. Think during exhalations that the hip, knee, and ankle joints are flexible rubber. Stand, walk, and sit with such joints. Let the hip and pelvic area be flexible like rubber.

Oiling Joints. To loosen up joints, imagine putting a drop of oil into each, and then move the joint in reality or in the imagination during exhalations. Feel how the oil distributes itself while it eases movement. This has worked for arthritic joints as well as for joints which were stiff after athletic movement, too much typing, cold, or playing an instrument.

Yogic Stretching. Never strain to go into any yogic position. Where tension or resistance is encountered, stretch very slowly into an intermediate position. Hold this position for a few breathing cycles and adjust to it, especially during relaxing exhalations. Then, during subsequent exhalation, stretch a little more until again tension or resistance is felt, and adjust again to this position during relaxing exhalations. Repeat as long as possible. This is very useful for arthritics for extending their stretch to reach down to tie shoelaces or pick something up from the floor.

Flexible Spine. Certain parts of the spine may be more flexible than others. Stretching exercises are most important for the less flexible areas. No momentum should be used for stretching the spine. Gravity alone with a gentle extra stretch during exhalation is all that is necessary to make the spine in time very flexible. Work according to the instructions given above for yogic stretching.

Test the flexibility of the lowest, middle, and upper parts of the spine with the following positions. First, stand and bend forward from the waist, letting the arms dangle, and let gravity alone pull the arms and upper body down as far as possible. Allow the spine to give as much as possible during exhalations. Keep the head up if dizziness develops. Feel the flexibility of the spine and note any areas of special stiffness or discomfort. Stretch the stiff areas during exhalations, but do not stretch painful ones. Second, sit on the floor, arms stretched forward, knees straight, and let the weight of the head carry the upper body forward and down. Third, lie on the back, raise the legs, bring them slowly over the head and, with the knees straight, let the toes touch the floor or come as close to it as possible. The spinal stretches may also be made more effective without forcing by thinking during exhalations: "I wonder whether my right or my left hand will reach the floor first," "I wonder whether my nose or my forehead will touch my knees," or any other relaxing, encouraging, or diverting thought.

The spine is perfectly flexible when the following yogic positions can be attained without stress or strain: (1) the *Paschimothan Asana* or sitting head to knees pose; (2) the *Pada Hastasan* or standing head to knees or hands flat on floor pose; (3) the *Halasan* or plough pose, lying on the back with legs brought straight over the head until the toes touch the floor; (4) the *Karna Peedasan* or ear-knee pose, lying on the back, the legs brought over the head, and the knees bent, resting on the floor next to the ears; and (5) the *Poojiasan* or pill bug pose, lying on the back with legs brought over the head with the knees bent and pressed to the floor together just beyond the head.

Flexibility and Strength in the Pelvic Area

Flexibility of the lowermost spine and around the hip joints and strengthening of the deep lying abdominal psoas muscles is extremely important for good health. Easy locomotion and such activities of the upper body as carrying and throwing depend on these muscles. Flexibility and strength can be improved by the following exercises.

Curl. Lie on the back, the knees flexed comfortably. Lift the lowermost part of the spine and lower it in a slow, rolling motion, as if putting down each vertebra separately. Repeat. When this "curling down" becomes easy, start working at both, curling and uncurling the lowermost part of the spine.

Tuck. Pull the buttocks inward and upward and hold them there tensely as long as possible while relaxing the rest of the body. Do this as often as possible while sitting, standing, lying, or walking.

Pelvic Lift. Sit in a comfortable chair with your legs well supported and knees bent. During inhalations thrust the tailbone forward and tense the muscles of the buttocks and lower abdomen. Relax during exhalation. Repeat often. Do this also while lying down or standing.

Tailcurl. Imagine the spine ending in a tail. Slowly curl the tail forward and upward during a relaxing exhalation. Keep breathing relaxedly. Release the created tension during a subsequent relaxing exhalation.

Tilt. Tilt the pelvis forward and upward during an exhalation and then continue breathing relaxedly. Do this often while sitting, standing, or lying down.

Crease. In any position, form a crease across the upper abdomen by holding the chest up and forward and elevating the front of the pelvis. Repeat this often in case of swayback or back pain.

Pelvic Rocking. Rock the pelvis forward and backward at a slow pace. Imagine breathing in and out through a hole in the small of the back in rhythm with the rocking. Find your own rhythm. Find out whether you prefer to inhale while rocking forward and exhale while rocking backward or the opposite way. Do it as it feels most comfortable at the moment. Keep the mind blank while rocking. Avoid hyperventilation.

Muscle Tonus

Muscles move body parts and act as shock absorbers. Adequate muscle tone economizes energy, aids the circulation, and prevents accidents. For instance, the activity of good leg muscles aids circulation by pumping blood upward to the heart. On the other hand, if the back muscles are not in tone, the alignment of the spine can be adversely affected, resulting in pinched nerves and consequent pain.

Diverse muscle relaxation exercises were described in previous chapters, but a distinction must now be made between beneficial and detrimental relaxation. Flabbiness and laxness may be relaxed, but are not beneficial for the health of body and mind. Muscle tonus and alertness require a healthy tension, but not the energy-wasting kind.

Methods have often been developed during periods of

mental and physical decline to keep mind and body in better condition. Examples are the exercises of Hatha Yoga, T'ai Chi, Kung Fu, and later the physical training for monks of different religions, and also the development of the Swedish Massage by Pehr Henrik Ling and German Gymnastics by Turnvater Jahn for the populations of repressed Europe during Napoleonic times when military service in the subject nations was prohibited.

All kinds of calisthenics and gymnastics will improve muscle tonus. The following exercise is given as an example since the abdominal muscles often lack tone. The instructions are from Relaxation and Toning-Up Exercises to Facilitate Pregnancy and Childbirth (Jencks and Rosenthal 1973), but this exercise is beneficial for both sexes at any age.

Toning Abdominal Muscles. Kneel with both hands and knees firmly on the floor. While exhaling relax the abdomen and let the back cave in. Then, slowly, while inhaling, tense the abdominal muscles and arch the back. Repeat four to eight times.

Eutony

G. Alexander in Denmark (Stokvis and Wiesenhütter 1971) developed a special method for improving muscle tonus, called Eutony, which means good or most advantageous tonus. It is outlined below since it has not been described to date in English.

Eutony is an optimal balance of tonus with least energy expenditure within the dynamic equilibrium necessary for unhampered blood circulation, respiration, and muscle tone during movement and rest.

Beginning with Jaques Dalcroze's rhythmic-musical education (see Table 8, chapter 4), G. Alexander developed the Eutony method through her experiences with healthy and sick children and adults during the past forty-five years in Denmark. Eutony training is now used in the elementary school system in Denmark as well as in the preparation for practical or artistic professions and in therapy.

Eutony training induces tonus changes, so that body and mind can be in tune with internal and external physical, emotional, and mental events. It changes posture and behavior, promotes physical and mental equilibrium, and brings about a frank and relaxed manner. Repeated new adjustments which improve and enrich the personality are a constantly satisfying aspect of this method.

Eutony training utilizes the fact that sensory awareness of a body part will usually locally increase the circulation and alter its muscle tonus, and that directing the attention to different tissues of the body results in basically different sensations. For instance, directing the attention to the skin as the outermost limit of the body produces sensations different from those produced by giving attention to subcutaneous tissue.

Training Procedure. There are no schematized repetitions, and no direct corrections of posture and tensions are made. The initial states of mind and body determine how the training begins, and changes are made indirectly, by constantly monitoring and adjusting the body image and physiological tensions. The most diverse, often apparently insignificantly small changes are sensed and objectively compared with the body image and best possible equilibrium of muscle tensions. During the following outlined general training course, any newly discovered facts will be integrated into the developing personality.

1. Control positions are used to reveal shortened muscles and inhibited joint movement.
2. Passive movements are used to test regulation and control of innervation and reflex tonus.
3. The human figure is modeled to test the body image.
4. Sensory awareness of the body in the surrounding space is developed in order to normalize the body image.
5. The autonomic nervous system is consciously influ-

enced toward establishing a healthy dynamic equilibrium of blood circulation and respiration during rest and work.

6. The tonus of the contracting and relaxing muscles during the same movement is harmonized to avoid wasting energy.

7. Stretching is practiced by brisk general stretching, by stretching away from the floor or a partner with maximal strength but without exertion, and by stretching away from the floor at different angles with normal strength but minimal energy expenditure, simultaneously allowing harmonization of muscle tonus, circulation, and respiration.

8. Control of shifting the body weight is practiced while lying, sitting, standing, and walking.

9. Keeping balance and equilibrium is practiced on a moving ground.

10. Free eutonic movements of the body in space are made alone, with a partner, and in a group.

This latter way of moving, as some of the preparatory exercises, is similar to the ancient Chinese T'ai Chi movements, of which examples are given below.

Equilibrium and the Center of Gravity

Physical equilibrium is affected by the position of the center of gravity, which in turn depends on the alignment and position of the body. The center of gravity of the human body, while standing straight or sitting, is in the lower abdomen. Occidentals usually feel or imagine their center of gravity too high: in the chest or even as high as the head. Orientals, on the other hand, generally feel and imagine their center of gravity correctly in the lower abdomen.

The yogic sitting posture or *asana*, which means throne, seat, or manner of sitting, is characterized by a broad base with a low center of gravity. Its forms, according to the oldest instructions in the Upanishads are: the Lotus,

Swastika, and Bhadra (Deussen 1899). All three are in India usual ways of sitting on the ground, the first two with the lower legs crossed, the last with the soles of the feet pressed together. All that is said about these positions with their natural low center of gravity is that they should be comfortable and the chest-neck-head axis must be straight. All other yogic asanas were later developments. The emphasis on the low center of gravity is illustrated by the heavy, broad base of Buddha effigies. Special terms for the lower abdomen, enclosing the center of gravity, are the Chinese T'ai Chi *"tant'ien,"* the Japanese Zen *"hara,"* and the Islamic Sufi *"kath."* In Japan, a toy doll is given to children which vividly demonstrates the effectiveness of the low center of gravity. It has a round, lead-weighted belly and bottom, causing it always to return to the vertical position when it is knocked over. It is painted as an image of Boddhidharma, or Ta-mo, the supposedly white, blue-eyed monk, famous for his imperturbable sitting, who brought Buddhism from India to China about 520 A.D. and founded the Zen sect.

In the yogic meditation positions the low center of gravity is static. In T'ai Chi and the martial arts it is a moving center. It is in both the reservoir of strength and vitality.

Better physical balance will bring about better mental balance. This has been repeatedly observed in psychotherapies which include physical balancing exercises. Shallow breathing, on the other hand, reduces relaxation, flexibility, and mobility, and seems to "raise the center of gravity to the chest," inviting feelings of insecurity and a precarious equilibrium of body and mind.

The following exercises are designed to lower the center of gravity and improve equilibrium.

Equilibrium Exercises

Feeling the Center of Gravity. Imagine all your weight concentrated in the abdomen, just above the pelvis. Feel it at first during relaxing exhalations, but then allow the abdomen to remain expanded during diaphragmatic breathing and let the center of gravity remain at its low level also during inhalations.

Raft. Imagine the buttocks supported by a broad, anchored raft or platform, carried by ocean waves. Feel the broadness and resilience of the base. Feel the flexibility and ease of the upper body.

Spinning Top. Imagine a focal point or weighted center of gravity from which to balance or move in the lower abdomen. Let the center hold you. Inhale for lightness, exhale for heaviness. Feel the spine as vertical axis. Imagine spinning and dancing like a top, always holding your balance, always with a straight axis.

Center of Gravity. Establish such center at the equilibrium point between the feeling of being held up from above and supported from below. For doing this, combine the String Puppet during inhalation, with Gravity or Sitting during exhalation; see chapters 4 and 6. Or just "feel out" your center of gravity during exhalations and inhalations, allowing the floor to completely support your weight while the spine is perfectly aligned vertically.

Balancing Circus Man. This is a toy which demonstrates the physical principle that, in general, the lower its center of gravity, the more stable is an object. The toy consists of a straight stick, balanced on its point, which supports an arch with a heavy marble at each end. The stick may be dressed like a little man who carries the half-circle arch with its marbles. Since the weights are lower than the point of the stick, it easily balances and pivots on its point.

Imagine being a Balancing Circus Man, or having two heavy water buckets suspended from a bar that goes through your body just above the hips. Feel the increased balance especially during exhalations, while you walk as though balancing on a rail.

Hands on Hips. Having the hands on the hips and the feet squarely on the ground is a posture which not only increases self-assurance, but also enhances physical balance. Assume or imagine the posture during exhalation. For balance with an authoritative feeling, the hands are placed on the hips palms down. For solid defiance the backs of the fists rest on the hips. For well-balanced self-support or self-assurance the palms with the fingertips downward and the thumbs to the front support the hips from the back.

Tree. Sensory feedback for achieving better balance may be achieved by standing on one foot only, as in the yogic tree posture. Proprioceptive sensitivity of being balanced should be acquired by doing exercises standing on one foot with closed eyes.

Kung Fu Riding Horse Position. This exercise lowers the center of gravity, improves equilibrium, and increases muscular strength.

First, stand erect, well aligned but relaxed, feet parallel and close to each other, hands hanging loosely at the sides. Keep the toes stationary and turn the heels out. Then, from this position, keep the heels stationary and turn the toes out. Keeping the toes stationary turn the heels out again, and finally turn the toes out once more until the feet are parallel and wide apart. While this is done with the feet, the relaxed hanging hands are clenched into fists which are raised to the abdomen, facing toward the body. Then they are planted firmly on the hip bones, still facing the body. This sequence of movements is called Opening the Horse. Beginners should open it only to as wide a stance as is comfortable. With practice, the end position can be achieved in one jump to a much wider stance.

Second, as soon as the opened position is achieved, do the following all at once: draw the elbows back, let the fists face forward and upward, and bend the knees as if sitting down on a chair, keeping the back straight and vertical.

At this point the Kung Fu Deep Breathing (see chapter 5) is added. Beginners should practice the Riding Horse Position and Deep Breathing separately before adding them. Do the Deep Breathing in the Riding Horse position initially for two minutes. Concentration on the breathing distracts the attention from the strain of the position. As strength and skill increase, breathing in this position can be continued for as long as one wishes, but about five minutes a day are sufficient for keeping in good condition.

If the Kung Fu Deep Breathing in the Riding Horse position is performed in front of a mirror, the face may be observed to appear masklike, with wide-open, staring eyes. This is a sign of a state of deep concentration or altered consciousness which should be maintained until the end of the exercise. If the face is relaxed, the concentration may be disturbed.

Movement

Body movements can be active, that is, initiated by the voluntary muscles, or passive, that is, moved by an outside agent. See Passive Movements, below. They can be free, without a resisting force, or forced against a resisting force. Movements may be made with relaxed muscles during exhalations, or with tensed muscles while holding the breath or during inhalations. See Counterbreathing, chapter 5.

A muscle contraction may be isotonic, the tone remaining constant, with movement depending on outside forces. Passive movements are an example of this. As soon as muscle tone changes, the even flow of passive movements is disturbed. Therefore such movements provide the best indication of complete muscle relaxation and may be used as an excellent biofeedback indicator. A muscle may also function isometric, without changing its length or thickness. In this case its tension may change, but no movement occurs.

For any given movement there is only one pattern which is the most economical, and this will also be the most graceful. Balanced arm motion begins with movement initiated from the elbow. Balanced walking is initiated by the psoas muscles inside the trunk with the knees moving parallel to each other and straight forward. Movements should flow evenly in their natural course and not be disturbed or interrupted by unnecessary tensions which waste energy. Muscular movements which are the most efficient mechanically are not only graceful and harmonious, but also result in a relaxed voice, unobstructed circulation and digestion, and relaxed breathing.

Thinking of a movement of a body part arouses neural impulses related to it, and executing a movement in the imagination before carrying it out in reality facilitates its execution.

The spine and the psoas muscles are the fundamental anatomical bases of support and movement. The strength of the arms and legs depends on their connections with the strongest parts of the spine, where the psoas muscles, which bind pelvis and legs to the spine, reach high up into the thorax and are attached to the spine at a level opposite the lower end of the sternum. Apparently simple activities like walking, running, throwing, carrying, and so on require extremely complex interactions between the nervous, muscular, and skeletal systems. The even flow of naturally well-balanced movement is one of the miracles of the human body and depends on the healthy condition of all the nerves, muscles, skeletal structures, and their connections involved.

Locomotion

Locomotion must be viewed as an activity of the entire body, that involves a complex set of interrelated behavior. Adult human locomotion combines forward and rotational movements about the trunk and hip, knee and ankle joints, with the feet supporting the entire body.

The flexible pelvic area accommodates the twisting, turning motions of locomotion, but it is also a stable center

with large joint surfaces and ligaments to bear the stresses
generated by body weight and motion. Any decrease in
the ability to rotate the trunk from the hips because of
overweight, stiffness, or weakness, impairs the ability to
maintain equilibrium. This results in a compensatory toe-
ing out for providing a broader base of support, resulting
in misaligned hip and knee joints which are vulnerable
to injury. To compensate further, the steps are shortened
and the feet placed wider apart, in a walking pattern re-
sembling that of small children. A child cannot yet maintain equilibrium or make smooth, forward motions involving rotation of the body from the hips. It also helps
keep its balance by stretching its arms out. When walking skill is improved, the feet are kept closer together,
longer strides are taken, and the arms become less important for maintaining balance and tend to swing to counteract the rotation at the hips. Because of their precarious balance, it is easier for humans to walk fast than
slowly, and it is more fatiguing to stand than to walk since
the human locomotor system favors walking and carrying
over standing and sitting.

Dissipation of Tension Through Movement

Excess energy, released by action of the sympathetic
nervous system, if not immediately dissipated by muscular action, produces muscular or nervous tension. This
tension may then be dissipated by muscular action, such
as chopping wood, jogging, gymnastics, garden- or house-
work, dancing or T'ai Chi, and by certain psychotherapies
as, for instance, Bioenergetics or Terpsichoretrancetherapy (see Table 6, chapter 3).

Following are exercises for facilitating movement, increasing the effectiveness of calisthenics, and movements
to preserve, increase, or release energy.

Facilitating Movement

Movement and Balance. Balance is made easier if
movement of the body or body parts is carried out during

exhalations only. During inhalation stand firmly or halt the movement momentarily. This is especially important on insecure ground or for old persons who have broken a hip and must learn again to walk.

Movement and Breathing. Move from the center of breathing: the diaphragm. This is at the same time the anatomical area where the psoas muscles attach to the spine. "Breathed" movement seems to preserve energy and tire less. For forward movement exhale, for backward movement inhale. Imagined or real downward movement is enhanced by exhalation, upward movement by inhalation. This holds for an actor advancing or retreating on stage as for a serve in tennis or a swinging back in golf, and it aids the movements of an invalid as those of a dancer.

Movement and Gravity. Control lightness or weightedness of movements by incorporating the breathing rhythm. Exhale for heaviness or weight and feel the attraction of gravity. Inhale for lightness and lift. Take advantage of the counter force of the solid ground. The harder you push against it, the harder the ground pushes up against you. When you move against gravity, imagine that the ground pushes you up during exhalation.

Climbing. For climbing stairs or a steep slope, exhale and inhale normally at rest before starting, then start climbing during exhalation. Continue climbing as long as the normal exhalation lasts. Halt for inhalation. Allow the breath to stream in passively, as with Rubber Ball, chapter 5. Continue climbing with the next exhalation. The number of steps climbed per exhalation varies according to condition from only one or two in the very weak and old to a flight of stairs in the young and healthy. Usually the number of steps climbed during one exhalation will diminish with climbing. Do not adjust the breathing to the climbing, but the climbing to relaxed breathing. The idea of climbing stairs during exhalation may sound contradictory to upward movement during inhalation. However, the downward push of the legs is the most important lifting factor for climbing, and that is done during exhalation. The muscle relaxation of the upper body during exhalation also preserves energy for the climb. *Horizontal Movement of the Vertical Axis.* Initiate horizontal movement of the vertical axis of the body by a very slight upward extension of the head. This movement results in coordination, resilience, and speed.

Imagined Movements. Executing a movement in the imagination before carrying it out in reality facilitates its later performance. Try this with several different ways of getting up from bed, chair, or floor. Practicing movements in the imagination is very important for athletes for improving accuracy, speed, and coordination. Arthritics can limber up by imagining movements.

Increasing the Effectiveness of Calisthenics

Up and Down. Let the hands hang at the sides. Then, during inhalation, raise them to shoulder height in front of the body. Allow them to sink to the hanging position during slow exhalation. Repeat, raising the hands sideways. Continue slowly and relaxedly as long as pleasant.

Arms and Knees. Raise the arms and bend the knees during inhalation, lower the arms and straighten the knees during exhalation. Work very slowly with flowing movements.

Ribcage Stretching. Sit cross-legged on the floor with the hands resting comfortably on the ankles or legs. Curve one arm over the head and bend and stretch as far as possible in the direction of the curved arm during exhalation. Bring the arm down during inhalation. Repeat with the other arm.

Rolls. Raise the arms horizontally sideways and very slowly make large or small circles from the shoulders. Exhale while lowering the arms and inhale while raising them. Then do many downward and inward rolls during one exhalation, and many upward and outward ones during one inhalation. "Scoop up energy" with outward and upward movements during inhalations, and "pour it into yourself" with downward and inward movements during exhalation.

Jumping Jack. Imagine doing the jumping jack. Move the arms down and legs together on exhalation, legs apart and arms up on inhalation. End with an invigorating inhalation.

Tree in the Wind. Stand easily, legs about three fists apart, arms raised above the head. Move the whole trunk and the arms to right and left in the measure of Triple Time Breathing, chapter 5. Feel the counterstretch of the stretched side during inhalation. This stretch does not occur when doing side bends without triple breathing. This exercise seems simple, but it is very effective. Do not repeat it too many times in the beginning.

Rowing. Sit or stand and imagine rowing a heavy boat against the wind. Alternately pull the elbows back forcefully while bending backwards and stretch the arms while bending forward. Use Triple Time Breathing, chapter 5.

Skiing. Imagine being on a cross-country ski tour. Lower the hips and walk with very long steps, grazing the floor with the soles of the feet. Let the arm swing in the alternate direction of the moving leg as if pushing with a ski pole. Use Triple Time Breathing, chapter 5. How long can you walk in this manner without skis, snow, and poles?

T'ai Chi and Similar Movements

T'ai Chi movements (see Table 6, chapter 3) are not repetitious and structured, as are calisthenic and gymnastic movement exercises. Each teacher of T'ai Chi teaches differently, and any practitioner carries the exercises out according to momentary need and fancy.

Amoeba. Imagine being an amoeba. Begin making flowing motions in any direction with any body part or parts. Follow the motions with your center of gravity, as if letting your substance flow into the created space. Continue without pause to make very slow, flowing, balanced movements.

T'ai Chi Circular Breathing. Practice this first lying, sitting, or standing. Later breathe in this manner also while moving freely, inhaling during upward and outward movements and exhaling during downward and inward movements.

Focus on the lower abdominal area, and observe the breathing movements. Let the breath flow continuously, so that the "letting go" of exhalation is the beginning of the "coming in" of inhalation. Think of the flow of the breathing cycle and imagine it as a flexible, circular pattern in your own way. Expand, contract, and change the circle. Let it originate in the center of the lower abdomen and return to this center.

Continuous Movement. Play a phonograph record of not too familiar music. Imagine throwing a ball back and forth from one hand to the other and move accordingly until the body feels like moving otherwise. Continue moving spontaneously while the music lasts, but do not dance, prethink, or structure any movements. Repeat throwing the imagined ball from hand to hand if spontaneous motion ceases. Move slowly and flowingly.

Pulling and Pushing the Air. During inhalation imagine, and act out, pulling in the air with the arms from the front. Push it away during exhalation. Repeat slowly and rhythmically as long as pleasant. Practice this also with sideways arm movements, bringing the hands together on the chest at the end of the inhalation.

Unknown Footing. Walk as if the footing were absolutely unknown and you could not see it. There could be water, grass, air, or even space under the feet. There could be steps, thorns, rocks, pitfalls. Test the ground for safety with the soles before daring to step, but remember that in the imagination you can also walk on water or air.

Floating Grass. Sit in a cross-legged position in water

up to the neck or imagine doing so. Imagine the spine floating upward as grass or water weeds float up. Allow the
arms to "float upwards" in reality and feel or imagine
them resting on and supported by the water. Then let the
elbows sink down again. Allow the arms to float or sink
and move with the breathing.

Thin Line. Sit up straight and imagine a thin, vertical
line inside the spine, supported at its base. "Feel" the line
rise from its base support during inhalation, and then settle back down onto its support during exhalation. Repeat
as long as comfortable.

Willow in the Wind. Imagine the spine and head to be
a willow in the wind. The wind may change its direction
and strength at any time. Allow the branches and trunk
to sway or move with the wind, always returning to easy
straightness when the wind abates.

Quiet Pond. Sit in a comfortable position and imagine
being a pond that has been stirred up. Feel it become stiller and stiller, until the surface is calm and smooth. When
something stirs it from inside or outside, feel the ripples,
but always let it return by itself to its innate calmness,
its deep, quiet center.

T'ai Chi Sphere. Stand with bare feet and sway a little
to become conscious of the center of gravity of your body
in the lower abdomen. Adjust the feet as necessary. Feel
the movement under the soles of the feet as the body
sways. Inhale and feel the lift. Exhale and settle back
down. Allow the arms and body to move with the breathing. Then form the shape of a circle with the inside of the
hands and arms and imagine encircling a sphere. Imagine
it to be slippery: if it is held too tightly, it will slip away;
if it is held too loosely it will escape. Let it be very heavy
or as light as a soap bubble. Keep moving it around. Play
with it and imagine that it changes slowly. Let it grow
large or shrink, expand one part to make it egg-shaped.
Lift it, lower it, let it move around you. Let the movement flow easily and continuously as you curve and ro-

tate. Move very slowly. Always center the motions along the spine, keeping it flexible, but as vertical as possible. Keep centered around the spine while doing the free-form moving with the sphere.

Moving the Space. Make any movement with arms, legs, or any other body part, and while doing so imagine displacing or moving the "space" away, as though it were water, and in this manner "swim through space."

The Technique of Passive Movements

Movement of relaxed body parts, without the active participation of the subject, has been found to be a very effective means of inducing both physical and mental relaxation. The subject should lie or sit comfortably.

Relaxation is initiated progressively by the repetition of a series of slow, monotonous, rhythmic but random movements. An assistant supports with one hand one arm of the subject, while he freely moves the hand, wrist, and fingers of the supported arm with his other hand. Then he progresses to moving the forearm and finally the upper and/or entire arm of the subject, and especially also the elbow and shoulder joints. The assistant must make sure that he supports the subject's arm well wherever necessary during movements, so that the subject can remain relaxed.

The subject must not initiate any movement, but must allow the assistant to do the moving and must again and again release any resistance against the movements with an exhalation.

This is a good technique to enable both subject and assistant to notice when and where resistance to the passive movements occurs, thus increasing sensory awareness.

The assistant must see to it that the limbs which he moves are perfectly relaxed. He may also gently "shake out" any resistance of a limb, or "move it out" of a joint. But all movement must be within the range of motion of joints and should never be forced.

After the first arm, the head and neck are moved, then the other arm, and finally the lower limbs. After passive movements, the subject should remain relaxed for a few minutes and then begin raising his limbs, and letting them fall heavily with all muscles relaxed, in the same sequence in which the passive movements were made.

Passive movements differ from the passive stretching in physiotherapy, in which the goal is the lengthening of muscles, tendons, ligaments, and soft tissues which have become shortened due to a pathological cause. The physiotherapist often disregards the relaxation of the part with which he works, and he may even ask the patient to inhale in order to increase a passive stretch (Thomsen, 1970).

The technique of Passive Movements requires the absolute cooperation of the subject of "doing nothing" to ensure the complete relaxation during random movements. This is necessary to bring about the desired combination of deep physical and mental relaxation. It produces at the same time an increased range of movement and flexibility.

During passive movements the subject can be instructed to hum, sigh, gargle, or vocalize slowly and lazily at different frequencies. This ensures deep, slow exhalations which promote better relaxation; it gives the subject a pleasant feeling of vibration; and it serves the assistant as an audible feedback of the subject's state of relaxation.

Relaxation Through Movement. Lie on a comfortable, not too soft mattress, close the eyes, exhale for relaxation, and ask your body where or which part it wants to move. Allow any part to move in any way, but do not allow repetitious patterns to develop, nor make prethought movements. Repeatedly exhale for relaxation. Take your cues from the body and keep moving until complete relaxation results.

This exercise is the motor equivalent of the sensory Relaxation Through Attending to Internal Sensations, chapter 4. It also quiets restlessness and clears the mind. It is the most similar to passive movements which can be done without an assistant.

Jogging: Free and Easy!

Jogging should not be hard work, but easy, leisurely, limbering up, releasing excess physical and mental energies, stimulating the circulation and respiration, freeing the mind, and promoting pleasant thoughts.

Feedback from sensations of body and mind and techniques of breathing and imagining are important. Feel and sense what body and mind are doing, and imagine the light, free, and easy movements of a child running leisurely, just expending excess energy. Allow the body to run at the speed it wants to. Do not try to keep up with somebody else or outdo yourself.

Breathe in only through the nose. Breathe out through the nose or through the mouth around the tongue, which is held relaxedly curled or flat against the roof of the mouth to slow the exhaled air stream. This keeps moisture and warmth in mouth, throat, and lungs.

Allow the legs to run as they want to, and breathe to fit the motion of the legs. The important thing is that breathing and steps are attuned, without one forcing the other into a pattern. Breathe out slowly for as many steps as comfortably possible and breathe in shortly and deeply.

Find your own rhythm of movement. It may change from time to time. Think a jingle, imagine a conversation, or hum in the rhythm of the jogging. Notice and enjoy nature.

During inhalations "inspire" pleasant thoughts, strength, courage, delight. During exhalations breathe out used up air, anger, disgust, discouragement, or just enjoy the leisure of relaxed jogging.

Allow body parts to become loose and relaxed, one by one, if they tense up. Imagine jogging with Rubber Joints and Pulling Cord, chapter 6, or anything that makes the jogging easy and aligns the posture. Leisure and limberness are important, not power and speed.

Conclusion

The exercises in this chapter increase awareness of flexibility and muscle tone. Good flexibility and muscle tone are necessary for proper balance and easy, graceful movement. These exercises also assist in adjusting bodily misalignments and repairing damages which are incurred in daily life due to ordinary and special stresses. As a result, energy is conserved, and better mental balance and equanimity are achieved.

Muscle tone and flexibility may also be improved by self-massage, which is discussed and described in the next chapter.

7. Self-Massage and Sport Massage

Self-massage antedates any health-promoting exercise outside the activity incurred routinely in food-seeking. A cow "licking her calf into shape," a cat washing her kitten, or any animal rolling on the ground or rubbing against a hard object is using massage techniques. Pummeling, kneading, and stroking have been used in primitive human society and were made into arts by the Indians, Chinese, and Mediterranean peoples. By 400 B.C., the Greek physician Hippocrates had described four different massage techniques: a "soft" one for loosening up and relaxing muscular as well as nervous tension; a "hard" one for toning up, conditioning, and strengthening; an "extensive" one for breaking down tissues and reducing weight; and a "moderate" one for building up tissues and gaining weight.

When the classical ideal of excellence of body and mind was replaced by Christian preoccupation with the soul and the hereafter, the art of massage was forgotten. It was rediscovered during the Renaissance. The Kung Fu was first translated from the Chinese into French by the Jesuit Father Amiot in 1779 (Nebel 1886). In the early 1800s P. H. Ling in Sweden (Ling 1853) laid the foundation of modern health gymnastics and massage, based on the knowledge of anatomy and physiology.

Self-massage and sport massage have been practiced in Europe for at least half a century (Ruffier 1921, 1963; Surén 1928). They are not much known in English-speaking countries. A survey revealed that, of fourteen books on these subjects, written between 1955 and 1971 and listed in the National Library of Medicine Catalog, four were in German, two each in French, Russian, and Italian, and one each in Dutch, Portuguese, Czech, and an unidentified language. Not one was in English.

Purpose

Self-massage and sport massage aid the circulation in tissues and organs. They increase metabolism, release substances back into the circulation, and help return the lymph into the bloodstream. All body cells benefit from them. They help remove waste products from intercellular spaces and around joint capsules, stretch the tendons, loosen muscle knots, and increase suppleness.

Self-massage and sport massage are designed for conditioning the healthy and for compensating for minor dysfunctions. Acutely inflamed tissues should be massaged only upon instruction by an expert, and any conditions related to illness or major dysfunction must be treated under medical supervision by a specialized masseur.

An outline of different types of sport massage is given below. They can be administered by another person who is well informed about self-massage or as a self-massage by the athlete himself.

Self-massage can be used in addition to or as a substitute for exercising. A good, thorough conditioning massage of the whole body takes one to two hours. It will refresh the body for two to three days. If time or strength for a whole body massage are lacking, parts can be massaged in sequence on successive days. Muscle massages should be interspersed with lymph drainage massages. An advantage of self-massage is that it gives the body a good workout as well as the massage. It is an efficient method for conditioning the body and is not as exhausting as most calisthenics.

Self-massage can be learned easily, can be performed anywhere at any time, and needs no special clothing or equipment. It may be used as a complete massage, or selected body parts may be massaged for special purposes. The body should be used as its own feedback instrument for finding out what should be treated where, and how. For tiredness, a refreshing and invigorating massage is indicated, for nervousness a calming and gentle one. For stiffness and tense muscles and tendons much stretching and loosening-up must be included. For muscular or nerve weakness strengthening is indicated, and for aiding body weight reduction a very strong and vigorous massage must be administered. In time, new personal ways of massaging for accomplishing special purposes will be developed. Examples are massaging one foot with the other, using hard objects to roll on for massaging the back, or finding new positions in which a limb can be comfortably supported.

Types of Massage

The classical Eastern massage, which originated in China and was refined in Japan (Serizawa 1972), and the traditional Western massage are mainly muscle and joint massages which can easily be administered as self-massage.

There was also developed long ago in the East a massage which stimulates "nerve points" for the treatment of illnesses. Such a massage was first described in Europe by A. Cornelius (1902, 1909). It is related to nerve reflex zones and requires expert knowledge of anatomy, physiology, and pathology. A similar massage was reinvented by E. Dicke in Germany through self-experimentation while treating her leg which was in danger of needing amputation because of imminent necrosis. Her massage was called Reflex Zone Massage (Leube and Dicke 1951) or Connective Tissue Massage (Ebner 1962, Dicke et al. 1968). It too is a branch of nerve therapy and is important for treating certain internal illnesses, but it is much too complicated to be understood or applied by the layman.

Shiatsu (Namikoshi 1972), on the other hand, a Japanese technique of finger pressure, is supposed to be suitable for self-massage. It is discussed below only briefly, since it has been well described in English. Lymph drainage massage (von Mengershausen 1972), which has recently been developed in Europe, is described at length since there is to date no description of it in English. It is simple and efficient and can be administered by anybody.

Massaging Technique

The body part which is massaged must be well supported and relaxed. Generally, every stroke is repeated three to five times. Strokes should be circular around toes, fingers, and small enough joints and limbs, followed by strokes toward the heart. On large limbs much kneading and pressing is followed and preceded by lengthwise stroking toward the trunk. On the trunk all strokes are heartward, unless circling is indicated. Massaging should alternate between stroking the skin lightly, kneading the muscles thoroughly, and stroking deeply between muscles and along tendons. For massaging muscles which lie deep, the muscle is pressed against the underlying bone with pressure by the palm of the hand. A massage is always ended with long, soothing strokes along the surface of the skin. For relaxation, long, soothing strokes are made. For invigoration strokes are short and vigorous with rubbing and tapping. In order not to tire one part of the massaging hand too much, different strokes are used alternately and different parts of the massaging hand, such as knuckles, fingertips, or the balls and sides of the hand, or even the elbows are employed. The arms should be intermittently relaxed and shaken during exhalations.

The skin may be massaged with or without oil or a soap leather. If done in the shower or bathtub, the warmth of the water will stimulate the circulation and relax the muscles, increasing the effect of the massage. A final cold rinse should be taken.

Massage should be administered daily or even more often for limbering up, relaxation, invigoration, or lymph drainage. A thorough, complete body massage should not be administered more often than twice a week, so the body has time in between to rid itself of the liberated waste products. Periodic light loosening and stretching of muscles and joints by shaking or passive movements should always accompany massaging of body parts.

If there is no time or strength for a whole body massage but one is desired, the following sequence is suggested for successive massages: feet, ankles, and lower legs; knees and upper legs; hips and buttocks; hands and lower arms; upper arms and shoulder; chest and neck; back; face and head.

The breathing rhythm plays an important role in massage, and disregarding it may counteract the action of the best massage stroke technique. To test this do the following. Massage your own or another's large neck or arm muscles during slow, relaxed exhalations of both subject and masseur. Pause during inhalations. Then massage the same muscles while the subject and/or masseur inhale or hold the breath. Both should notice how much more effective and deep the massage is during exhalations.

Breathing should never be halted or interrupted during self-massage because of mental concentration or other unintended tensions. For best results, certain strokes should coincide with exhalations, others with inhalations, and a "creative pause" (see chapter 4) is as important for the effect of massage as it is during respiration exercises. The following coordination of strokes with breathing is generally useful. Any strokes which knead, press, wring, roll, hack, slap, and all deep strokes along and between the muscles are administered during exhalations. Any strokes which create friction, pick up, lift off, or loosen the skin, rub, vibrate, or shift and displace the skin are administered during inhalations or while holding the breath. Stretching of muscles, tendons, and joints is done for relaxation during exhalations and for invigoration during inhalations. See also the use of counterbreathing, chapter 5.

Self-massage instructions follow for diverse body parts and for different purposes.

Muscle Relaxation Test. A tensed, hardened muscle is an obstruction for the circulation and can thus hinder its own nourishment. A healthy muscle is very soft when relaxed. Test different muscles during varying stages of tension and relaxation and learn to detect unnecessarily hard places and tissue deposits in and between the muscles and around the joints. The hardness in muscles can be massaged away. For this only the hardened places should be massaged. Muscles which are not in good shape are often shortened; therefore stretching exercises must accompany the massaging. Any massage is incomplete if it is not accompanied by active and passive stretching and loosening exercises.

Hand and Arm Massage. Rub the forearm briskly with the fingers during exhalations. Inhale deeply. Rub one finger after the other in circular movements during exhalations. Knead each finger knuckle. Stroke slowly and deeply along the fingers toward the palm during exhalations. Repeat with the other arm and hand. Stroke along the sides and between the bones of the hand toward the wrist during exhalations. Encircle the wrist with the thumb and fingers and rub in a circular motion. Squeeze each muscle of the forearm separately from the wrist to the elbow at about ten adjacent points, followed by slow, deep stroking of the muscle in the same direction during exhalation. Either massage the same muscles on both arms alternately, or massage first all muscles of one forearm and then all of the other.

Massage the upper arm by squeezing each muscle between the fingers or in the palm of the hand, from elbow to shoulder, and stroke upward along each muscle slowly and deeply after squeezing it. Shake arm and neck loosely, exhale deeply, and relax.

Massage the shoulder joint by pressing around it with the fingertips while rotating the arm backward and forward.

Massage the muscle between the neck and the shoulder by squeezing and pummeling it with either hand. Then, while exhaling, stroke it deeply, in either direction or both. Bend slightly forward and backward, loosening the muscle, and relax while exhaling. Shake shoulder and arm loosely and relaxedly. Exhale and feel the relaxation. Inhale and feel the invigoration. Work alternately on both arms or finish one arm first and then the other.

Foot Massage. Hold a toe between thumb and forefinger and rub in a circular motion three to five times. Repeat for all toes. Stroke, stretch, and rub the toes from above and below. Stretch, flex, and rotate one toe after another with the fingers. Then stretch and flex all toe and foot joints in all directions. End by "cracking" the joints of the toes by pulling and stretching them.

Rub the sole of the foot and squeeze the sides together. While holding or supporting the toes and ball of the foot with one hand, stroke the sole toward the heel with the fist of the other hand. For a deep massage of the sole, use the second knuckle of forefinger or middle finger and press into the sole, twisting the knuckle to right and left, slowly sliding it from the toes to the heel. Repeat three times each: along the inside, midline, and outside of the sole of the foot. Give a special knuckle kneading to spots which are tender or hurt. Fist-beat the sole and especially the bottom of the heel. Massage the heel with the inside of the whole hand.

Massage the bones on both sides of the ankle. First rub briskly, then press deeply with a knuckle. End by stroking the tissues first deeply, then gently upward along the leg.

Massage upward along the Achilles tendon, using the fingertips or knuckles. Rub gently upward to the shin, calf, and sides of the lower leg. Make circular movements with the ankle, first in one direction and then in the other, and finally shake the foot loosely. In time, become inventive and learn to massage one foot with the other instead of with a hand.

Leg Massage. Flex and stretch the toes. Move the ankle and rub around it. Make clockwise and counterclockwise movements with the foot. Stroke deeply between the bones at the ankle. Exhale and relax.

Position the leg well-supported as high as comfortably possible in order to take advantage of gravity to aid the circulation. Stroke the calf briskly, then knead it with both hands, hand over hand. Chop it from ankle to knee with the fists or sides of the hands. Roll it with the balls of the hands. Stroke deeply from ankle to knee. Stroke several times slowly and deeply along the Achilles tendon.

Rub the shin, then knead both sides of it with the fingertips. Finally stroke slowly and deeply from ankle to knee.

Massage deeply around the kneecap in circular movements with a knuckle or fingertip, moving spiral fashion from point to point. Shove the kneecap back and forth in all directions. Squeeze the tissues and tendons behind the knee between the fingers and balls of both hands and then stroke them gently sideways and toward the upper leg.

Divide the upper leg into at least four longitudinal parts for massaging and work along one at a time. The upper leg needs much more vigorous massaging than the arms and lower legs. Pound with the fists, chop with the sides of the hands, stroke with knuckles or elbows. Relax occasionally, exhaling deeply. First rub one part briskly, then squeeze, pummel, and hack as hard as possible. Finally stroke slowly and deeply toward buttock and groin. Make the long strokes during exhalations. Work slowly and deeply, either on the same part of both legs alternately, or finish one leg first and then the other.

Stand up and shake the leg loosely and relaxedly. Exhale and feel the relaxation. Inhale and feel the invigoration.

Back and Neck Massage. The back is the most difficult for self-massage, yet it is not out of reach for the fairly limber. It can be massaged in at least four positions: (1) Lying on the back, feet on the floor, knees bent to relax the upper legs, shoulders or head well supported, the back arched slightly upward. (2) Lying on one side. For this position, sides should be alternated frequently to prevent fatigue. (3) In a half-sitting position, feet on the floor, knees up, shoulders or head supported by a wall or chair. (4) Sitting on a stool which is comfortably high in order to keep the legs well relaxed.

The back is massaged in three parts: lower, middle, and upper. The areas should somewhat overlap. The body parts adjoining the part of the back to be massaged must be relaxed and supported as well as possible. In the first lying position the back can be massaged on a mattress or bed to keep the body as relaxed as possible. Any support for the arms while massaging will help to keep them from tiring so quickly.

First stroke all areas lengthwise with strong, rubbing strokes. Then massage them with the knuckles with short, strong, pushing movements. Squeeze them between the fingers, poke and circle with the fingertips, shake and vibrate the tissues. End by rubbing with the flat hand.

Next massage the buttocks by first pinching with the fingertips or poking with the knuckles, then pummeling

with the fists or slapping, and finally stroking upwards
with the fists or knuckles.

Rub along the spine and then make strong, flipping
movements with the fingertips toward it or push toward
it with the knuckles. Next make long, stroking movements down from the neck and up from the bottom, all
along the spine.

Massage of the back of the neck is especially important
since it is often one of the tensest parts of the body. Massage it like the back, but do also the following. Make
small circling or pressing movements along both sides of
the spine, both sides at once or alternately, from the bottom of the neck to the base of the skull. Relax often by
exhaling. Knead the muscles between neck and shoulders
and stroke them in both directions. Then stroke toward
and across the spine alternately from right and left, beginning at the base of the skull and working down the
neck. End by stroking down the back of the neck toward
the shoulders. Move the head slowly in all directions while
massaging. Give special attention to any knots and hard
places by kneading and stroking them. Begin and end any
neck massage by a lymph drainage massage along the
throat, see below.

Abdominal Massage. Different techniques of massaging must be used for the surface layer of the abdomen
and for the contents of the abdominal cavity. For the abdominal contents, two techniques are used according to
whether toning-down or toning-up are required. For reduction of tension, calming and relaxation are necessary.
For toning-up, invigoration and strengthening are indicated. In the first case the relaxing massage is done with
one hand flat on the abdomen while the other hand grasps
the wrist of the first and slow, circling strokes are made
in a clockwise direction, starting around the navel, pro-
gressing outward in a spiral, finally reaching the lower
right abdomen, continuing up the side to under the right

ribs, from there to under the left ribs, and finally down the left side of the abdomen to the pelvis.

For toning-up, the massage is started similarly, but then the spiraling strokes become rougher and faster, with stronger pressure, accompanied by strong pumping movements. Next the whole abdominal surface is vibrated with the flat hand horizontally, first parallel to the surface of the abdomen, moving it to right and left, and then vertically, deep into the tissues, by tapping and punching the whole abdomen harder and harder with the fingertips. Also deep finger pressure massage or slow, deep, clockwise strokes should be made during exhalations, especially in places where discomfort is felt. And finally, it is especially beneficial to press and massage the lower right abdomen approximately in the area of the appendix.

Deep Breathing should follow any abdominal massage. For this the hands are placed on the abdomen, one above and one below the navel, and the abdomen is expanded outwards as much as possible during inhalations and pushed inward and upward during exhalations. This is repeated eight to ten times. The deep breathing aids the blood and lymph circulation and acts as an "internal massage" for the intestines.

The technique for the surface layer of the abdomen is the following. Between the abdominal muscles and the skin there is a layer of fat. This must be massaged thoroughly on a hard surface, almost as if rubbing the washing on an old-fashioned washboard. To provide the hard surface, the abdominal muscles are tensed as much as possible and the legs are stretched to increase the tension. This provides the base for the massage and at the same time protects the internal organs from too strong pounding. The abdomen and flanks are first rubbed briskly with both hands. Then, strong, alternating counterstrokes are made with the flat hands, first from right and left across the abdomen and then up and down. This is repeated with fists and knuckles. After this the breath is held and the tensed abdomen is pounded with the fists. Finally, calming surface strokes are made over the whole abdomen, followed by Deep Breathing.

Face and Head Massage. Breathe calmly while massaging and repeat all strokes about five times. Stroke sideways with the fingertips of both hands from the middle of the forehead to the temples; then from the middle of the nose along the cheekbones to the temples. Massage the temples with circular motion. Vibrate the skin of the forehead with the fingertips loosely and relaxedly.

Make gentle, circular strokes around the eye sockets above and below the eyes, then stroke gently above and below the eyes along the eye sockets from the nose to the temples. Stroke from right and left over the bridge of the nose between the eyes, and then make small strokes upward from it toward the forehead. Stroke down from the bridge of the nose to both sides. Stroke from below the nose out and down, around the mouth; then up, along the sides of the nose; then from under the chin to the temples.

Drum lightly with the fingertips on the forehead, cheeks, and neck. Stroke slowly and deeply up the neck in several places: under the chin, on the sides, and on the back. Massage with circular strokes along the vertebrae of the upper spine, then stroke gently down the back of the neck. Use deep finger pressure along the base of the skull in the back of the neck. Stroke upward with short strokes against the base of the skull at the back of the head. Continue such strokes along the hairline above the ears and to the forehead.

Press the scalp with the fingertips and move the skin vigorously to loosen it. Accompany the massage with deep, relaxing exhalations and invigorating inhalations. Steaming and creaming the skin, exposure to a sunlamp, and muscle stretching by yawning and other facial movements should be added to the massage to stimulate the circulation.

Relaxation Massage. Work very slowly. Massage with deep, slow strokes along and between the long muscles of legs, arms, and back during exhalations. Stop the massage during inhalations. Rub gently with circular strokes around joints, then stroke the area gently toward the trunk. Squeeze muscles very gently during exhalations. Work very slowly. Tap body parts which need loosening gently during exhalations, then let the breath stream back in passively, as with the Rubber Ball exercise, chapter 5. End by gently stroking the skin with long strokes toward the heart.

Invigoration Massage. An energetic, invigorating massage not only increases the tonus of tired muscles but also promotes mental invigoration, especially if it is combined with self- suggestions of invigoration, enlivenment, encouragement, and exhilaration.

Rub the skin briskly. Inhale while pounding the muscles fast. Exhale quickly and deeply. Then rub briskly while inhaling in short breaths. Exhale deeply. Make vibrating or drumming strokes. Tap the skin very fast with the fingertips. Rub it vigorously, and end by stroking it gently. Especially the face and neck should be massaged in this manner. Feel the refreshed circulation in muscles and skin.

Strengthening Massage. This massage is designed to strengthen the muscles and increase their efficiency by removing accumulated fluid and useless deposits, increasing tonus and elasticity, and reducing stiffness.

Massage the muscles firmly, but not so as to cause discomfort. Pound lightly and refreshingly, knead and roll the tissues lightly, and end with a general soothing massage. Deep Breathing, see above, is important for general strengthening. This massage should be administered frequently, but for relatively short times.

Weight Reduction Massage. Besides the obvious, superficial fat deposits, the overweight have increased pressure in the abdomen due to accumulations of fat, gas, and feces. This hinders the blood circulation and lymph flow. The connective tissue is clogged with deposits of waste products, the abdominal muscles are weak, and usually the breathing is not the healthy diaphragmatic type. A low calorie diet, good excretion, breathing and movement exercises, sweating, strong complete body massage, and lymph drainage massage must all be combined to counteract these symptoms and correct malfunctions. Massage promotes the mobilization of the contents of fat cells, aids the liberation of waste products, and brings them into the lymph and blood stream. It also keeps the skin well supplied with blood for regeneration and firming as the fat layer is being removed.

This must be an extensive massage, hard to the point of pain and prolonged to the point of exhaustion. It should never be administered within three hours after eating. Start by fast rubbing, hand-over-hand. Knead all the muscles slowly and deeply, as hard as possible. Pound the fat tissue and then stroke it hard, always toward the heart. Knead again, pound again, press in circles, slap, press the muscles against the underlying bone wherever possible, and stroke again to increase the metabolism as much as possible. Keep breathing deeply during the massage. End with Deep Breathing, see above. It is good to begin and follow up a weight reduction massage by a lymph drainage massage.

Shiatsu. This Japanese finger pressure massage uses deep pressure or compression. It is perpendicularly applied with no rubbing motion, with the soft bulbs of the first three fingers or thumbs, or with the palm of the hand. The duration of pressure is up to three seconds around the neck and five to seven seconds in other places. The pressure should cause a sensation midway between pleasure and pain. Main Shiatsu pressure points are on both sides of the vertebrae along the spine, in the spaces between the ribs, on the buttocks, in the regions of internal organs, around joints, and along the limbs, especially all bones of hands and feet.

Sport Massage

All the techniques above described can be used in sport massage whenever needed. Sport massage is divided into training massage, warm-up massage, regenerative massage, and between-events massage.

Training Massage. This increases the efficiency of the body while it is being prepared for the athletic season. It must be strong and deep and may be so strong that muscle pains result, which may momentarily rather decrease than improve performance. It helps to rid the body of waste products which accumulate during periods of lowered activity. It reduces the fat surrounding the muscles, loosens muscle knots, and generally limbers up joints and muscles for faster and more precise action. Training massage must be followed by several days of relative rest during which the body can eliminate the dissolved metabolic waste products.

Warm-Up Massage. This is administered directly before an event for increasing the blood circulation, loosening the muscles, and increasing elasticity. At this time muscle action should be tested by a few activation exercises. Heavy massaging with the production of metabolic waste products must be avoided before an event.

Regenerative Massage. The purpose of this massage is to remove the metabolic waste products from the tissues. In addition it tones down the muscles and calms the nerves. Gentle stroking and lymph drainage massage are indicated. It does not always prevent the muscle soreness which may occur one or two days after an event, but it is very beneficial since it acts thoroughly on the warmed-up body, after physical exertion.

Between-Events Massage. This is important for reestablishing the efficiency of certain muscles between events.

A regenerative massage is administered to those muscles which were just used and a warm-up massage to those which are especially important for the next event. This kind of massage is especially important between the events of the pentathlon or decathlon.

It is advisable that athletes learn the skill of self-massage first, and then also practice with each other so that, if necessary, they can aid each other when skilled sport masseurs are not available.

Lymph Drainage Massage

This technique was developed by the Danish biologist E. Vodder and his wife in Cannes about 1932 and has been demonstrated repeatedly at international health congresses. After about 1958, it became more widely known in Germany and has been described by G. Quilitzsch (1967), W. Thomsen (1970), and J. von Mengershausen (1972). Manual lymph drainage self-massage is a simple and efficient health-promoting measure.

Since little has been published to date about lymph drainage massage, and apparently nothing in English, an introduction to the subject is necessary.

The lymphatic system plays the important role of a major "sewage system and treatment plant" in the body. The body is two-thirds liquid, and all substances, such as oxygen and carbon dioxide, foods and waste materials, hormones and enzymes, and other substances necessary to life, are constantly flowing from one place to another. Substances are transported to the cells by the arterial blood, and from them by the venous blood and the lymph. The low pressure flow in the veins and the lymphatic system is conducive to clogging.

The Lymphatic System

This system consists of a branched arrangement of vessels and capillaries with wider meshed walls than those of the blood vessels and their capillaries. This makes possible the absorption of larger particles, especially protein fractions and bacteria. The lymphatic capillaries have a surface available for absorption as great as, or greater than, that of the blood capillaries. They are present in almost every tissue and especially numerous in the skin, and they join to form numerous larger vessels.

Figure 4 shows the paths of the larger lymph vessels in the body. The lymph flows through the vessels of the limbs toward the trunk, and in the trunk from all sides to the large lymph nodes at the armpits and groin. All lymph from the legs and abdomen below the diaphragm collects in the large thoracic duct through which it flows up through the chest, and empties, together with the lymph from the upper left side of the body, into a large vein under the left collarbone. The lymph from the upper right side of the body joins with the venous blood in a large vein under the right collarbone.

Lymph vessels, like veins, have valves which allow flow in one direction only. Many filters are interspersed along their path in the form of lymph nodes. These filter the lymph, freeing it of foreign particulate matter, especially bacteria and other toxic matter. The nodes also produce lymphocytes, which play an active role in combatting infections.

Contractions of consecutive sections of the lymph vessels produce a wave of contraction heartwards, and thus pump the lymph toward the heart. This pumping is aided by the pulsating of the arteries, which has a massaging effect on the neighboring valved lymphatic vessels and veins. Warmth promotes the movement wave of the lymph vessels, while cold hinders it.

Clogging of the Connective Tissue. All the substances of the metabolic processes pass through the connective tissue: the salts, acids, and small-moleculed substances on their way between the cells and blood capillaries, and the large-moleculed substances and protein fractions on their way between the cells and the lymph capillaries.

Figure 4
Lymph Vessels

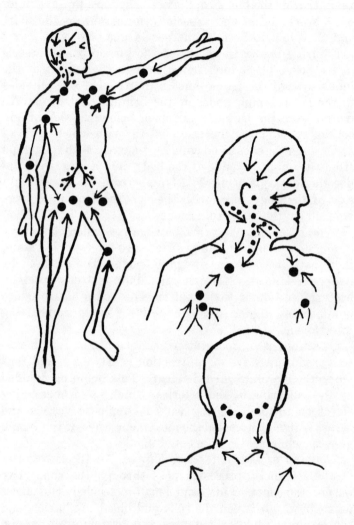

Lymph flow is in the direction of the arrows

Lymph nodes ●•

Good lymph drainage is especially important for the transport of the large-moleculed proteins. If these are not transported rapidly through the connective tissue, the system will become clogged and deposits of proteins, calcifications, hardening, and sclerosis with lack of oxygen and tissue acidosis will result.

The flow of substances through the tissues continues in a healthy manner if one maintains a diet of just sufficient and healthful food and much physical movement. However, Western man's eating habits generally flood the tissues with large-moleculed waste products, and excessive food intake and reduced physical activity lead to an accumulation of transit substances with clogging of connective tissue and lymph vessels. Any reduction or interruption of the lymph flow interferes with the healthy life of the tissue cells and leads to inefficiency and illness.

Besides the deposits in the connective tissue due to excessive food and poor lymph drainage, there are those which form after stresses, as, for instance, after chronic or acute inflammations. Such deposits cause grinding and creaking in the joints.

E. Vodder compared the clogged tissues to a "soggy meadow." In such a meadow the oxygen in the ground is displaced by water; it is cold and full of morbid growth, and only sour grass grows, which cattle do not like. Drainage must be established to make the meadow sweet and healthy again. So must the surplus substances in the connective tissue be removed. Unnecessary accumulations of fluid and fat and creaking around joints indicate the need for better lymph drainage. Unless an acute inflammation exists, the application of warmth, increased movement, deep breathing, and lymph drainage massage can safely be undertaken.

The Lymph Drainage Self-Massage Technique

Technique. Stroking is done very lightly and loosely, in slow, circular movements, generally with all four fingers of the outstretched hand at once. Movements can be clockwise or counterclockwise, but the direction must not be changed during a massage, to prevent counteracting the induced lymph flow. This stroking can best be practiced on the upper legs, one hand on each leg. During the stroking, the skin should be moved lightly over the tissues below it. About five circles should be made at any one place, one circle per second. The pressure of the circling fingers should vary, so that a pumping effect results. After the five circling movements, the fingers are moved one-and-a-half to two inches in the heartward direction and the circling is repeated. In this manner the lymph is pumped or stroked along its vessels toward the center of the body, and the subsequent lymph flow will pass more easily into the partially emptied vessels. Thus the massage of the surface lymph vessels produces a mild suction which affects also the more deeply located ones. Only occasionally and at certain places is the pumping, circling motion done with a single finger or the thumb instead of with the four fingers together.

Any lymph drainage massage, no matter whether it is applied to arms, legs, trunk, or head, starts and ends with the lymph gland chains which are located at the sides of the neck, from below the ears to the collarbone pit. This massaging should be done in a comfortable, relaxed position, such as lying on the back, with the massaging hands crossed over to massage the opposite sides of the neck.

The duration of any lymph drainage massage should be five to fifteen minutes, repeated one to three times daily. For acute and painful conditions the massage should be shorter and more frequent; for chronic conditions less frequent and longer. The areas massaged should be elevated, so that gravity can aid the flow of the lymph toward the heart, and the underlying muscle groups should be as relaxed as possible. Painful places should be treated gently.

Arm Lymph Drainage Massage. The lymph flows from

the palms along the inside of the forearms and upper arms to the lymph nodes in the armpits. The massage begins at the armpits with gently circling, pumping movements, repeated about ten times. Next the area inside the elbow is treated in a similar manner, and finally, with the arm well supported, it is continued step by step the length of the inside of the arm from palm to armpit.

Leg Lymph Drainage Massage. This begins with a gentle, circular massage of the lymph glands in the groin. Then, starting at the knee, the massage continues heartward, using both hands on the same leg in the following manner:

The hands are placed to clasp the leg lightly from both sides, with the fingers underneath and inside, the thumbs on top and outside. The circular movements of the fingers should be soft, broad, and flowing, pumping the lymph heartwards. The hollows of the hands can act as suction cups. The wrists should be held loosely while massaging. The leg should be raised and supported, so that gravity can aid the heartward flow of the lymph.

Next the hips are massaged with the same finger-circling movements, from buttock to hip joint and groin.

Massage of the knee joint follows next. First the glands under the knee are lightly pumped with all eight fingers while the thumbs circle around the kneecap. Then both sides of the knee are massaged, each side with the four fingers of one hand. The hollow spaces between the bones and the places where the tendons are attached should be massaged especially. The kneecap should be moved loosely sideways in any direction.

For massaging the lower leg, the knee is bent and the foot is supported, so that the calf muscles hang relaxed and loosely. Then the Achilles tendon, the calf muscles, and especially the inside of the lower leg are massaged with circular finger movements. Finally the whole leg is gently stroked out by first bending the knee and grasping the ankle lightly, and then straightening the leg, allowing the hands to glide gently up along it. The leg should be held high for this, so that gravity can aid the lymph flow. Varicose veins must never be massaged, whether with lymph drainage or any other kind of massage, since the danger of thrombosis or embolism exists. If pains occur in the course of lymph drainage self-massage, or if existing pains become worse instead of better, the massage should be discontinued or only the circumference of the painful spot be massaged very gently. Often pain will disappear if this is done.

Blood-Surge Exercise. A variation of the lymph drainage massage, for increasing lymph flow and blood circulation in the limbs when massaging is inconvenient or should be avoided, is the Blood-Surge exercise by Helmel (von Mengershausen 1972).

One arm is stretched and tensed maximally, the hand in a fist, during a short, sharp exhalation through the lips. Then the arm is completely relaxed and allowed to hang loosely during an inhalation. This is repeated about twenty times, once per second. Then the other arm is similarly exercised, and then both arms alternately. The Triple Time Breathing, chapter 5, may be reversed for this exercise, so that the exhalation lasts one count and the inhalation two.

The exercise for the legs should first be practiced while standing. The whole leg, on which the body weight should rest, is tensed maximally with the toes curled under. The movement should be as if stamping or pushing against the ground. The other leg is relaxed as much as possible. Again, short, sharp exhalations are made during the tensing. This exercise is done ten times with one leg, ten times with the other, and then ten times with both legs alternately. After it has first been practiced in a standing position, the exercise should be performed lying down, with the legs raised vertically, allowing gravity to aid the venous and lymph flows.

Increasing Lymph Flow Through the Trunk. This is more difficult and must be approached indirectly. It can be done by lying on the back and making bicycling movements in the air. The movements must be either parallel to the floor or vertical up into the air while lying only on the shoulder region of the back. Movements between these positions are not effective. The muscles deep in the abdomen will thus pump the lymph in the many abdominal lymph vessels. The efficiency of the exercise is increased if the respiration is rhythmical, so that cycling movements are made alternately during exhalations and inhalations. Cycling should be done about twenty times. This exercise is excellent before and after any leg lymph drainage massage.

Also, for aiding the lymph flow in the trunk, long stroking movements can be made upwards along the spine, and long broad strokes up the sides of the back. This will move the lymph to the large glands under the armpits.

Diaphragmatic breathing will also aid the lymph flow in the trunk. For this the reader should review Deep Breathing, above, and the pertinent exercises in chapter 5.

Joints and Muscles. Lymph drainage massage aids the body fluid circulation by increasing the speed and ease with which the lymph is returned to the blood stream, and it is useful for removing the deposits of waste substances after any acute inflammation or poisoning has subsided. It can be used for relieving different pains and swellings due to such diverse causes as chronic joint afflictions, or the immediate treatment of sprains, pulled muscles, or mosquito bites.

Sinuses. For treating the sinuses during hayfever and other acute or chronic rhinitis or sinusitis, lymph drainage massage is applied at least two times daily: first to the lymph glands along the throat; then to the upper rim of the cheekbones, circling gently with the four fingers from the nose toward the ears; and then to the bridge and top of the nose. Each is repeated about twenty times.

Eyes. For treating pain or swelling around the eyes or tiredness of the eyes, the fore and middle fingers should tap very gently around the eye sockets, and then make little circles above and below the eyes outward to the corners.

Headaches. For treating a frontal headache, the four fingers of both hands should circle gently, broadly, and slowly, spiraling from the middle of the forehead to the temples, about twenty to thirty times. This is also a good tranquilizing and sleep producing procedure.

For alleviation of pains in the back of the head and the neck, the lymph gland chains along the sides of the throat should be massaged gently, then the back of the neck, then the back of the head, and then again the lymph gland chains along the throat. Next, the back of the neck should be kneaded thoroughly, alternately with the right and left hand, and then massaged with the four fingers, with slow, gentle, pumping, circling strokes.

The neck muscles must be as relaxed as possible during this treatment. This can be achieved by tilting the head backward or by lying on the back.

Conclusion

Animals use massage regularly by reflexive licking and rubbing. Man, too often, applies it only in therapy to the sick or damaged body. It should be more appreciated and used by the healthy. A diversity of techniques and applications are described in this chapter, including massages for different parts of the body, for relaxation and invigoration, muscle strengthening, weight reduction, and especially sport massage and the new, extremely effective lymph drainage massage. Massage improves the automatic biofeedback of the body by increasing circulation and metabolism, removing waste products, helping to return the lymph to the blood stream, stretching tendons, loosening muscle knots, and increasing suppleness. The health-promoting effects of massage bring about feelings of well-being, and self-massage increases the feelings of self-sufficiency and satisfaction.

8. Managing Everyday Concerns

Stressors are normal in everyday life and should be met as challenges rather than negative factors. Coping with stress in general was discussed in chapter 3. This chapter is specifically concerned with the unavoidable stresses of tiredness and pain, with anxiety, which is an unnecessary habit, and with coping with the environment.

Invigoration and Improvement of Wakefulness

For invigoration and improving wakefulness, any or all of the following can be done. First, alert the sympathetic nervous system (see chapter 2) by inhaling; by pinching, slapping, or tapping the neck, face, and around the ears; by putting ice or cold water on the back of the neck; by stretching the limbs periodically; or by an invigorating self-massage (see chapter 7). Second, allow inner reactiveness to mobilize the energy necessary for staying awake and aware of the task or situation at hand. Third, correct misaligned postures and environmental situations which induce drowsiness by straightening and stretching the spine; by using firm, straight chairs to sit on; by keeping the room at a moderate temperature and well ventilated; by being relaxed, yet well aligned; and by taking advantage of the supporting environment (see chapter 4). Fourth, increase psychological stimulation by becoming intellectually interested in the task at hand, by becoming emotionally involved in it, or by becoming sensory aware of it. Fifth, reduce external or internal substances which induce drowsiness by avoiding allergy- and hypoglycemia-producing substances; by removing body wastes by good elimination and lymph drainage massage (see chapter 7); and by avoiding overeating. Sixth, improve sleep by using diversion and relaxation techniques for falling asleep, such as, relaxing with exhalations, relaxing the limbs at the joints (see chapter 5), adjusting the sleep posture during exhalations, and using Autogenic Training (see chapter 4); by eating only moderate amounts of food before sleeping; and by using comfortable, quiet sleeping quarters.

Invigoration Exercises

Invigoration is related to upward movements, vibrations, exciting rhythms, and to a lightness of the spirit. It is the feeling of being very alive. For invigoration exercises the eyes should remain open, unless meditation is used for mind invigoration, and generally, exercises must be kept short.

Simple Invigoration. Imagine stretching the arms and legs and feel very much alive during inhalations. Also just inhale with an invigorating thought, such as "alive and anew," "aware and awake."

Energizing. Stretch and flex the limbs during inhalation while imagining energy rising up along the spine. Relax, and repeat.

Alertness. If the attention lapses during mental work, inhale and imagine that oxygen comes as energy into body and mind, and that it sweeps away all tiredness and "cobwebs of the mind."

Awake Breathing. If you are not alert enough to be adequate to an occasion or job at hand, your breathing may be too shallow. Allow the breathing to become as awake and aware as the task or situation demands, but at intervals revert to your natural rhythm, allowing sighing or yawning to occur naturally. Again and again enliven your breathing with refreshing inhalations.

Sweeping Out Tiredness. Exhale forcefully and deeply and imagine that you are sweeping out, flooding out, or blowing out all slag, sludge, and foul air. Then inhale and imagine fresh, cool, vitalizing, invigorating air streaming in. Repeat as necessary.

Body Alertness. Make a short, quick, alert survey of your body and ask: Do the shoulders allow alertness, are the eyes alert? Are the ears fully awake and attentive? What about the chest, the arms? Drive out drowsiness where it lingers. Do groins, hips, and buttocks interfere with the alertness of the upper body? Are feet and legs aware and awake? Check once more the head-neck-shoulder region. Inhale, and then resume your activity.

Energizing Walk. Do this in reality or in the imagination. Walk rhythmically, about four steps during inhalation, hold the breath for about four steps, and exhale during the next four steps. Adjust the speed of the steps to your physical and mental condition. However, take more steps during exhalations and/or holding the breath than during inhalations. Adjust the vigor of the inhalation to the need of the body. Very consciously end the real or imagined walk with a deep, refreshing, energizing inhalation.

Clean Air. Imagine walking through fog or smog during a long, slow exhalation. Then, during inhalation, imagine coming up and out of the fog or smog into clean, clear, snowy, sunny, cold mountain air.

Jogging. Imagine jogging leisurely on a good surface in a place which is pleasant and enjoyable. Let it have the right temperature, the right surface on which to run, the right landscaping. Breathe in rhythm with the imagined jogging.

Manhole. Imagine jogging happily along or walking rather fast. Suddenly step into an open manhole. Let this surprise take away the breath. No harm was done, but you are really stirred up and awake.

Counterstretching. Strengthen and energize the head and neck region by turning the head slowly right or left, the chin toward the shoulder, inhaling while turning the head and lowering it toward the shoulder and exhaling while bringing it back to the starting position. Do this so slowly that the motion is barely visible. Breathing in this exercise is opposite to that for relaxing the head and neck and is invigorating.

Double Door. For invigoration of the shoulder and neck region, imagine a double door in the region of the shoulder blades. Allow its two parts to swing open widely during inhalations. Let them close during exhalations. Imagine that a cool, fresh breeze enters while it opens. Become calm and self-possessed while it closes.

Face Treatment. Imagine an invigorating massage of the skin of the face. Imagine drumming on it with the fingertips. Feel a water massage from a refreshing shower or raindrops, or feel little hailstones bouncing on different parts of the face. Feel the deeper tissues massaged during exhalations. Feel the fast, vibrating, exhilarating impact on the skin while inhaling in small, interrupted, almost gasping steps. End with a deep, refreshing inhalation.

Ice Plunge. Imagine diving into a pool cold enough to stop the breath. Imagine coming out of the pool and relax. Inhale for new vigor and energy.

Cold Shower. Inhale deeply in short steps and imagine the cold water of a shower beating on shoulders, head, chest, and neck. Feel the vibrations and the sting of the cold water jets. End with a deep, invigorating inhalation.

Climbing to Awareness. Imagine climbing stairs or a mountain during inhalations. With each step imagine climbing into greater and greater wakefulness and alert-

ness. Keep the exercise short to prevent overventilation.
Light Bulb. Imagine a little glowing, warm light bulb
on top of your head. Make it float down the back of the
head and along the spine during consecutive exhalations
while allowing it to warm every vertebra and melting any
tensions. Then let it ascend during consecutive inhalations,
filling the spine with energy and invigoration.
Finger and Arm Invigoration. Invigorate the fingers
with about five small, strong, flexing movements during
a stepwise inhalation. Exhale while letting the hand relax, then repeat. Initiate movement of the arm, hand, and
fingers from the shoulder blade region and imagine that
the forearms or fingers, like those of a string puppet, are
supported and moved by means of strings from an outside force. Remember that lifting and lightness are associated with inhalations. Permit the fingers to be soft, light,
liquid, and sensitive, or heavy, precise, and hard like little hammers according to the work they must perform.
Experiment with the breathing while doing this, so that
it aids the actions.
Integration Breath. Imagine or do the following. Hold
the arms straight down in front, hands folded, palms down.
Raise the outstretched arms slowly above the head during inhalation. Feel the invigoration. Bring the folded
hands behind the head and press the palms together about
five times while holding the breath. During exhalation
raise the arms with the folded hands to full height and
slowly lower them to the starting position. Repeat three
times.
Mental Invigoration. Try any or all of the following.
Imagine during an exhalation "shaking water off the fur,"
or "shaking dust off the mind." Then, during the following inhalation, allow clarity, order, and invigoration to
enter body and mind.
   Imagine during inhalations that coolness and vitality
flow into the head. Relax the body during exhalations.
End on a refreshing inhalation.

Relax completely during an exhalation. Allow the limbs to become heavy and the mind empty and floating. Then, during the ensuing inhalation, imagine or feel vibrations and think of physical and mental invigoration and renewal. Repeat about three times. Do the Long Breath, chapter 5. Then after an exhalation, inhale deeply and "send the invigoration up into the mind."

Awakening. For awakening after sleep, or for coming out of a relaxed altered state of consciousness, inhale and make small stretching movements with fingers and toes. Either move several times during one long inhalation, or inhale stepwise while moving the fingers. Relax during exhalation. Lengthen the spine during inhalation. Feel it stretch and become longer. During exhalation relax again, but in a more refreshed manner. Then, during the next inhalation, imagine plugging yourself into your new battery for recharging. Repeat this for several inhalations. Then stretch and flex the limbs, inhale, and start getting up. If young and healthy, get up with an inhalation to increase vigor and vitality. If weak and not so healthy, get up during an exhalation in order to preserve strength and avoid wasting energy.

Conserving and Increasing Energy

In general, intersperse as many rest periods into your life as possible: in elevators, while walking to or from a job, or while warming up the car engine. Use Third Leg, chapter 4, and the other exercises described in the section on the supporting environment, and use Climbing, chapter 6, and the other exercises described for facilitating movement. Remember that one main aspect of economizing energy is to keep the body as relaxed as possible whenever indicated, and that for this slow, relaxing exhalations are of utmost importance. Following are some useful examples of exercises.

Golden Thread. For being calm and relaxed, yet feeling

alive, imagine a golden thread through the crown of the head and down the spine. Imagine that this thread is your center of calmness.

Solar Plexus or Storage Battery. The solar plexus is a network of nerve fibers, located at the level of the sternum, behind the stomach, in front of the spine. Its fibers radiate like a sun. The solar plexus region is a very good place for storing and conserving energy in the imagination. Inhale and exhale while imagining charging a battery there, or filling a reservoir with energy.

Reservoir of Energy. Create a reservoir for conserving and holding energy in the lowermost abdomen, in the region of the navel, or in the chest. Get energy during inhalations. Hold it, and possibly increase it while holding the breath. Think of endurance during long, slow exhalations. Imagine during inhalations that something starts glowing within you, or imagine a beam of light in the reservoir. Relax those parts of the body which are not involved in the building of the energy reservoir during exhalations. Use the reservoir as a place from which to draw energy in an emergency. Energy can thus be built up and "preserved" for several days before some event, in order to reach a peak of energy for a game day, a contest, or a special event.

Calm Base. For being still and calm, inhale and exhale a few times deeply. Then find a comfortable balance between relaxation, tension, and real or imagined support for the limb, the whole body, or the mind, whatever is to be the "calm base." From this base let well-aimed aggression proceed, be it in pistol shooting or in an argument.

Pumping Strength. Breathe in and out sharply and imagine pumping energy and strength directly into any body part or limb which needs it. End the pumping with an inhalation. If an exertion follows, hold the breath for this.

Athletic Warm-Up. The efficiency of a warm-up is increased and muscles remain more relaxed and invigorated if movements are consciously made as follows. For greater flexibility make forward movements and stretch, or overstretch, during exhalations. For invigoration make forward movements and stretch, or overstretch, during inhalations. Mix the two consciously during the warm-up. Inhalation also develops tension, and stretching during inhalation should alternate with relaxtion during exhalation, so that the proper balance between the two is maintained.

Partial Relaxation and Invigoration. Relaxation or invigoration alone may not be appropriate. Learn to combine invigoration of one part of the body, or tension of one part of the body, with relaxation of other parts. Remember that exhalation produces relaxation and inhalation produces invigoration or tension. Learn to bring a specific part of the body to the required state of invigoration or tension, and then relax the rest of the body. For example, relax shoulders and neck during exhalation, and during inhalation invigorate an arm for special movement, such as playing an instrument or a throw in athletics. Unnecessary tension in shoulders and neck hinders the freedom of the arm for easy, yet controlled movement and must be released with exhalations.

Endurance. Endurance may be increased by alternate relaxation and invigoration. If, for instance, an arm must be held for a prolonged time in a raised position, feel it light and invigorated during inhalations, feel it relaxed and easy during exhalations. Design your own exercises for increasing endurance using the entries of Table 10, chapter 5.

Efficient Hands. To prevent tension while writing or working with the hands, imagine initiating the movements from the shoulder blade region or the elbows, not from the forearms or hands. Let the shoulders sink and relax the arms and hands repeatedly while working. Invigorate the fingers periodically by making small flexing and stretching movements.

Delegating Energy. Imagine the Rubber Joints, chapter 6, for relaxation and balance. Then, during an inhalation, gather the full breath and imagine during the next strong exhalation forcing all the inhaled oxygen into back, arm, fingers, or wherever energy is needed, for forethought, energetic action.

Pain Reduction

Pain is a stressor. Coping with diverse stressors was discussed in general in chapter 3. The sensations of and reactions to pain vary widely individually and are greatly influenced by the beliefs, values, and mores of a society. Buddhism, for instance, with its nirvana concept, teaches emancipation from and oblivion to pain, care, or external reality. The difference between the cultural attitudes of American Indian and Judaeo-Christian women with respect to childbirth was mentioned in chapter 3.

Much can be learned from those who are capable of coping with pain in an adequate manner. The fifteen-year-old Japanese World War II fighter pilot and prospective Kamikaze, Yasuo Kuwahara (1957) instinctively counteracted excruciating and prolonged pains during his extremely hard training in at least five ways: he induced relaxation and relief by prolonged groaning, that is, exhalation; he tensed every muscle in his body and thus interfered with pain perception by a strong counterstimulus; he used rhythmic breathing and thus diverted his attention; after a bull whip lash over face and eye, he gently stoked the burning skin, diminishing the perception of one sensation by gentle additional sensory input; and finally he used an ASC of total dissociation by plunging into black oblivion, "the wonderful, blessed, great dark hole."

The best approach for coping with pain is first to try to analyze its peculiar characteristics, differentiating it from other possible pains; then to decide what might change or alleviate it; and finally to experiment with ap-

propriate imagery, relaxation, diversion, dissociation, or
physical treatments like heat, cold, or massage.

Alleviation of Diverse Pains

It must be remembered that all the following suggestions work with some, but not with others. Different exercises should be tried, and those which bring relief be
conscientiously practiced.

Dull Aches. These have been relieved by imagining during exhalations a hot water bottle which warms and relaxes, or by treating the aching area with warm water or
alcohol, or even by imagining receiving a painkilling shot
into it. Thinking of softening the area or feeling the pain
"evaporate" during exhalations also proved helpful.

Sharp Pain and Stabbing Pain. These have been partially relieved by imagining that the painful area was icy
and very rigid, or by imagining that it was very soft, like
foam rubber, so that the stabbing met with no resistance.
This did not work for stabbing pains so strong that they
halted the breath.

Burning Pain and Pains from Burns. These can be relieved by thinking coolness and soothing lotions being applied during inhalations, and relaxtion during exhalations. However, thinking coolness for burnt soles of feet
may make it possible for a burn victim to walk, but the
tissues will suffer additional damage. Common sense
must always be a guiding factor for deciding whether
pain reduction is beneficial or not.

Cramps. These can be handled in at least three ways:
relax as much as possible, tense as much as possible, or
relax and tense alternately. Time the tensing with inhalations and the relaxing with exhalations. A cramp can
also be waited out by concentrating exclusively on relaxing the body during exhalations in places which are not
affected by the cramp. This has proven very helpful for
getting rid of cramps without changing the position during yoga practice and for continuing swimming with a

cramp. Lymph drainage massage is good for prevention. *Local Warmth.* Warm a hand, for instance on the abdomen or chest, and then put it on the painful area. Imagine during inhalations inhaling the warmth into the painful area and pain streaming out through it and away from it during exhalations.

Coolness. Coolness or warmth can be attributes of one kind of pain and may be remedies for another kind. Usually the opposite is required for relief. Experiment while remembering that coolness, rigidity, and tensions are enhanced by inhalations, the opposites by exhalations.

Anesthetic. Imagining strongly having a body part immersed in ice water or snow, or having been injected with a numbness-producing anesthetic, can evoke an effective anesthesia in dentistry and otherwise.

Arthritic Pains and Stiffness. Arthritic pains can be eased by imagining a warm shower over the shoulders and neck during exhalations, or a warm blanket over the knees. Cupping a painful area with a warm hand increases the effect. Imagine further that the afflicted area loosens up and becomes soft and warm during exhalations.

Before any movement, imagine moving the body parts involved in the movement, be it an arm for reaching or the legs for walking. Limber up the body in the imagination before getting up in the morning. Invigorate the limbs during inhalations while making imagined movements and relax during exhalations. Only then attempt to move in reality. Move then only during exhalations, since this avoids unnecessary body tensions and increases limberness. Inhale between movements. Hold the breath during movements only if the pain is excruciating. Lymph drainage massage (see chapter 7) is also helpful before getting out of bed. Also, get up from sitting and climb stairs during the exhalation phase. Halt during inhalations.

For bending, as for instance for tying shoelaces, bend as far as possible during one long exhalation. Wait and relax during several breathing cycles while the body adjusts to the position it reached. Then stretch a little further during another long exhalation. By thus bending stepwise, one may extend the reach a great deal.

Anticipation of relief is also helpful. If a hot bath or a hot whirlpool can ameliorate the pain, imagine going to the hot water. Imagine the anticipation very vividly during exhalations. Then imagine being in the hot water.

Headaches. Distinguish the features of the headache. It can be in different places and have different qualities. It may be general, frontal, or one-sided, pressing, stabbing, nagging, dull, or pounding. Next, find body areas which are tense. Tension headaches can be due to tensions in the head itself or in the neck and shoulders, the spine, the small of the back, or even the legs. Do appropriate relaxation exercises and experiment to see if relaxation of certain body areas will reduce the headache.

For pressure headaches try the following. If the pain feels like a "board before the forehead," think of the area softening and becoming relaxed or warm during exhalations. During inhalations think that the bony walls of the skull expand or that coolness streams into the head. The thought of opening the head at the crown to "let fresh air in" also allayed or ameliorated pressure headaches. Experiment whether this works better for you during exhalation or inhalation. It differs. Also experiment whether coolness or warmth is better to ameliorate the headaches. For sharp or stabbing pains, see above. See also chapter 7 for lymph drainage massage to ameliorate a headache.

Back Pain

Complaints about back pain are common, but more often than not, those who keep complaining do not faithfully perform the exercises prescribed by a physician. Such exercises must be performed regularly and conscientiously. The pain should be a constant stimulus to do something about it, and the back pain sufferer must learn to live twenty-four hours a day without a hollow in the lower part of the back and must avoid standing as much as possible. Hole in Small of Back, chapter 5, should be performed for relaxing muscle strain at any time and in any position. Any or all the exercises for flexibility and strength in the pelvic area (see chapter 6) can be used. Low heels must be worn, and standing or walking should be done with the toes straight ahead and most of the weight on the heels. The buttocks should be "tucked under" and tightened as often as possible, so that the hollow in the back is eliminated. When possible, the knees should be elevated higher than the hips while sitting. This is especially important while driving and can be accomplished by moving the car seat forward. While you are sleeping, lying on the back with propped up knees or on one side with one or both knees drawn up is best.

Review also the exercises for hips, pelvic area and legs, chapter 4, and do Light Bulb for easing the whole spine. If this is used for a pain spot in the spine, work first below and above that spot inducing relaxation and warmth. Then imagine the light bulb during inhalations and exhalations at the place where the pain is felt. Concentrate on the breathing phase which best relieves the pain.

Attention to Bodily Malfunctions

Body and mind are malfunctioning when sensations or reactions are outside the normal range of a continuum: if, for instance, instead of adequate emotional involvement, overexcitement or apathy is felt, or if diarrhea or constipation occurs instead of normal excretion. Many malfunctions are less obvious, but attention to them can aid in relieving them before conditions become worse.

Mouth, Tongue, Throat, and Nose

Exercises for the mouth and throat are especially necessary for those who locate momentary or prolonged general stresses in that area; for those who use it much, like singers and lecturers; and for relieving distress due to pathological changes.

Review the exercises in chapter 4 for the mouth and throat and those for the head and neck region. The following sequence proved very effective for special work at the mouth-throat junction. Choose any or all, and take time to sense, feel, and experience the relaxation and moisture, the widening, and the comfort which this series evokes.

Dish. Find a comfortable position for the jaw during an exhalation. Relax the tongue and, while exhaling, lay it down into the framework of the jaw as if in a dish, or bring it to any other comfortable position in the mouth.

Relaxing the Tongue. During an exhalation, relax the palate and the root of the tongue. Wiggle the tongue by "shaking" it loosely, as a swimmer may shake his limbs to relax them before beginning a race, or by any imagined loosening up movement. This should be done mainly in the imagination and with a minimum of physical movement.

Floating Tongue. During exhalation, allow moisture to flow around the root of the tongue and the palate, and imagine that the tongue is floating, or imagine that it rests pleasantly relaxed on a cushion of air.

Throat Temperature. Imagine the most comfortable temperature and moisture at the palate, the root of the tongue, and in the throat.

Holes Under Chin. Imagine two openings under the chin, to the right and left of the root of the tongue. Imagine breathing in and out gently through these openings. Feel the air stream up into the nose. Feel it open up the sinuses. Feel it stream out again under the chin.

Waterfall. Imagine water streaming down inside the throat like a waterfall during exhalations. Allow it to have the most comfortable temperature. Imagine a little lake where it ends, into which the water flows. Then find an outlet from there, so that the water can descend to yet a lower level. Repeat a series of waterfalls, until the imagined lake is located in the lower abdomen. Success with this exercise depends also on body alignment and relaxation. Straighten the spine during an exhalation and loosen up the lower back and pelvic area.

Following are exercises for special difficulties in the throat, mouth, and nose areas.

Swallowing. For swallowing, be it medicine or a tube, first fixate on some object or sound during a deep inhalation. Then exhale deeply and relax while, or just before, swallowing.

Sore Throat. A dry throat can be moistened and at the same time relaxed by the thought of moist, comfortably warm air streaming through it during exhalations. If the throat is sore and dry, thinking of soothing coolness during inhalations may help. Waterfall and Opening Flower also bring relief.

Counteracting Coughing. A cough or a tickle in the throat may be controlled by using both exhalations and inhalations. Let thoughts like "calm, warm, moist, relaxed, or comfortable" accompany exhalations, and thoughts like "cool, fresh, or very still" inhalations.

Clearing Sinuses. Shiatsu pressure, chapter 7, on the sides and bridge of the nose, the middle of the forehead, top of the head, and temples, will relieve sinus troubles, and so will lymph drainage massage (see chapter 7). Yogic practice described the following: if the right nostril is congested, sit or lie in a slightly reclined position with the head a little back to the left. Press on the left, free nostril without closing it entirely. Breathe calmly, and the congested nostril will be free after a few minutes. Reverse the position for a congested left nostril.

Teeth Gritting. To counteract gritting of teeth, allow the lower jaw to become limp and relaxed during an exhalation. During the next exhalation feel what happens to the jaw when it becomes limp and relaxed. Feel whether the teeth remain clenched during exhalations. Loosen, let go of, release, relax the jaw repeatedly with exhalations. Feel the space which opens up when the jaw relaxes. Let everything in the mouth become soft, comfortable, and relaxed during exhalations. Disregard the inhalations or let your mind be invigorated by them, but do not pay attention to the mouth during inhalations. Practice the sequence for special work at the mouth-throat junction (see above). Allow the lips to become soft and full during exhalations. Become aware of the teeth gritting as soon as it occurs and immediately release the jaw. Release the jaw and repeat some of the mentioned exercises especially before falling asleep at night.

Relieving Eye Discomfort

Sit back comfortably and work slowly. Exhale gently and close the eyes. Feel coolness gently streaming up the nose during inhalation. Exhale gently and relax the tissues around the cheekbones and above the eyes. Permit the eyes to move under the closed lids. Relax completely during a deep exhalation. Imagine during an inhalation that the inhaled air streams in through the closed eyelids, and think "my eyes are getting cool." Relax with an exhalation and repeat. Feel the forehead widen and expand above the eyes during inhalation. Relax during exhalation. Repeat. Sit back, relax for a moment, and allow the breathing to resume its natural rhythm.

Follow the above routine as close as possible, and incorporate whatever feels best from the following list of thoughts to be used during inhalations and exhalations respectively. The items in the two columns are interchangeable according to individual needs. Use any or all.

Thoughts During Inhalations	Thoughts During Exhalations
My eyes are getting cool. My eyeballs shrink.	My eyes are getting warm. The pressure around my eyes feels relieved.

The space inside my
forehead expands.
My eyes feel light.
The space between my
eyelids and my eyeballs
increases.
My eyesockets expand.
My eyelids become light
and thin.
My eyelids float.
The visual center in the
back of my head seems
refreshed.
The top of my head
seems to become wide
and open.

The space behind my eyes
seems to enlarge.
My eyes become soft.
Moisture fills the space
between my eyelids and
my eyeballs.
My eyeballs are floating.
My eyelids become soft
and warm.
My eyes sink back softly.
My eyes become very
relaxed.

My chest and abdomen
relax comfortably.

For relieving eye discomfort, see also lymph drainage
massage, chapter 7.

Relieving Discomfort in the Chest and Abdominal Area

Start the relaxation at the throat. Exhale a few times
slowly and deeply and imagine making the throat wide
and open. Relax and think during exhalations "soft, gentle,
wide, open," and so on, with respect to places inside the
throat, chest, and abdomen. Do any or all of the following
exercises according to need.

Opening Flower. Feel whether and where there is nar-
rowness or tension in the throat. Imagine a flower bud
opening in it, as in a time lapse film. Repeat this during
two or three exhalations. Feel what happens to that throat
region during the next two or three exhalations. Is there
a widening? Softening? Moisture flowing?

Inverted Funnel. Imagine an inverted funnel, narrow
above, wide and open below. Imagine this funnel starting
at the mouth-throat junction. Feel during exhalations a
widening, softening, and opening up toward the lower,

wide open end of the funnel. Ascertain the place down to which the throat or chest opened up. Then start the narrow top of the funnel about an inch or two above that place, and repeat the widening, softening, and opening up during exhalations. Imagine that some liquid of pleasant temperature and consistency streams down the funnel. Relax in this manner the throat, chest, and abdominal cavity.

Guide Rope. Imagine the exhalation to be a guide rope along which you can glide, slide, or feel your way down into the chest cavity. Repeat this for about three consecutive exhalations. Relax while going down. Continue down into the abdominal cavity along the guide rope of the exhalation.

Elevator. Imagine riding down an elevator within yourself from the throat into the chest during exhalation. Make a stop at the place the elevator has reached at the end of the exhalation. Allow the inhalation to stream in passively. Then descend further during the next exhalation. Repeat, starting and stopping as necessary, and go down through the chest into the abdomen.

Knot Dissolves. Remember the feeling of a "knot in the stomach," or actually create it by holding the breath and tensing inside. Then gently release the tenseness, or, for that matter, tenseness which was there without creating it, during successive exhalations by thinking "the knot dissolves." If no relief is felt, check if the jaw or base of the tongue are tense. Such tension is often related to stomach discomfort. Release these tensions.

Setting Sun. Internal tensions can be reduced in the chest as well as in the upper and lower abdominal area by thinking of a setting sun during exhalations. Feel the gentle warmth, the red glow, the slow sinking, and allow the "inner space" to expand like a horizon, while the body walls seem to soften and expand elastically.

Relaxing the Lower Abdomen. Repeat first the widening of the chest and abdominal cavity. Then observe passively where discomfort makes itself known. Give such places a gentle, but deep finger pressure massage (see chapter 7) during deep exhalations. Wait passively, but attentively, until the body reacts. The abdomen usually "makes known" its reaction by air movements and pressure changes. Wait passively and then massage again where necessary.

Relief of Heartburn. Think "cool" during inhalations and "calm and relaxed" during exhalations, or imagine drinking soothing cool milk with the thought of coolness during inhalations.

Counteracting Nausea. Imagine inhaling "coolness" into the stomach area and exhaling through a place in the body as far removed from the stomach as possible. Then try to talk to the stomach and tell it to relax and calm down. Nausea is evoked by the PSNS. Do anything possible to divert the mind at the same time as stimulating the SNS (see chapters 2 and 3). Shiatsu pressure points, chapter 7, for counteracting nausea are on the bones behind the ears, in the middle of the back of the neck and along the bone there, and around the shoulder blades.

Excretion. The excretion of urine, feces, and menstrual flow can be influenced by the imagination and the breathing rhythm. The general rule is that increased excretion is evoked by thoughts of warmth, relaxation, or flow during exhalations. Decrease is effected by thoughts of tension, stoppage, or cold during inhalations. Depending on the purpose, inhale, tighten the muscles, and think "hold!" or "cold!" or relax during repeated exhalations and think "warm and comfortable" or "movement and flow are easy."

Sleep Improvement

Never fall asleep in an uncomfortable or tense position. Take advantage of the supporting environment (see chapter 4). Release all muscular tensions, especially those of the eyes and jaw (see above and chapter 4). Relax mentally and emotionally by doing Waves or Tides, and Distance.

Use the time available for sleeping and waking to the best advantage. When going to sleep, do Long Breath and Lake. Observe the long, slow exhalations and allow yourself to be carried into sleep as if by ocean waves. Allow yourself to drift into sleep during exhalations. Allow yourself to feel the weight of the relaxed limbs. Readjust your position during exhalations to become perfectly comfortable before falling asleep.

Autogenic Training, chapter 4, is effective for falling asleep as well as for improving long-term sleep patterns.

Reducing Tension and Anxiety and Increasing Self-Assurance

Tenseness and anxiety are so common that they are often considered unavoidable and taken for granted or disregarded. They must be reduced or eliminated before self-assurance and self-sufficiency can be felt or effectively displayed.

Anxiety

Anxiety is a mental and/or emotional state with psychological and physiological manifestations. The Latin *angere,* and the Greek word from which it was derived, means "to make narrow," "to bind tightly," or "to strangle." These meanings of the term *anxiety* are its perfect operational definition since they express what happens physiologically, mentally, and emotionally during a state of anxiety. Psychophysiological techniques for eliminating or reducing anxiety attempt to counteract conditions of constriction by "widening," "opening," and "expanding" narrow passages and by "softening," "loosening," and "letting go" of tensions.

A mental state of anxiety involves a cognitive concern about the future and the unknown, an inability to think clearly, and preoccupation with imagined or actual disturbing factors. The emotional state includes unpleasant alternations or mingling of dread, apprehension, uncertainty, fear, and hope. Psychological manifestations of anxiety are, for example, irritability, bad temper, and ineffectual behavior. Anxiety may also manifest itself as a flight from reality.

Physiological manifestations of anxiety are sensory, motor, autonomic, and hormonal. The throat may become tight and feel "choked," the chest is pulled in and narrowed, the abdomen tightens, diaphragmatic breathing is halted or shallow, and thus the respiratory and digestive passages are "made narrow" while the autonomic nervous system reactions become thoroughly upset by the dilemma of an evoked fight-or-flight reaction, chapter 2, without an appropriate physical response. As a result, the voluntary muscles of the limbs tense or move nervously without purpose in order to counteract "being bound tightly."

A state of anxiety may have few physiological though many mental manifestations. For example, during physical tiredness, when there may be little muscle tension and no involvement of the sympathetic nervous system, the mind may "race." On the other hand, a state of anxiety with few mental and many physiological manifestations may occur during the excitement after successes, with excited, jittery nervousness of the limbs, a feeling of being "high," sympathetic nervous system activity, and possible muscular tension. Such a state may also be induced simply by the release of certain hormones in the body or by the injection of certain chemicals.

Anxiety is felt individually in diverse ways. Some notice mainly its mental manifestations, others autonomic reactions, and others muscle tensions. With respect to the muscles, the tensions may be felt in the neck, the limbs, the jaw, or even the bridge of the nose. Psychosomatic and neurotic patients feel anxiety predominantly located inside the abdomen and chest, suggesting autonomic nervous system involvement, while the psychologically healthy, but overstressed, like business executives and athletes, feel it predominantly as muscle tensions in the limbs and neck, suggesting somatic muscular involvement.

Techniques for the Reduction of Anxiety

Anxiety is neither necessary nor beneficial. It is a habitual stressor which can be greatly reduced or eliminated. Much of the advice given in chapter 3 for Coping with Stress is also valid for reducing anxiety, and so are the exercises for relaxing and widening the respiratory and digestive passages and those for taking advantage of the supporting environment.

The most effective procedure for reducing anxiety depends on counteracting the specific manifestations of the state. All kinds of tension, as well as being manifestations of anxiety, may also produce or increase anxiety of themselves. They can be reduced immediately upon noticing them by relaxing exhalations. The mental manifestations can be reduced by diversion or dissociation. The somatic muscular manifestations can be reduced by either muscle relaxation or physical activity. The sympathetic autonomic nervous system manifestations can be reduced by exercises which increase the parasympathetic action of the autonomic nervous system, such as Schultz's Standard Autogenic Training or Benson's Relaxation Response. These will also bring about a long term reconditioning of the parasympathetic responses and will thus prevent future anxiety reactions. The emotional manifestations of anxiety will be reduced or disappear with elimination or reduction of the mental, somatic, and autonomic manifestations.

Reducing Nervous Tension

Fidgeting or Trembling. The simplest way to reduce fidgeting or trembling is to think "calm," "heavy," or "restful" with respect to the afflicted part during several consecutive, long, slow exhalations. This calms trembling hands and legs and reduces biting the fingernails, picking the face, and other nervous habits.

Facial Tension. To counteract nervous tension in the face, put the hands up to it and feel the comforting warmth or calming coolness, but mainly the support of the hands against the skin and bones. During exhalations think "relaxed, calm, comfortable." If it is not possible to raise the hands to the face, exhale gently through slightly opened lips, letting the cheeks puff out lightly to smoothe any wrinkles and letting the lips become soft, full, and relaxedly alive. Let the eyes relax and forehead wrinkles fade.

Internal Tension. Repressed anger and aggression result in internal tension. Release and relieve these feelings by conscious exhalations while sighing, singing, whistling, or other ways of exhaling.

Tension Release by Abreacting. The strong-willed competitor pushes his body and mind to the limits. This is a great stress on the nervous system and may result in anxiety and apparently irrational emotions and behavior. A sudden remembrance of past stresses may intensify such states, and fits of anger or depression may occur. Regression to primitive, infantile feelings and behavior may result. Irrational behavior should be avoided, but the evoked emotions must be relieved. They should be abreacted as soon as possible in an appropriate manner. The term *abreaction* refers to the process of working off pent-up emotions and disagreeable experiences by living them through in speech, actions, or feelings. Physical actions can be replaced by using the imagination coupled with the breathing rhythm.

Experience the upsetting emotions and imagine doing whatever seems an immediate, spontaneous reaction to the evoked feelings. For instance, for relieving great anger imagine stamping repeatedly with one foot making angry shouts, while in reality sitting in some meeting and just letting the breathing come out in short bursts. For great joy imagine shouting or gasping by just breathing in that pattern. Release pent-up resentment by uttering extensive curses or swear words subvocally during exhalations. After all, the tension release is the important factor, not the effect of nonsense profanities.

Quiet Fixation. For regular, long-term conditioning of the autonomic nervous system, sit relaxedly in a quiet environment, fixating passively on a fairly neutral thought or image for five, fifteen, or thirty minutes. This is the basic procedure used in Indian and Chinese ancient meditation techniques, Schultz's Standard Autogenic Training, Transcendental Meditation, and Benson's Relaxation Response. No transcendental, esoteric, or medical admonition is needed to reap the beneficial results of such quiet, passive, concentration.

Increasing Self-Assurance and Self-Sufficiency

Ground. Stand, exhale, and feel the support from the ground. Get confidence by feeling the feet squarely on the supporting floor or earth. Inhale to increase strength and power. Then walk, feeling both the support and your own power.

Great Calm. Inhale and exhale to find your center of balance somewhere in your lower middle. Inhale deeply and let the air out slowly until there is a natural stillness. Use this moment for squeezing the trigger in target shooting, for making a foul shot or a golf putt, or for any hand-eye coordination task which is better achieved from a calm and steady center. This has also been used to make verbal statements of utmost importance with great calm.

Preparedness. For being prepared for an impending stress, such as having a tooth pulled or some painful intervention, inhale deeply, hold the breath, and then exhale deeply. During the exhalation the muscles relax and stress is less noticeable. The opposite is to tense the muscles so hard that the stress is not noticed. Both work.

Changing Moods. Feel free to use the imagination and breathing rhythm for changing or adjusting your mood or temper, so that they are most appropriate to a situation or need. For instance, the thought of being considerate is enhanced by exhalation, the thought of being brave by inhalation. See Table 10, chapter 5, for other mental states which are enhanced by the breathing phases.

Freedom. In order to preserve energy and vigor, but reduce hostility and inappropriate aggressive feelings, think during inhalations "live!" and during exhalations "and let live!"

Hero. Imagine being a hero or gladiator or somebody you greatly admire for his strength, endurance, and self-assurance. Imagine strength flowing into you during inhalation. Stay relaxed during exhalation. Straighten during inhalation and feel held from above during exhalation.

Loner. If you must live or work by yourself and have difficulties doing this, practice being a loner. Inhale and feel increased strength and self-containment. Exhale and stand solidly on your own feet.

Self-Assurance. Become conscious of the swinging of the diaphragm during relaxed breathing. Feel the relaxed action of the diaphragm which works by itself. Rest within yourself within the rhythm of the not always regular, but self-sufficient diaphragm and feel your own self-sufficiency. Think "fit" during inhalation and "calm" during exhalation, or "Free from fear and fright" during inhalation and "I meet my troubles calmly" during exhalation.

Mountain. Imagine during inhalations becoming big and strong. During exhalations think "I am a mountain of patience, and all disgust and despair runs off my shoulders like little mountain streams." This image has been used in many different settings, with many variations.

Eagle. Imagine being an eagle. Imagine soaring high in the bright blue sky during inhalation. During exhalation glide easily on the air currents with the world far below. Think during inhalation "I sail..." and during exhalation "...on the stream of success." Feel the lift which this gives and the confidence it inspires.

Prolonged Exercises

The following exercises are more extended imagery exercises, and beginners may want to read them slowly on a tape, and then listen at leisure, or have them read by another person aloud. Ample time should be allowed between sentences.

Lotus. Imagine the blossom of a lotus flower within you, somewhere below the diaphragm, approximately at the level of the navel. This flower, when closed, looks like two hands held together, palm to palm. Imagine the flower in this bud stage. During exhalations, imagine that the petals open slowly. They open wide and lie down on the water. They float on the water. Feel the beauty of the flower. Let it fill the whole body. Feel the flower floating on the water. Imagine being the flower, floating on the water.

Observe the beauty and purity of the white petals. Observe their glow. Feel the glow of the petals as they reflect the energy from the sun. Feel how they also acquire energy from the sun. Feel the vibrantly alive energy. Feel it during inhalations and exhalations. Then, during an inhalation, imagine that the petals close again. While they close, absorb the energy and vitality they have gained. Gather yourself, gather something into yourself, hold on to yourself. Let the petals open again during an exhalation. Feel calmness, serenity, security, and quiet.

Repeat the opening and closing of the lotus flower. Feel the energy and strength, the security and serenity. Finally, with an exhalation, delegate security and serenity, strength and energy to the limbs and other parts of the body, especially also to the head.

Organ Concert. Imagine that you are playing an organ, a very old one, which has a strong, beautiful tone. Improvise according to your emotions. Play in all moods and registers.... Play pianissimo or pull all the stops. Skillfully supply just the right amount of air for the right tones and variations.... Play very softly.... Then allow the emotions to rise into joy or anger, exultation or defiance.

But, alas, the bellows begins to tear. It is old and its leather is brittle, and it has borne much wear and stress. As the air starts leaking out, the organ loses its power.... Feel the waning of energy.... Feel the frustration, especially if the emotions are still strong.... But there is still enough pressure to play a soft, gentle tune. Be skillful. Adjust to the situation. Don't give up. Continue the melody with full, rounded tones at as full a range of pitch and power as possible with the reduced pressure.... Become a master at managing and adjusting to the situation.... Skillfully finish playing for the pleasure of the audience and your own satisfaction.

And then set about getting the bellows repaired. Use new, flexible leather. Play again and try, at first carefully but then more and more daringly, how the old organ can be played anew in all its registers and power.... Exult over the beauty of the tone.... Feel proud of your achievement of having managed during the period of breakdown and weakness without giving up.

Allow the tune to end according to your desire.

Bones. Think about your bones and how superbly their construction serves their purpose. They are the supporting elements of the body and must be rigid, but not too rigid, since they must yield to a certain extent under stress and not break.

Imagine carrying two heavy suitcases and feel the bones of the arms stretch and draw apart at the joints due to the weight. Imagine this during an exhalation. During inhalations breathe in the strength for carrying the heavy load.

Imagine during exhalation running down a flight of stairs, two steps at a time, and feel the bounce of the compression, yet the elasticity. Try the same during an inhalation and feel the difference. Allow yourself the relaxed bounce during exhalations.

Bones must be strong. Imagine them being made of steel or stone, and feel the weight in the body. Imagine them being made of wood, having suffered permanent compression and wear after a lifetime of walking, running, jumping, and moving.

Now think of their porous structure with a total weight of only about twenty pounds. Feel the lightness and appreciate the relatively weightless strength of your superbly sturdy, supporting structure.

Think of the articulation of the bones at the joints, one after another, and feel looseness, flow, and movability.

Finally, remember the metabolism in the bones, their aliveness. Imagine the cells and blood vessels which aid in the self-repairing power. Think of the marrow as a factory for red blood cells.

Feel very strong, very elastic, very alive "in your bones" from meditating on your bones.

World Within. Permit yourself to go, during exhalations, to your center, your center of gravity, the middle of your body. Imagine going down into it in an elevator, climbing down a ladder, sliding down a rope, or any other way that appeals to you. Exhale and go down along the guide rope of the exhalation. Go down and down, stepwise or in one swoop, to the lowest place where you can imagine the center to be. For most, this is somewhere below the level of the navel.

And there, in the center, make room during exhalation. Create your place of privacy, a place all your own, within yourself; a place to go to, to turn to, whenever and wherever you need it. Have there what you need. Remove from it all that is useless or disturbing. Allow in, or exclude, anybody you wish. Be with others or alone.

If your outside world seems too big, too exhausting, too confusing, make the inner world cozy and comfortable, small, simple, safe, secure, secluded, and still. If your outside world is too small, too restricted and restricting, too depressed and depressing, too dark and dreary, make the inner world wide and open and expanded, elaborate and elegant, light and bright, elating and inspiring. Use your fantasy, your desires, your wishful thinking in order to fashion and furnish it according to your needs. Make it the right temperature: let it be warmed by the sun or a fireplace; cool it with fountains or fans. Make it comfortable with pillows or mosses. Get flowers, fruits, plants, anything that pleases you. Provide books and objects of beauty. Make it the place of your edification, where you build yourself up and grow. Make your center serviceable and useful to relax and refresh body and mind. Make it absolutely your own. Become perfectly secure, perfectly satisfied within yourself; be yourself; become one with your center. Experience your inner world and take from it into the outside life satisfaction and strength, security and courage.

And when you practice this exercise again and again, allow the place to change, to develop, to serve according to your needs; according to the needs of your senses, your body, your mind, your emotions, your feelings. Let the world within serve your needs, and let it prepare you for handling the world without.

After practicing this several times, experiment with bringing persons into your World Within. Examine your feelings toward them and their actions toward you. Use this exercise for analyzing your relationship to others and for trying out vicariously future behavior for the real world.

Adjusting to the Environment

Conducive Environment. Imagine being in an environment most conducive for what you have to do, be it studying, conversing, listening to a lecture, or attending a conference. Construct the environment in your imagination and use the breathing rhythm appropriately. If you are in a room where you think you cannot work or study well, remember or imagine a place where you could do it well. Imagine the details of that place. Imagine how the body would feel in that place. Keep that feeling. Relax with exhalations and invigorate yourself with inhalations. Then go about your work in the real environment, while your mind dwells in the most appropriate environment.

Fresh Air. If the room in which you are is stuffy, inhale and imagine breathing fresh mountain air, sitting by a stream, or being in some other refreshing, invigorating place. Review relevant entries of Table 10, chapter 5, and design your own exercises as needed.

Wall. If there is tension in your immediate environment, first relax with an exhalation. During the next inhalation imagine a protective wall rising between you and the environment. This might be a bullet-proof glass wall through which stress cannot reach you, but from behind which you observe the actions and reactions of others and react leisurely from your place of safety.

Distance. Imagine during exhalations that the distance between you and whatever stresses or disturbs you becomes greater and greater. Or, during exhalations, imagine the troubles or difficulties becoming smaller and smaller, or fading away and dissolving.

Air Cushion. While sitting, sense the downward movement of muscle relaxation in the wake of an exhalation. This should feel as if the body were moving down, until it comes to rest on the seat of the chair. Feel sitting thus on the chair. Then feel the buttocks and imagine their tissues "being blown up" like an air cushion. Make this cushion soft, but of partial tension. Relax onto and rise slightly from the imagined cushion ever so often.

Long Sitting. When sitting for a long time, especially in a stuffy room, invigorate yourself by tensing and relaxing the buttocks. Tense while inhaling or holding the breath. Release the tension during exhalation. Practice this first with the actual movement. Then learn to do it so slowly, or almost in the imagination, that no movement is visible. Keep the upper body relaxed.

Stop and Start. For physical as well as for mental action coordinate stopping and starting with the breathing rhythm. For sudden action, stop and start the breath together with movement or thought. For smoothness, carry on movement or thinking during long exhalations. For instance, a business executive, dictating, is interrupted repeatedly by disturbing telephone calls and becomes nervous. He can during an exhalation "disengage" from the dictating, "gather strength" during an inhalation while lifting the receiver, and be relaxedly ready for the telephone conversation with the next exhalation. Upon finishing, he again disengages with an exhalation and "gathers his thoughts" with a refreshing inhalation for continuing the dictation.

Rolling with the Waves. For adjusting to a distasteful situation in which you must remain, imagine "rolling with the waves." Do so in rhythm with exhalations and inhalations. Relax during exhalations, and gather energy to stay in the situation during inhalations.

Selective Sensory Awareness. Reduce stressful environmental stimulation whenever possible by Wall or Distance. Then use selective sensory awareness by paying attention to the necessary and enjoyable. Enjoy the colors of nature, art, or artifices. Observe others with their needs and foibles.

Sensible Speed. When in a hurry, relax your walk. Do the String Puppet, Clothes Hanger, and Rubber Joints. Slow down to an efficient pace, the one achieved without excess tension or energy output. Become aware of the environment. Use the walking time to prepare mentally for the next business.

Time Expansion and Contraction. When you are in a hurry or under time pressure, exhale slowly and deeply and imagine that time is expanding. When you are waiting or impatient, and time seems too long, inhale and think it passes more quickly.

Patience and Endurance. Do Long Breath. Then, after an inhalation, exhale very slowly and deeply and think of great patience and endurance. Inhale for strength. Relax the limbs and chest during the next exhalation. Repeat and feel your capacity for patience and endurance increase and accumulate in a reservoir in the lower abdomen.

Equanimity. For reducing fear of persons or for interactions with unpleasant individuals, first do Distance. Then inhale and think "courage." Finally, exhale and inhale calmly, think of equanimity, and approach your relationship from this new vantage point.

Efficiency for a Purpose. Remove the qualities of a job or situation which are negative factors for achieving your aim by Distance. Magnify those which are important to the task to be performed during inhalations and at the same time gather the strength and courage for achieving your aim.

Cooperation. Imagine the cooperative actions of animals. If working with teammates, imagine being one of the cooperative pack animals, such as wolves or any of the dog family. Move in and out of the pack cooperatively, aided by appropriate breathing. Get out of the way when you are not needed, move in when of use.

Aggression. Prepare for aggression with inhalation, carry it out with exhalation. For strong aggression imagine being a very aggressive animal, like a taunted tiger. For reducing aggressive feelings practice Patience and Endurance, or Equanimity. If you must be aggressive for an argument, a proposal, a match, or a performance, prepare by doing Calm Base, Ground, Hero, and Toad.

Communication

The word communication comes from the Latin *communicare*: to have in common, take part, or share. Animal communication depends on the development of the muscular system, the nervous system, the senses, and the excretion of certain substances. Human communication is extremely complicated, involving not only all factors of communication in other animals, but intellectualized verbalization. Movement or cessation of movement, muscle tone, breathing, and all variations and combinations of these may either enhance or confuse the meaning of a verbal message.

Communication can be improved when sender and recipient are aware of their own and each other's facial expressions, gestures and other movements, tension or relaxation patterns, expressed emotions, breathing, tone of voice, and general demeanor, which may all either reinforce or contradict the verbal message.

Mature communication includes all possible factors for improving the sending and receiving of clear messages (Beier 1966; Pemberton 1969). Under stress, regression can occur, and communication may revert to less mature patterns or stereotyped role playing, such as: the playful patter of small children without expectation of a meaningful answer; the parentlike admonishings without permitting any chance for a response; the sullen silence of a stubborn child; the infantile acting out of joy or anger; or the purposely confusing word and behavior patterns of teenagers. Primitive, one-way messages create confusion and increase tension and misunderstanding. Communication is the give-and-take in which sender, recipient, and a clear message are involved, and the effects of messages must be observed and answers patiently awaited.

The manner in which a message is given or received is important. The giving may be related to exhalation, the receiving to inhalation.

Readiness. Wait for the other's message in a relaxed, attentive, "exhaled" manner. If necessary, gather strength and courage during an inhalation to be able to wait until the other has finished his message. Relax with an exhalation and analyze the message. Then, during inhalation and exhalation, prepare the appropriate response. Give it in a relaxed "exhaled" manner, or emphasize it by an inhalation before putting it forth with force.

Response. Decide whether the response should be approach or withdrawal, permission or denial. Emphasize approach and permission with exhalation. Emphasize withdrawal or denial with inhalation or holding the breath. Incorporate the breathing rhythm into movements and words in communication.

Conclusion

Small, unavoidable, everyday stresses, such as tiredness or lack of energy, pains or bodily malfunctions, tension or anxiety, and adverse influences of the environment may add up to a rather annoying level of stress. This can be greatly reduced by using any of the large number and diversity of exercises in this chapter. The most suitable and effective ones should be selected, and the index may be consulted for additional ones. Stress-reducing behavior should become a beneficial habit through the constant practice of these exercises in the daily routine.

9. The Use and Uses of Psychophysiological Techniques

Most societies, in the course of becoming civilized, developed some philosophical system which included health-promoting measures: Yoga in India, T'ai Chi in China, Mazdaznan in Persia. Hippocrates and the Greek and Roman physicians knew the healthful effect of exercise and massage. Celsus wrote about special exercises to be used by the physically inactive before going to bed.

Changes in behavior patterns depend on the intellectual theory on which programs for change are based, on the psychological motivation for change, and on the human physiology which is involved. Little can be done about the physiology of man, which has remained the same for ages. But theories and practices which are based on the idea of individual responsibility for a healthy body and mind differ from those which are based on the medical or psychoanalytical models, like Selye's or Freud's, which were derived from observation of medical and psychotherapy patients. Psychophysiological methods developed from psychoanalysis, such as those of W. Reich, A. Lowen, M. Feldenkrais, and F. Perls, do not have as sound and sensible a basis as the self-help and training methods that have been developed for general individual improvement, or for specific purposes like perfecting performance in the performing arts and athletics, or to overcome physiological difficulties, such as J. H. Schultz's Standard Autogenic Training, C. Atlas' Dynamic Tension, E. Gindler's Sensory Awareness Training, M. Fuchs' and B. Jencks' respiration methods, G. Alexander's Eutony, and diverse calisthenics and self-massages. These all have their basis in physiology, in which behavior is firmly rooted, while psychoanalysis derives from a theory which lacks empirical support.

The Importance of Sensory Awareness

Conscious awareness, in the context of this book, means consciousness of the body, its functions and malfunctions, and it may be divided into intellectual and sensory components. For instance, intellectual awareness of a bad posture, overweight, or anxiety includes knowledge of the physical and psychological bases and the harmful results of these conditions, whereas sensory awareness is the sensory perception of the physical misalignment or excessive bulk and weight and their physiological effects, and the physiological components of anxiety, such as restricted breathing, tensed muscles, or increased heart rate. Conscious sensory awareness is most effective within the specific modality to which a problem is related. For instance, perception of posture and overweight are primarily proprioceptive and somesthetic (see chapter 2). Intellectual awareness is less effective for initiating change than the continuous feedback of sensory awareness of the physical impediments caused by misalignment and excessive weight.

Body and mind are indivisibly interrelated and constantly interacting with each other in the most intricate ways. Usually this happens subconsciously and only the results are observed. In order to consciously control these interactions, an increased conscious awareness of bodily and mental reactions, to be used as a biofeedback indicator, must be developed and techniques to induce beneficial changes must be learned.

Sensory awareness varies greatly individually from oversensitivity to insensitivity. Knowledge of the degree of one's sensitivity or lack of it is necessary for protection from both physical and mental overstimulation. Oversensitivity may be either beneficial or deleterious. It is detrimental if it results in anxiety or an upset physiological system. For example, those with psychosomatic difficulties may suffer because of stimulation of an oversensitive sense of taste or smell. On the other hand, a chemist or wine- or food-taster will use the same sensitivity professionally for identifying substances, disregarding it when it serves no useful purpose. Relative insensitivity may also be beneficial or detrimental. It is not uncommon to be so involved with some task, interest, or pleasure as not to notice cold, pain, hunger, or fatigue. Such insensitivity may act protectively unless such stimuli become stressors capable of doing serious physiological damage. Thus, a proper degree of both intellectual and sensory awareness is required in order to correct detrimental conditions before they cause damage. Over- and undersensitivity to stimuli may be detected by carefully observing bodily and mental reactions as passively and objectively as possible. A decision must be made as to whether a change in sensitivity is advantageous, or whether what is needed is rather a decrease of anxiety or an increase of apprehension with respect to a stimulus. Sensory sensitivity may be either increased or decreased as the situation demands. For example, it may be increased by sensory awareness training, or decreased by dissociation. Chapter 4 describes the development and use of sensory awareness.

The Use of Psychophysiological Techniques

The inner and outer environments must be accurately perceived and correctly assessed, so that decisions about necessary changes are based upon facts instead of assumptions. The purpose of the use of psychophysiological techniques is the attainment of physical and psychological stabilization of the individual within the environment. Some changes are extremely simple to make, others require conscientious, regular training. Some changes must be initiated by physical means, others by mental or a combination of the two. Most changes are not accomplished easily, and the ancient Chinese, writing about the control of body and mind (Wilhelm 1935), were aware of the primary deterrents to success when they wrote: "This means work and self-discipline, and individuals have always had difficulties with these two."

The three Great Ts of athletics: Training, Technique, and Tactics, that is, diligent practice of a repertory of techniques to acquire proficiency in them, and the use of the right one for the right purpose at the right time, are essential for making corrective changes in the most effective manner. Particularly important in applying any technique or method in the most effective manner is the use of the body as its own biofeedback instrument by means of increased sensory awareness. This ensures more sensitive self-regulatory control over body and mind through continuous monitoring of sensations, and appropriate modifications of behavior.

Decisive for the choice of technique to be used are the time and place of use, the degree of need, and personal preferences. Often similar results can be attained by different means. Some may prefer imagery exercises, others more physical, mechanical, and structured ones. Some of the exercises described in this book may be done in any situation; others involve altered states of consciousness and require special conditions and precautions (see chapter 2).

If success is not attained with one kind of exercise, others should be tried. Individuals differ. For instance, one may best succeed in relieving muscular tension by relaxing the joints, another by exhaling, a third by using the imagination, and a fourth by doing calisthenics or yogic exercises. Also, one technique may be the best at one time, and another one at another time or place. Techniques should be selected and modified to maximize benefits, and whatever is useless or detrimental should be eliminated.

Occasionally, while working with body and mind, a hindrance or impasse is encountered. This may be due to boredom, to the use of an inadequate or incorrect technique, or to some psychological or physiological difficulty or condition. To overcome such hindrances the following is suggested: investigate the cause of the impasse and increase the determination and motivation or change the technique as required.

Most instructions in this chapter refer back to exercises described at other places in this book. All exercises are listed in the index either under topics or under names of the single exercises, and frequent use of the index is recommended for finding special topics.

The mentally healthy, whether or not physically handicapped, can often help themselves by learning and then conscientiously doing the appropriate exercises. Those experiencing psychological stress with psychosomatic difficulties and those in need of psychotherapy are often unable to do so and, to reiterate earlier advice, they should learn the exercises under the supervision of a therapist.

Usage

The following instructions serve as examples for usage of the techniques and exercises described in the text.

Physical and Mental Relaxation

For immediate physical or mental relaxation, exhale! It is amazing what this simple procedure, repeated as necessary, will do.

Physical Relaxation. Build relaxation exercises into all

daily activities, combining as much relaxation with work as possible. Relax not only during breaks, but while standing, walking, or jogging, when sitting down and when getting up. Remain relaxed when not stressfully occupied. Become aware of mounting tensions in jaw, forehead, and throat. Release tensions of the throat by Opening Flower, Waterfall, or Holes Under Chin. For relaxation of the neck and shoulder region use Warm Shower, Complete Neck Roll, or any others of the exercises for the head and neck region in chapter 4. Much tension is located in this region, therefore use also self-massage and lymph drainage massage. For releasing tension in chest and abdomen, recall Knot Dissolves, Setting Sun, and Relaxing Lower Abdomen. Relax the face by doing Infant's Lips or review Facial Tension. For leg relaxation review Standing and Walking, Third Leg, and Tail. Let the upper trunk be supported by a flexible hip and pelvic region; review Raft and Rubber Joints.

Tensing the diaphragm is coupled with a narrowing of the throat, while a free-swinging diaphragm produces relaxation of the voice. Relax the voice by relaxing the throat not only by the exercises for mouth, tongue, throat, and diaphragm, but also by Loosening Joints. For increasing the breathing capacity do Long Breath, Extinguishing the Candle, and Filling and Emptying the Bottle. Also practice all the ways of breathing depicted in Figure 2, chapter 5, and use those which best serve your requirements.

Mental Relaxation. For mental relaxation review Concentration, chapter 2, and Table 2. Also do Sound Meditation. For long-term reconditioning of the autonomic nervous system toward the relaxed, parasympathetic side, the methods of choice are Quiet Fixation or Standard Autogenic Training.

Use relaxation exercises especially before falling asleep. Falling asleep with a tense jaw or tense eyes interferes with deep, relaxing sleep. Review Sleep Improvement. Relax similarly during bus or airplane travel.

Invigoration. Review the invigoration exercises and choose those which seem most adequate. Do also Water Jug, and Wings. Induce invigoration locally where needed. Also, give an invigorating massage to those parts of the body which need it, especially the face. Keep arms and fingers invigorated for work or play while the rest of the body remains as relaxed as possible.

For counteracting fatigue, practice especially Simple Invigoration, Ice Plunge, Double Door, Face Treatment, and Fresh Air. After you have been sitting for long hours, invigorate body and mind with Energizing Walk. Do this either during a short real walk or simply vividly imagine the walk. Also do Jogging, and Jumping Jack.

When you are working against a deadline, conserve energy by interspersing many short rest periods, but keep the mind as alert as possible with invigoration exercises.

Conserving and Increasing Energy. Most tasks require much less energy than is expended. Adjust the energy to the demands of the task. Learn to release tensions which serve no purpose as they develop. Good posture preserves strength and keeps the body relaxed. Practice Clothes Hanger, and Pulling Cord.

Be conscious of the supporting environment. Review the section in chapter 4. The exercise Climbing has proven especially energy saving for those whose work is distributed on several floors, and for the elderly or sick who have difficulty climbing.

For increasing energy use exercises and imagery related to strength and power, such as Energizing, Pumping Strength, and Solar Plexus or Storage Battery. Construct reservoirs of energy for different purposes (see chapter 8). For extra strength during heavy work or mountain climbing invigorate the legs or any body part which needs it by Pumping Strength.

Posture, Flexibility, and Movement. Effortless, graceful movement from a well-balanced center is not only beautiful, but it saves energy and is healthful for body and mind. Practice especially Clothes Hanger, Pulling Cord, Link Chain, and Fountain. Practice these exercises sitting, standing, and walking.

For better balance practice Center of Gravity, Raft, Calm Base, Balance, and Balancing Circus Man. The Circus Man is as useful for youngsters balancing on a tree trunk over a stream as for a stroke patient who must learn again to find his balance.

For promoting relaxed movement, move during exhalations and remember Rubber Joints. For retarding or breaking movements make them during inhalations. In general, the breath should not be held during movement unless for a special purpose, such as a strenuous effort. Skills for attaining flexibility and relaxation must be acquired before those designed to increase strength and speed, otherwise torn muscles or ligaments and back injuries are more likely.

Counteracting Minor Ailments

Minor ailments often interfere with work efficiency. When the eyes are tired or burning, choose from the index listings under Eyes. For tension headaches, backaches, a sore throat, and similar afflictions, see the exercises described under Pain Reduction. If extremities swell or become stiff, perform a lymph drainage massage. For cold hands or feet, see Warmth in Extremities or do the Blood Surge Exercise. Decrease discomfort after muscle strain by performing a relaxing massage.

The chronically ill may find it useful to divert the mind by World Within. Thus they may dwell in the past or in pure fantasy, and while the time away pleasantly instead of complaining and fretting. They may also profit by doing imagined calisthenics, such as Jogging, Jumping Jack, or Climbing.

Coping with the Environment

Review the exercises for Influencing the Mind and Coping with the Environment. For building confidence in relationships with superiors and for interactions with coworkers, students, or family, choose appropriate exercises from Increasing Self-Assurance and Self-Sufficiency. Also review Communication. Determine your difficulties and improve communication by doing whatever is necessary. When the environment becomes oppressive or offensive, practice Wall, Endurance, or Distance. Under mental pressure remember Calm Base, Mountain, and Rolling with the Waves. For reducing indecisiveness, use ideomotor finger movements, chapter 3, for making decisions. For increasing the power of concentration, practice the first two exercises, Heaviness and Warmth, of Autogenic Training or the Kung Fu Riding Horse with the Kung Fu Deep Breathing.

At different times, different exercises will be most appropriate. Use whatever is needed, but practice the exercises also in advance at leisure, so that they may be available for recall in time of need. Choose whatever brings the best results, and do it often.

Note to Therapists

A therapist who plans to use psychophysiological exercises for patients must learn to do them himself first and become familiar with some of the reactions which may occur. He should also gather experience by teaching group courses in order to observe the diverse reactions which may be evoked in different individuals by identical instructions.

Group courses, with the opportunity of learning about others' reactions, are often useful for patients and give the therapist a chance to discuss material which might otherwise not have been discussed. However, each patient reacts differently and will have to work according to his own imagination, needs, and rhythms. Ample time must be allowed in groups as well as in individual sessions for patients to react, to sense the results, and to discuss reactions.

Psychophysiological exercises related to the mucous membranes and skin have proven helpful for patients with allergies, burns, sore throats, and the like. The exercises for pain reduction and conserving or increasing energy have the most diverse uses with patients.

Breathing Therapy. The breathing exercises, especially those for relaxed breathing and slowing the respiration, are useful for retraining patients with either psychosomatic or physical breathing difficulties, such as asthma, emphysema, just a simple cold, or hay fever. They have also eased the breathing of those with broken ribs or physical restrictions like a cast or a corset.

Respiration functions on the borderline between the conscious and the subconscious and can be influenced by either. Conscious breathing exercises are useful for those with healthy, relaxed breathing rhythms, but disturbed breathing is more effectively changed by the circuitous route over the imagination. Direct, conscious effort and mental concentration add tension to an already strained function and may be more of a hindrance than a help.

Psychotherapy. Psychotherapists who use psychophysiological techniques must be well acquainted with the actions and reactions of the autonomic nervous system. The information in this book is not sufficient to provide the necessary background, and outside sources should be consulted for additional information.

Psychophysiological exercises are not a cure for malfunctions, but a means by which an upset autonomic nervous system and inadequate habits can be reconditioned and retrained. The exercises are excellent for physical relaxation, for reducing anxiety, and for increasing self-sufficiency.

The therapist must decide what a patient needs: relaxation, invigoration, or both; an increase of reality relatedness, diversion, or dissociation; physical or mental abreactions, or ego-strengthening. The therapist can then try different techniques with the patient and choose which work best. Psychophysiological exercises have the advantage that the patient must participate actively and can usually do "homework" between sessions.

Neurotic, heavily stressed, and psychosomatic patients benefit from all relaxation exercises and retraining of the breathing rhythm. The technique of passive movements has proven especially helpful for relaxation of overactive children and with patients of low intellect. It not only induces good relaxation, but also increases the cooperation of the patient.

Psychophysiological exercises should not be used with borderline schizophrenics and others who have difficulties relating to reality. Such patients may become extremly anxious by being forced to confront the reality of their own body, with a consequent worsening of their mental condition. Research with psychophysiological exercises for schizophrenics is being done, but no data for reliable success exist to date.

A therapist should know diverse psychophysiological methods for immediate interventions as well as for long-term conditioning. He must be aware of a patient's individual differences and needs and act in terms of the present situation, not in terms of previous sessions. He must get clues from the patient's body messages, such as general and local tensions, and should be able to diagnose arousal of anxiety by observing obstructed or upset breathing. Holding the breath often signifies anxiety or resistance, or that an important thought crossed the patient's mind. Intentional synchronization of suggestions with the appropriate respiratory phases greatly improves the effectiveness of the therapist.

The immediate need of a patient is of utmost importance. Anxiety may be increased by relaxation when the real need of the moment is to abreact physically. The therapist should use his own psychophysiological reactions as indicators of what a patient's message is, but must disengage emotionally from his reactions before responding. He must minimize his assumptions about the patient and rather inquire about the patient's assumptions. A therapist must know about the occurrence, importance, and usefulness of hallucinations and abreactions, since these are frequently evoked in the course of psychophysiological therapies. Patients may become anxious about spontaneous or induced abreactions, especially during a deeply relaxed state, and the therapist who uses potent relaxation therapies must know how to handle such situations, being permissive, and yet a strong guide. Finally, the therapist should supervise the patient in designing his own exercises, suggestions, and practice schedule.

Most of the exercises in this book were originally developed for self-training of body and mind, without purposely inducing altered states of consciousness. However, many patients slip spontaneously into such states during relaxation or other body-related therapies. Therefore, therapists using psychophysiological techniques must be thoroughly familiar with such states and know their usefulness.

Final Note

A *short program* for mental and physical fitness is often requested. However, no such program is described in this book. Individual differences and requirements vary too greatly. Life is a dynamic equilibrium between a constantly changing environment and the psychophysiological system, and man must try to do the best with what is available to him mentally and physically.

Keeping body and mind in the best condition possible is a twenty-four hour task. An important aid in this task is the conscious use of biofeedback: the utilization of physiological sensations for the purpose of modifying behavior in the most efficient and effective manner. For this purpose, sensory awareness must be increased and skill must be acquired in the use of as many psychophysiological techniques as possible in order to be able to apply the most appropriate at the right time in the best way.

References

Akstein, D. "Terpsichoretrancetherapy." *The International Journal of Clinical and Experimental Hypnosis* 21 (1973): 131–143.

Alexander, F. M. *The Use of the Self.* London: Re-Educational Publications, 1910.

Alexander, G. "Eutonie." In Stokvis, B., and Wiesenhütter, E. *Der Mensch in der Entspannung* (3rd ed.). Stuttgart: Hippokrates Verlag, 1971.

Atlas, C. "System of Health, Strength, and Physique Building." Correspondence Course. New York: Private Office, 1945.

Barber, T. X. "Suggested ('Hypnotic') Behavior: The Trance Paradigm versus an Alternative Paradigm." Harding, Mass.: Medfield Foundation, 1970.

Beier, E. G. *The Silent Language of Psychotherapy.* Chicago: Aldine Publishing Co., 1966.

Benson, H. *The Relaxation Response.* New York: William Morrow & Co., 1975.

Benson, H., Beary, J. F., and Carol, M. P. "The Relaxation Response." *Psychiatry* 37 (1974): 37–46.

Bernard, C. *Leçons sur les phénomènes de la vie communs aux animaux et aux végétaux. 2 volumes.* Paris Bailiere, 1878–1879.

Bezzola, D. "Zur Analyse psychotraumatischer Symptome." *Journal für Psychologie und Neurologie* 8 (1907) : 204–219.

————. "Elementar-Autanalyse." *Zeitschrift für die gesamte Neurologie und Psychiatrie* 43 (1918) : 27–33.

Brooks, C. V. W. *Sensory Awareness.* New York: Viking Press, 1974.

Cannon, W. B. *Bodily Changes in Pain, Hunger, Fear, and Rage.* New York: D. Appleton & Co., 1929.

Cheek, D. B., and LeCron, L. M. *Clinical Hypnotherapy.* New York: Grune & Stratton, 1968.

Cohn, R. C. "An Approach to Psychosomatic Analysis." *Psychoanalysis* 3 (1955) : 58–67.

Collins, J. K. "Muscular Endurance in Normal and Hypnotic States: A Study of Suggested Catalepsy." Honors Thesis. University of Sydney, 1961.

Cornelius, A. *Druckpunkte.* Enslin Balin, 1902.

————. *Nervenpunkte.* Leipzig: Thieme Verlag, 1909.

Deussen, P. *Allgemeine Geschichte der Philosophie.* Leipzig: Brockhaus, 1899.

Dicke, E., Schliack, H., and Wolff, A. *Bindegewebsmassage.* Stuttgart: Hippokrates Verlag, 1968.

Dürckheim, K. *Hara.* London: George Allen & Unwin, 1962.

Ebner, M. *Connective Tissue Massage.* Edinburgh: Livingstone, 1962.

Ehrenfried, L. *Körperliche Erziehung zum seelischen Gleichgewicht.* Berlin: Heenemann KG, 1957.

Erickson, M. H., and Rossi, E. L. "Varieties of Double Bind." *The American Journal of Clinical Hypnosis* 17 (1975) : 143–157.

Eyring, H., and Dougherty, T. F. "Molecular Mechanisms in Inflammation and Stress." *American Scientist* 43 (1955) : 457–467.

Feldenkrais, M. *Body and Mature Behaviour.* New York: International Universities Press, 1949.

————. *Awareness through Movement.* New York: Harper & Row, 1972.

Frazer, J. G. *The New Golden Bough.* New York: Criterion Books, 1959.

Fuchs, M. "Über Atemtherapie und entspannende Körperarbeit." *Psyche* (Stuttg.) 3 (1949/50): 538–548.

————. "Atemtherapie oder rhythmisierende Entspannungstherapie?" *Praxis der Psychotherapie* 4 (1959): 173–178.

————. "Eigenrhythmus über Entspannung und Atmung ohne Selbsthypnose." *Zeitschrift für psychosomatische Medizin und Psychoanalyse* 10 (1964): 141–145.

————. "Atemrhythmisierende Entspannungstherapie bei psychosomatischen Störungen." In D. Langen (Ed.): *Schriftenreihe zur Theorie und Praxis der medizinischen Psychologie.* Stuttgart: Hippokrates Verlag, 1971.

————. *Funktionelle Entspannung.* Stuttgart: Hippokrates Verlag, 1974.

Hanish, O. Z.-A. *Mazdaznan Health and Breath Culture.* Chicago: Mazdaznan Press, 1914.

Hess, W. R. "Funktionsgesetze des vegetativen Nervensystems." *Klinische Wochenschrift* 5 (1926): 1353–1354.

Huang, A. C. *Embrace Tiger, Return to Mountain.* Moab: Real People Press, 1973.

Illich, I. *Medical Nemesis: The Expropriation of Health.* London: Calder & Boyars, 1975.

Jacobson, E. *Progressive Relaxation* (2nd ed.). Chicago: University of Chicago Press, 1938.

Jahn, F. L. *Werke.* Neu herausgegeben von Karl Euler. Hof: G. A. Grau, cie., 1884–1887.

Jencks, B. "Influence of the Environment in Preparing an Animal to Meet Stress." Doctoral dissertation. Salt Lake City: University of Utah, 1962.

_____. "Self-Rhythmization. Part I.: Instructing a Person in the Basic Concepts." A 25-minute teaching film. Salt Lake City: University of Utah, 1970a.

_____. "Self-Rhythmization. Part II.: Instructing a Group in Finding and Adjusting Self-Rhythms." A 26-minute teaching film. Salt Lake City: University of Utah, 1970b.

_____. "Self-Rhythmization. Part III.: Self-Rhythmization Therapy with a Psychosomatic Patient." A 26-minute teaching film. Salt Lake City: University of Utah, 1970c.

_____. "Self-Rhythmization: A Psychophysiological Therapy." Paper presented at 50th WPA, Los Angeles, Calif., 1970d.

_____. *Basic Self-Rhythmization Exercises: Instruction Manual for Trainees.* Salt Lake City: Jencks, 1971.

_____. "Ausgewählte individuelle psychophysiologische Kombinationstherapie (AKT)." In H. Binder (Ed.): *Zwanzig Jahre praktische und klinische Psychotherapie.* München: J. F. Lehmanns Verlag, 1973, 131–149.

_____. "Einführung in die Hypnose." In H. Binder (Ed.): *Zwanzig Jahre praktische und klinische Psychotherapie.* München: J. F. Lehmanns Verlag, 1973, 13–17.

_____. *Exercise Manual for J. H. Schultz's Standard Autogenic Training and Special Formulas.* Salt Lake City: Jencks, 1973.

_____. "Problem-Oriented, Psychophysiological Combinationtherapy." Paper presented at 53rd WPA, Anaheim, Calif., 1973.

_____. *Respiration for Relaxation, Invigoration, and Special Accomplishment.* Manual. Salt Lake City: Jencks, 1974.

_____. "Relaxation and Reconditioning of the Autonomic

Nervous System for Children: The Autogenic Rag Doll." Paper presented at 18th Annual Scientific Meeting, ASCH, Seattle, Wash., 1975.

————. "Utilizing the Phases of the Breathing Rhythm in Hypnosis." Paper presented at the 7th International Congress of Hypnosis and Psychosomatic Medicine, Philadelphia, Pa., 1976.

————, and Rosenthal, E. S. *Relaxation and Toning-Up Exercises to Facilitate Pregnancy and Childbirth.* Pamphlet. Salt Lake City: Jencks, 1973.

Johnson, S. *A Journey to the Hebrides.* Troy: Parfraets Press, 1903.

Junová, H., and Knobloch, F. "Psychogymnastik als eine Methode der Psychotherapie. *Praxis der Psychotherapie.* 11 (1966): 63–76.

Kuwahara, Y., and Allred, G. T. *Kamikaze.* New York: Ballantine, 1957.

Leube, H., and Dicke, E. *Massage reflektorischer Zonen im Bindegewebe bei rheumatischen und inneren Krankheiten* (5th ed.). Stuttgart: Piscator-Verlag, 1951.

Ling, P. H. *The Gymnastic Free Exercises.* Boston: Tichnor, Reed & Fields, 1853.

Lowen, A. *Physical Dynamics of Character Structure.* New York: Grune & Stratton, 1958.

————. *Breathing, Movement, and Feeling.* New York: Institute for Bioenergetic Analysis, 1965.

Luthe, W. (Ed.). *Autogenic Therapy.* 6 volumes. New York: Grune & Stratton, 1969–1972.

Majno, G. *The Healing Hand.* Cambridge, Mass.: Harvard University Press, 1975.

Mengershausen, J. von. *Bewegungsübungen und Selbstmassage.* Bad Homburg vdH: Bircher-Benner Verlag GmbH, 1972.

Mensendieck, B. *Körperkultur des Weibes.* München: F. Bruckmann, 1906.

Meyer, J.-E. "Konzentrative Entspannungsübungen nach

Elsa Gindler und ihre Grundlagen." *Zeitschrift für Psychotherapie und Medizinische Psychologie* 11 (1961): 116–127.

Michaux, L., Lelord, G., Lauzel, J. P., and Wintrebert, H. "La relaxation chez l'enfant par le mouvement passif. Etude E. E. G." *Revue de Médecine Psychosomatique* 3 (1961): 53–56.

Minick, M. *The Kung Fu Exercise Book.* New York: Simon & Schuster, 1974.

Morgan, C. T. *Physiological Psychology.* New York: McGraw-Hill, 1965.

Namikoshi, T. *Japanese Finger Pressure Therapy–Shiatsu.* San Francisco: Japan Publications, 1972.

Nebel, H. "Über Heilgymnastik und Massage." *Innere Medicin* 98 (1886): 2641–2660.

Nietzsche, F. *Ecce Homo.* Frankfurt am Main: Fischer Bücherei, 1968.

Palos, S. *Atem und Meditation.* München: O. W. Barth Verlag, 1974.

Pemberton, W. H. "Talk Patterns of People in Crises." In: *Pemberton Papers.* Berkeley: University Extension, University of California, 1969.

Perls, F. S. *Gestalt Therapy Verbatim.* Lafayette: Real People Press, 1969.

Pulos, L. "Hypnosis and Think Training with Athletes." Paper presented at 12th Annual Scientific Meeting, ASCH, San Francisco, Calif., 1969.

Quilitzsch, G. *Taschenbuch für Massage.* Heidelberg: Haug-Verlag, 1967.

Read, A. D. *Childbirth Without Fear.* New York: Harper Brothers, 1944.

Reich, W. *Character Analysis* (3rd ed.). New York: Orgone Institute Press, 1949.

Rolf, I. P. "Structural Integration." *The Journal of the Institute for the Comparative Study of History, Philosophy, and the Sciences* 1 (1963), Number 1.

Ruffier, J.-E. *Traité Pratique du Massage Sportif.* Abbeville: F. Pallicut, 1921.

———. *Traité Pratique de Massage Hygienique, Sportif, Medical.* Paris: Editions Dangles, 1963.

Schultz, J. H. *Das Autogene Training.* Leipzig: G. Thieme Verlag, 1932.

Schultz, J. H., and Luthe, W. *Autogenic Training. A Psychophysiologic Approach in Psychotherapy.* New York: Grune & Stratton, 1959.

Selver, C. "Sensory Awareness and Total Functioning." *General Semantics Bulletin* 20 & 21 (1957): 5–17.

Selye, H. *The Physiology and Pathology of Exposure to Stress.* Montreal: Acta, 1950.

———. *The Stress of Life.* New York: McGraw-Hill, 1956.

———. "How We Adjust." Television Show. Montreal, 1973.

———. *Stress Without Distress.* New York: Lippincott, 1974.

Serizawa, K. *Massage, The Oriental Method.* San Francisco: Japan Publications, 1972.

Speads, C. Unpublished Lecture in 1944. Cited by R. C. Cohn. "An Approach to Psychosomatic Analysis." *Psychoanalysis* 3 (1955): 59.

Stephan, P. M. *The Secret of Eternal Youth.* New York: Arco, 1971.

Stokvis, B., and Wiesenhütter, E. *Der Mensch in der Entspannung* (3rd ed.). Stuttgart: Hippokrates Verlag, 1971.

Stolze, H. "Selbsterfahrung und Begegnung mit dem anderen durch konzentrative Bewegungstherapie." *Du und der Andere.* Biel: Verlag Institut für Psychohygiene, 1967, 47–58.

———. "Selbsterfahrung und Bewegung." *Praxis der Psychotherapie* 17 (1972): 165–174.

Surén, H. *Gymnastik für Heim, Beruf und Sport.* Stuttgart: Dieck & Co., 1927.

────. *Selbstmassage—Pflege der Haut.* Stuttgart: Dieck & Co., 1928.

Thomsen, W. *Lehrbuch der Massage und manuellen Gymnastik.* Stuttgart: Georg Thieme Verlag, 1970.

Todd, M. E. *The Thinking Body.* New York: Paul B. Hoeber, 1937.

Toynbee, A. *A Study of History.* New York: Oxford University Press, 1947.

Vishnudevananda, S. *The Complete Illustrated Book of Yoga.* New York: Julian Press, 1960.

Wilhelm, R. *The Secret of the Golden Flower.* New York: Harcourt, Brace & Company, 1935.

Wilhelm, R. "Elsa Gindler. Eine grosse Pädagogin besonderer Art, 19. Juni 1885 bis 8. Januar 1961." *Heilkunde Heilwege* 11 (1961), Heft 5.

Index

Proper names and page numbers of exercises, page numbers of definitions, and the most important references to a subject are in *italics*.